The Anarchist's Guide to Grammar

Val Dumond

The Anarchist's Guide to Grammar
Copyright © 2011-2012 Val Dumond
All rights reserved including the right of reproduction in whole or in part in any form.

First Edition

Printed in the United States

ISBN-10: 978-0-9797466-0-4

EAN-13: 978-0979746604

Muddy Puddle Press
P O Box 97124
Lakewood WA 98497

Library of Congress Cataloging-in-Publication Data
Available from publisher.

Dumond, Val

The Anarchist's Guide to Grammar
Exploding the Myths of U.S. Language
Guidebook to improved writing
English/Val Dumond
ISBN: 978-0-9797466-0-4
1. U.S.-English language — Usage
2. Grammar
3. Punctuation
4. Writing guidelines

OTHER BOOKS BY VAL DUMOND

Grammar For Grownups
Elements of Nonsexist Usage
Just Words
Mush On and Smile: Klondike Kate
Ahlam's Stories
How We Fought WWII at
　　William T. Sherman Elementary School
Doin' The Puyallup
The Sun Never Rises (compiled and edited)
Dream Makers (compiled and edited)

TABLE OF CONTENTS

Introduction	ix
Part I: The Four Parts of Grammar	1
Things	3
Nouns and Stand-in Pronouns	3
Verbs	39
Action and Stop-action	39
Modifiers	65
Adjectives, Adverbs, Phrases, Clauses, Verbals	65
Little Words	97
Conjunctions, Prepositions, Articles, Interjections	97
PART 2: Punctuation — Grammar's Road Signs	125
Commas, Commas, Commas	129
The Reflective Pause	129
Colons, Semicolons, Periods	141
Headlights, Dots with Tails, Full Stops	141
Question Marks & Exclamation Points	153
The Voices of Writing	153
Parentheses, Brackets & Quotation Marks	161
Enclosures of the Word Kind	161
Apostrophes, Ellipsis, Hyphens, Dashes & Diagonals	173
Dots and Dashes	173

PART 3 : Putting It All Together — Assembling the Parts	193
Words	197
Wimpy and Wonderful	197
Sentences	209
How To Structure Them	209
Paragraphs	223
How To Build Them	223
Spelling	229
Four Ways To Do It Better	229
Numbers	237
How To Write Them	237
Unbiased Language	245
Include "Them"	245
Writing Style of Your Own	251
Your Style Manual	259
Grammar Glitches—A To Z	265
English Terms	275
About The Anarchist	277
Acknowledgments	279
Index	281

This book is written for all who struggle with words... and wouldn't have it any other way!

—Val Dumond

"*Nothing happens until you break a rule.*"

— The Grammar Anarchist

INTRODUCTION

WHAT BOLLOCKS!

Question authority; You have been duped into believing there are grammar "rules"... somewhere. It's time United States writers take a close look at the "rules of proper English" and ask a few questions. When you were just a kid, you learned to communicate, first by throwing a wobbly, crying and screaming, and sometimes cooing. Then by talking and reading and writing. At home, you learned from Mom and Dad; in school you learned from Teacher. What you learned was what they knew.

Now you are a writer, whether you do it for solace, for entertainment, or for profit. Are you still working with that stuff you were taught as a child?

Maybe not.

Are you confused as you learn about other ways to talk and write?

Probably.

Do the "rules" you learned in grammar school still work for you?

Probably not!

So rise up! What do you fancy?

Grammar "rules" are rubbish! Throw the shambles away! Write your own brill rules!

Rise up, writers (whether you write emails or books, journals or office memos, blogs and Twitter messages, or magazines and novels)! Stone the crows! Rise up and declare your own style of writing.

BOB'S YOUR UNCLE!

Grammar purists claim there is a rulebook full of usage of "proper English". Yes, there are *rulebooks*, but do they offer only one way to use English? People who study language readily recognize the idiocy of knowing what is "proper". Purists choose a style of language and stick to it. "After all," they whine, "that is the way we were taught."

Is our language actually *English*? The nation's forebears escaped England and declared liberty from British laws. They changed their language, among other things, as they set out to live life their own way in a new country.

Still, they overlooked a few things. School children across the country once sang a song called "America" as our national anthem; the music is a direct steal from the Brits' "God Save the King". Even the President's theme song, "Hail To the Chief", comes from England. Every year thousands of U.S. high school and college graduates march down aisles to the British tune, "Pomp and Circumstance".

Even after a couple hundred years, the divergent fascination with things British continues, in everything from rock groups and actors to television sit-coms and mysteries. Posh and Becks are American royalty in the U.S. Some of us have even learned to love soccer and cricket!

We are awed by a British accent, which makes a speaker sound smart. Well, of course it does. The British use their English rules.

But we in the United States got rid of those "rules" — remember? — leaving us open to upstarts who want to lay out their own "rules". Now writers are befuddled with the mixed messages about language. It feels like trying to stuff a size 14 Brit into a size 2 pair of made-in-the-U.S. jeans. It doesn't work.

After we told the Red Coats to go home, we changed a few things grammatical. We changed the second person pronouns from *thee, thou*, and *thy* to *you, you*, and *your*. We deep-sixed the "st" from words such as *among, amid*, and *do*. No longer do we spell some words with the superfluous "ue" (*analog, monolog, dialog, catalog*). We reversed the "re" to spell our own *center, theater*, and *miter*, and we removed the "u" from words such as *honor, glamor, favor*, and *color*.

We changed names of some British punctuation, using a *period* instead of a *full stop*, an exclamation *point* instead of an exclamation *mark*, and differentiating between the *parenthesis* and *bracket*. We even reversed the use of single and double quotation marks. The very word meanings changed with time: a *pram* became a *baby buggy*, a *lift* became an *elevator*, a *bonnet* became a *hood*, and a *bed-sit* (go figure) became an *apartment* or *pad*. *Bloody* and *bum* are two words not spoken in polite British company, but Americans have adopted them into common usage.

Still not a believer? Look at your computer listings under WORD / TOOLS / Language and find (at least) three English languages. Mine offers Australian, UK and US.

English in America is English-with-a-twist, different from Australian-English, Indian-English, Canadian-English, and all the other Englishes spoken around the world. Anyone who spends a little time in England or watches British sit-coms or listens to NPR's evening world news understands the difference between the English that is spoken in Great Britain and what is spoken in Great Bend (Kansas).

This book refers to U.S. language. Can it even be called *American-English*? There are too many other countries claiming to be "American" in the Western Hemisphere. Who do we think we are, anyway?

U.S. language is unique, a one-of-a-kind language that exists nowhere else because… the U.S. is comprised of your ancestors and mine, their customs, songs, food, and languages. Sure, that makes it difficult to learn, but consider the beauty of it. We each learn it in a different way — and then share with the next generation who change to suit "their" way.

WHY THROW A SPANNER IN THE WORKS?

Anarchy lets you be on your tod, but we can be on our own together. Let's do it our way! Only anarchy will move the purists who expound their "rules", refusing to accept any way but theirs.

Anarchy is a strong word, a scary, violent word. There's been "Anarchy in the UK" but what about anarchy in the USA? So before you get entangled with visions of bullying hordes plundering and raping, direct your attention to the peace-loving Greeks.

The word "anarchy" comes from the Greek word *anarkhos*, which means an "absence of any cohesive principle, such as a common standard or purpose", and that is what this book is about, exercising control over our own unique U.S. language.

Sherlock Holmes stated, through the words of Sir Arthur Conan Doyle (an Englishman), "I never make an exception; an exception disproves the rule." The implication is clear: a "rule" with exceptions is not a rule.

Here's another adage: *Nothing happens until you break a "rule"*. Do not be afraid. For a writer, breaking "rules" is tantamount to creating something unique. The best books on my shelf were written by authors who broke "rules", who wrote books with dialog but no quotation marks (E. L. Doctorow), who wrote each chapter in a different style (Robert Grudin, Ph.D.), who wrote stories without naming the protagonist (Ernest Hemingway), who wrote books in prisons and concentration camps (John Bunyan, Oscar Wilde, Ezra Pound, Miguel de Cervantes), who wrote books over a weekend (participants of a variety of websites that write-a-book-over-the-weekend or in 30 days or in a year). And how many "rules" did J. K. Rowling break by writing a best-selling, growing-up series of seven books for children (without pictures)?

Look what happened when these people broke some "rules": the Minutemen at Bunker Hill, Benjamin Franklin, Frederick Douglas, Abraham Lincoln, Clara Barton, Thomas Edison, Albert Einstein, Mahatma Gandhi, Rosa Parks, Major Margaret Witt, Dr. Martin Luther King Jr., Nelson Mandela. How much do you think Ichiro Suzuki would be worth in baseball if he had listened to "your swing isn't the same as the fundamentals, so fix it"?

Wherever you look, and listen, you'll hear unrest, confusion about grammar, and a call to make it go away. School kids just don't get it. "Rules" of any kind don't make sense to them, so they find ways to express their own anarchy.

Breaking rules has become a fascination; it's what keeps us glued to the television and the movie screen. Check your TV and movie schedules and notice the popularity of shows that feature grifters, con artists, reformed thieves, and hustlers.

Still afraid to attack the "rules"? One more adage: "Rules are meant to be broken"? Break them we do, every day. *Thou shall not kill* — governments kill regularly, even teaching citizens to kill in their armies and prisons. *Thou shall not steal* — citizens regularly "steal" from the government by misusing the welfare system. And financiers... ouch! *Thou shall not lie* — another regular among the broken "rules". As is (OMG) *Thou shall not use the name of thy god in vain* (which doesn't even specify which god).

WHICH UNI TAUGHT YOU THIS CODSWALLOP?

What you learned from your parents was the way words sounded, the way parents learned from their parents, who learned from their parents, who learned from their... well, you get the idea. However much you love your parents, they may not have learned passable grammar. Many of them came from other countries (and languages) and spoke their native tongue or *English* with heavy accents — and this is what you learned. If your parents spoke *good English*, you were blessed.

Problems arose when you got into school and faced teachers; teachers also learned language from parents. Furthermore, when teachers faced professors, they, like you, often had to deal with strange ideas. Teachers accepted the teaching from professors who teach from their own meager learning experience. Some el-hi teachers get through college without taking grammar courses. Where do *they* learn? Again, the answer may be two-fold: 1) from their parents or 2) from the textbooks they are given to teach.

WHICH PLONKER WROTE *YOUR* TEXTBOOK?

Teachers and professors must present course outlines for their classes. They are drawn from the textbooks with which they teach; few participate in the choice of textbook, especially in lower grades. If there has been confusion in their own learning, these teachers rely on the teaching guides to get them through grammar lessons.

Got it? So far nothing in your absorption process of grammar has suggested you have any choice in the matter. In fact, your teachers and professors constantly use the word "rule" to apply to *their* versions, as if what they teach is handed down from on high and therefore perfect.

In the words of Henry David Thoreau: "Any fool can make a rule, and any fool will mind it." Too many writers latch onto one of those "rules" made up by somebody else and refuse to let it go. Grammar Anarchy questions them.

WHY WINGE ON ABOUT THE RULES?

While you're in "Reference", take down a few dictionaries and look up the word "rule". You quickly learn such phrases as: "to decide or declare authoritatively or judicially decree" or "a directive issued by authorities" or "a set of established rules intended to minimize confusion" or "a prescribed law or regulation" or "a regulation or bylaw governing procedure" or "the exercise of control and authority".

Got it? A rule comes with authority and does not have exceptions, *cannot* have exceptions. As you recall Teacher's many exceptions to grammar "rules", consider how games rely on rules: baseball, football, soccer, Scrabble, bridge, and tag. Imagine playing them with exceptions ("Your Red Sox hitter wants a fourth strike? Okay." "Sure, quarterback, you can have a fifth down." "Of course, we'll call *zhtjchg* a word this time.")

Grammar in the U.S. language does not have hard and fast rules. It is full of exceptions, conditions, irregularities, ifs and buts, all spread untidily among our words. Who can unscramble this mess? Children?

WHAT ABOUT THE SPOTTY YOUTH?

When learning to drive a car, it helps to learn how the engine works, the effect of moving the wheel on how the car moves, and ways to safely handle a 2,000-pound mass of steel (sometimes as powerful as a pound of TNT). This is not a reasonable task for children.

Similarly, learning the power of words and how to control them will get you the grownup through many a traffic jam (literally) and into safe, comfortable traveling (literally). Not for children.

A very wise person once remarked, "We shouldn't teach grammar to a child — not until they are in their teens; teenagers question everything!" Furthermore, no child should be exposed to words like "interjection" or "conjunction" before learning what they do.

The same principle applies to such things as cooking, playing music or tennis, and sex. You have to try them out and make mistakes to find out what you need to learn. Then, when you review the basics, they make sense.

My earlier book, *Grammar For Grownups,* was put together with the premise that children should be encouraged to write, any thing, any way. Their writing will be based on what they have learned from reading, listening to others, practicing with words. A gentle, albeit understanding, parent or teacher can lead that sprog into improving their use of the language. Then, when they have been speaking, reading, writing for a few years, they will be able to digest the nuances of U.S. grammar — as a grownup. Nay, they will scream to pick up the fine art of using appropriate grammar.

KEEP YOUR PECKER UP!

Don't mistake *grammar anarchy* as a way to kill with words. Too many people already know how to do that. What is offered here are ways to use words to your advantage and to say what you mean.

Effective anarchists seek information, but we don't stop there. We offer ways to overcome a false sense of security, confusion about right and wrong, and a belief in something that doesn't exist. An effective anarchist has a plan: throw out the "rules" and establish your own guidelines.

Now, as a grownup, review the basics that you *should have / could have / may have* learned in school – and quickly forgot. As you progress with this book, you will quickly recall, "Blimey, I remember that. Now it makes sense." The reason is that you were too young to learn the difference between a "predicate" and a "participle" until you experimented with their functions as an adult.

You'll pick up guidelines for arranging the 26-letter alphabet into words and into messages. Like most creative fields, you'll harness the basics before attempting to mess with them. You'll review the parts of speech, but not necessarily to identify their names. You'll discover their *functions*, how they contribute to language. Don't think I've lost the plot; you'll find some real names for those parts of speech, but you won't be bogged down with them. After all, it's what they *do* that counts, not so much what they're *called*.

In this world of choice and possibilities, no successful writer blindly opts to follow someone else's preferences. When they become free to develop their own style, writers know how to reflect their own preferences?

Can you make up a word? Of course! Follow the people who have fun with words (Steven Colbert and his "truthiness" come to mind) and you'll realize how dictionary words sometimes fail us, and a new one is called for. You can make up words just as well as anyone else, like much of the British slang used with you here.

Once you understand how the parts of speech function, you write not only with greater accuracy, but with greater confidence, just as you drive more confidently by understanding the engine under the hood. You'll grab the wheel that guides your words when you claim your language for your own.

A good writer is blessed with the knowledge of language — the tools of the trade. A good writer uses that knowledge to impart meaning to the words on the page. A good writer gets results, positive attention, a new job, respect, praise — a publishing contract.

So here comes *The Anarchist's Guidebook to Grammar*! Stand back. Be prepared to look at the musty "rules", tear them apart, understand what they mean, suss the confusion, and take back control over your own words.

And yes, notice that I choose to place quotation marks around that nasty, nauseous word, except when it is an actual rule.

BITS 'N BOBS:

PART I, THE PARTS OF SPEECH:

Discover the reasons for capitalizing certain Nouns and Pronouns (things); you are given a simple lesson about how Verbs make things happen (Action) – or not (Stop-action). This is where you learn about the two kinds of *is*. You receive helpful tips on handling Modifiers (words that dress up and explain or describe those *things* and *verbs*). You pick up pointers for using the Little Words that tie things together to form sentences.

While real names are given for some parts of speech, you won't be overwhelmed with them. After all, it's what they *do* that counts, not so much what they're called. However, if you plan to go on "Jeopardy!" or get a better job or impress your friends, you'll need to know the difference between an *adjective* and an *adverb*.

PART II, PUNCTUATION:

This section reviews the dots, dashes, and squiggly things called *Punctuation* and what they do. It offers ways to use them effectively and how to change a meaning with just a little curly-cue.

PART III, PUTTING IT TOGETHER:

Finally, writers are challenged to look closely at the Words they select and receive help with fashioning Sentences and Paragraphs to form and separate ideas. Other odds and ends about this fabulous language are included in this section: how to write Numbers, how to use Unbiased Language, and how to Spell — oh absobloodylootly Yes! — four ways to improve your spelling... immediately.

Further help comes from sidebars that offer handy Grammar Guidelines for you to consider, examples of language usage, a few easy-peasy exercises to keep your language cells in good shape, along with a full set of Grammar Glitches.

Now, keep your hair on, leg it and chivvy along! No more British slang, promise! (Well, maybe a tad here and there. It's so expressive.) Be sure to look in the back of the book if you need translations.

— **Val Dumond**

Warning: Reading the ideas in this book may cause periods of depression resulting from the confusion in your brain. You may experience periods of nausea, light-headedness, disorientation, altered vision, feeling zonked, tightness of muscles, and extreme head shaking. Be patient. These are likely to result in writer's euphoria, hope, clarity, and uncontrollable excitement.

Part 1

The Four Parts of Grammar

Things
(Nouns and Stand-in Pronouns)

Verbs
(Action and Stop-action)

Modifiers
(Adjectives, Adverbs, Phrases, Clauses)

Little Words
(Conjunctions, Prepositions, Articles, Interjections)

Things

(Nouns and Stand-in Pronouns)

In the beginning came the names.

(Q) What do anarchistic writers write about? (A) Anything they want! Look closely at that word: any-thing. Writers write about *things* — and that's what this chapter is about. Look at the signs rebels scrawl onto cardboard:

> DOWN WITH (THING)!
> SUPPORT (THING)!
> GO FOR (THING)!
> (THINGS) FOREVER!

Things, in the world of grammar, are called "Nouns". Don't know why; don't know who started it, probably Adam and Eve. They named everything else.

Adam and Eve did it; your parents did it; you did it — and still do. Nouning! Naming things. We humans love to name things — people, places, and objects. Even ideas. The first thing we do when meeting people is ask their names. Parents name their children, often before they're born. Children name their pets, their toys, their spoons, and they're friends.

Grownups continue the exercise; grownups give each other special names (*Poopsie, Sweetums, Lovebird, Skipper, Dolly*); grownups name their cars, animals, computers, vacuum cleaners, boats, RVs and homes.

> ### Some Nouns Are Onomastic
> *Trivia: a special word defines the study of proper names of persons and places. It's called onomastics.*

Names are important. In language, those important names are given capital letters and referred to as Proper Nouns. A "daisy" is a flower; a "Daisy" is a person.

When taking a close look at the "rules" put forth by... who? (we don't know)... we soon discover dissention among the supposed solons of grammar. As with all parts of speech, they can't agree on the simplest of *things* — how to handle them.

In grammar, as with many other pursuits, identifying the players becomes important. The lead players are Things. In grammar language, they're called *Nouns* and *Pronouns*. These are the things talked about. The trick comes with knowing the many ways to add information and clarify meanings through such touches as capitalization and the use of the apostrophe — critical tools.

This review of Things provides what you need to know about nouns, the words that name people, places, and things. People, places, and objects are easy; they're Things; we can see them. But there are Things we cannot see, like *freedom, wind, peace, timing, ethics, popularity,* and *noise*, which are not as easily defined and named. Which leads many to create nouns by adding "ize" or "tion" or "ist" to verbs (*priority / prioritize, material / materialize, idol / idolize, prioritization, materialization, idolization*).

But don't knit your knickers in a knot with nouns. The stuff you can do with them imparts information about your things in special ways.

This chapter addresses capitalization of *proper* nouns (things that are important, special, or unique), looks at plurals (how many?) and possessives (who or what owns something?), the verbal change artists (verbs that pass themselves off as nouns), and noun / verb agreement.

Sometimes anarchists send stand-ins to do the work of nouns. These stand-ins are called *pronouns* — meaning "things standing in for the nouns". After all, who would expect the big old important muckety-muck noun-thing to do all the work?

Included in this chapter are *pronouns*, those often-small words that represent *nouns*. Somewhere in what you write (or read) sits a noun that is being referred to by a pronoun, and often is overlooked. A few pronouns may hide under strange identities (*somebody, anyone, they, who*). Some are compound or reflexive pronouns; yet all must agree with the verbs. Here readers learn to scope out the pronoun that replaces a noun — and identify the noun it replaces. The pronouns *they* and *it* are the big offenders. Once and for all, we'll settle the *who / whom* question, or will we? The Quick Pronoun Menu instantly removes most of the old pronoun problems.

NOUNS

What do you think of when you think of nouns? "People, places, and things." Your second grade teacher got that point across so well that you may find difficulty in repeating those nouns in any other order. Of course, your teacher preferred the grammar jargon word, *noun*, to the more functional word, *Things*.

Nouns are the naming words, the words to which we attach labels. U.S.ers take great delight in attaching labels to all kinds of objects, whether or not they can be seen. Nouns are the objects or ideas people talk about, the main part of sentences, phrases, and clauses.

> **Nouns**
>
> *Places to Go,
> Things to See,
> People to Meet,
> and Ideas to Contemplate*

Nouns can be generic, as in *city* or *child* or *park*, or specific, as in *Tulsa*, *Barbara*, or *Yellowstone Park*. When they are specific, they are called Proper Nouns, and are capitalized to show that you're talking about a certain city, child or park.

Capitalizing Nouns

Capitalized words command more attention than other words and can be confusing when they are used only for that purpose. This is why anarchists take such great care to use nouns that muddy up the issues. We aren't always sure whether or not to capitalize words such as *city police*, *childcare center*, or *park attendant*. The following guidelines will help.

Blame the British! The Brit rule was to capitalize most nouns, as in: *The Queen sent the Message to the Crowds outside the Palace.* Just read the U.S. Declaration of Independence to see capitalized nouns.

After the anarchist colonists rebelled against all things British, that was one of the "rules" they altered. Only the important — very important — nouns were capitalized (as in the Declaration). Following the War of Independence, the use of capital letters diminished. Much confusion remains, but the guidelines are clear.

Capitalize a word that refers to a particular person, place, or thing, when it has its own name. Not just "an island", but "Fantasy Island". Capitalize the words that refer to a specific company, city, or park (*The Company invites all members of the City administration to a picnic at City Park.*) If you work for the city of Boise, and wish to refer to other City workers, use the capital. The same guideline applies to other such government employers: company, state, county, federal. (The boss or supervisors will appreciate it.) In ordinary usage, do not capitalize such a term that precedes a proper name (city of Phoenix, state of Colorado). One exception might be Washington State when differentiating between the *state* rather and the District of Columbia. People who work for government agencies or groups often choose to capitalize the word all the time. That is a matter of choice by the agency or group.

> **Company Rules**
>
> *Whether you work for a company or a government agency, follow the guidelines that have been established for capitalizing certain words. Ask to see the Company Style Manual. If there isn't one, write it yourself.*

One simple guideline suggests capitalizing words such as *state, federal government, nation,* or *city* when it substitutes for the actual name of the state, federal government, nation or city. (*Since the State passed the law...; Members of the Federal agency agreed...*) However, generally use lower case letters when preceded by a possessive: *this company, our city, their organization.* Whether or not to capitalize a government (city, state, federal) is a personal choice unless you work for an agency that insists you always put it in caps — and many do.

PEOPLE

Ranks and titles are capitalized if they are used in front of a name: *Captain John Smith*, but not if used following a name: *John Smith, captain*, or *the captain*. *Judge Roy Bean*, but *Roy Bean, judge*, or *the judge*. The Anarchist claims one major exception. When referring to the President of the United States, the word *President* represents the office and is capitalized (my choice). Presidents of lesser organizations often feel the need to capitalize the term for reasons of aggrandizement, but that is a matter of personal or company policy. Some also like to capitalize other major offices, such as Governor or Associate Justice. This tendency reflects the belief that capital letters lend importance, but when and where to use them is optional. (Get out Your Style Manual and choose.)

Family members' names and titles are capitalized (*Aunt Jane, Dad, Mom*) unless the name is preceded by a possessive noun or pronoun (*Aunt Jane handed Mom her ultimatum.* But ... *It was my mom who handed the threat to my aunt.*)

PLACES

Geographical directions are capitalized only when referring to specific regions: (the *South* that survived a war, the taming of the *West*). They are not capitalized when indicating direction: (*The team headed north to the new stadium two blocks south of the city center*).

Names of states are capitalized, as are both of the two-letter postal abbreviations: Ohio, OH; Texas, TX; Florida, FL.

Of course you'll capitalize the geographical direction when it is part of the proper name: North Dakota, East St. Louis, East Greenwich. But omit the capital letters for the "ern" words, unless part of the actual name (*western Rhode Island, northern Alaska*, but *Southern Illinois, Eastern Washington*).

The entire company name of a business organization is capitalized: Boeing, ABC Company, The IBM Company. Some firms insist on capitalizing "The". Many don't.

Acronyms are capitalized: USA, FBI, CIA, MRI. Don't forget to explain the meaning at least once when using and re-using these shortcuts.

Countries are always capitalized, of course. So are the products that bear their names (*French fry, Belgian waffle, Danish pastry*). After repeated use, the caps sometimes get lost. Again, your personal preference can set your own "rule".

THINGS

Brand names are capitalized (*Folgers, Toyota, Macintosh*) even when they become part of everyday language. Early in the 20th century when automobiles were still new gadgets, people referred to all cars as *Fords*. A current trivia fad delves into the forgotten origins of some proper names attached to commonly used items. Bet you've forgotten that there was a Mr. Ferris (George Washington Gale Ferris) who invented the *Ferris wheel*, or there was a Frigidaire that preceded *fridge*.

Some proper nouns lose the capital letters after long usage. Many companies make a point of insisting that the capital letter be retained in their names: *Kleenex, Sanka, Coca-Cola, Xerox*, for example. Use generic names if you don't have the real thing: *tissue, decaffeinated coffee, cola, copier*. As usage of some proper names increases, the capital letter is often dropped. Hence, you may find yourself eating *french fries* and *cheese danish* one day while drinking a *sanka* or *coke*. Meanwhile, the choice is yours.

Other commonly capitalized words include the days of the week, months, and book titles. *Tuesday, Saturday, June*, and *October* are familiar. Books and other publication titles sometimes omit capitalizing certain words: conjunctions, articles and short prepositions. *The Rise and Fall of the Roman Empire* demonstrates the lower case conjunction (*and*), preposition (*of*), and article (*the*). Do you see the after-effect of the old British rule of capitalizing nouns? Always capitalize the first letter of title words. Be careful not to capitalize *the* when it is not part of a proper title (*the Bible*).

In school, names of study courses are capitalized only if they are derived from proper names: *French, Russian, Spanish*, but not *biology, history, chemistry*. Names of specific courses are capitalized: *Genetic Biology 101, Ancient History 202*.

Seasons are capitalized only when they are personified, that is, given a meaning that resembles a person: *When Summer smiles on us, we forget Old Man Winter, haul out our summer ammo, and put away our spring lasers*.

Historical events, historical eras, and holidays are capitalized: *the Dark Ages, the Iron Age, the Renaissance, the Days of Flower Power, the Summer of Love, Guy Fawkes Day, Labor Day*.

Always capitalize the first word of a sentence, the first word of a salutation and close of a letter (*Dear John, Sincerely yours*), the first word of a direct quotation that is a complete sentence (*She answered, "Of course, I understand."*), and the first word of a sentence fragment that substitutes for a complete sentence (*Such a shame!*).

Up for debate is the use of the lower case letters that begin the names for contrivances brought about by the Internet: email, ebook emag, iPod, iMac. Some say it's all right to begin a sentence with a lower case of this kind; others say, vehemently, "Absolutely not!" Another decision for Your Style Manual. Oh yes, do you use a hyphen in *e-mail* and *e-mag*?

Whether or not you capitalize a.m. or P.M. is a personal choice — unless the company style manual says otherwise. Whatever you choose, be consistent.

Making Nouns Plural

If there was just one shot at providing a guideline to make plurals out of nouns, it would be this: To make a noun plural, add a simple *s* or *es*. But then, teachers wouldn't be earning their meager pay, would they?

There are a variety of "rules" concerning plurals — most with tedious exceptions. But tackle the basics that follow and you can make plurals out of nouns your way. With repetition, your readers will easily discover your pluralization style.

SIMPLE *S* OR *ES* ENDINGS

To make plural most nouns, add an *s* — unless the noun ends with *s, z, x, ch*, or *sh*; then add *es*. Some people's names pose strange problems of their own. Take the Adams family, for instance. Writing about all of them, we write *the Adamses*. Writing about their house, we write: *the Adamses' house*. Certain grammarians insist we add *apostrophe-s ('s)* to produce any possessive, forcing us then to write the *Adamses's* yard. (This is a good topic for debate. Invite the Adamses.)

ENDING IN *Y*

Another problem arises with nouns that end in *y*. It becomes necessary to look at the letter before the *y*. If the *y* is preceded by a vowel (*a, e, i, o, u*) add the simple *s* (*keys, attorneys, buoys*). If, however, the *y* is preceded by a consonant (any other of the letters), change the *y* to *i* and add *es* (*companies, secretaries, alimonies*). Forget this guideline when pluralizing proper nouns (*Kennedys, Gettys, Canarys*).

ENDING IN *O*

If you want to open a real bag of trouble, start making plurals of things that end in *o*. There are no "rules", just exceptions, which offers a perfect target for anarchism to move in and make a point. Erase the many confusing, controversial, irritating, time-wasting "rules" for o-word plurals.

There seems to be no rhyme or reason why some o-word plurals end in *s* and some in *es*. In fact, most dictionaries provide two plural forms for most of the words. That leaves an anarchist free to choose, either *cargos* or *cargoes*, whichever you choose, you're right.

Can you think of a single o-ending noun that cannot be made understandably plural by adding a simple *s*?

Here's some good anarchistic news. Forget the option of inserting an *e* to make plurals of the o-words. When you find an o-noun that requires a plural, revert to the simple *s* guideline (*cargos, tornados, heros, torpedos, vetos, dynamos*). Simplify your life. There is no reasonable explanation for using *s* on some words and *es* on others. Oh yes, you'll catch flack from purists who insist that *tomatoes* with an *es* ending taste better than *tomatos* without, or that *potatoes* with an *es* ending are more edible than *potatos* without — but stand your ground! Remain firm! Eliminate the *e*!

If you use any of these words often, check a good (recent) dictionary, make your choice, and be consistent. (More in the Spelling Section.)

ALL THOSE OTHER PLURALS

After the trauma of words ending in *o*, you may be in a brave mood to approach other nouns that are made plural without sensible patterns. Change the vowels to pluralize these words: *foot, goose, man, woman, tooth* (*feet, geese, men, women, teeth*).

Some nouns require no changes at all to go from singular to plural: *deer, moose, sheep, fish*; they all remain the same, one or six hundred.

Only a couple of words fall into the category that requires *en* to make them plural: *child* (*children*) and *ox* (*oxen*). An archaic use of *brother* (*brethren*) is still used in some places.

Then there are a few words that change the *f* in a word to a *v* to make them plural: *wife, wives; knife, knives; life, lives*. Who knows why? Nor has anyone figured out why a lone *mouse* comes from a family of *mice*! (Although the use of more than one computer *mouse* is considered *mouses*. Go figure!)

SOME SINGULAR NOUNS APPEAR PLURAL

A few nouns that end in *s* are singular in meaning and require singular verbs. Consider: *civics, economics, corps, mathematics, news, phonetics, semantics, series, species*. And some nouns end in *s* and may be either singular or plural in meaning, and are used only with plural verbs: *goods, pliers, riches, scissors, thanks*. (See Verbs for more about the S-syndrome.)

Collective Nouns

Some nouns seem to be plural, but may be used as singular nouns. They are called *collectives* and require a close look. Such words — *group, team, gang, company, board, jury, family, number* — can represent either the individuals that make up the collective or the collective itself. Choose the verb form very carefully to express your meaning.

Both of the following sentences are correct, but they express different meanings.

The gang have until Monday to choose their targets.
The gang has until Monday to choose its targets.

In the first sentence, each member of the gang clearly will have a say in the choice. In the second, the gang will have to decide unanimously as a unit. Notice how the pronouns (*their, its*) offer clues to identify the number.

Compound Nouns

Compound nouns are combinations of two or more words that vary in plurals according to the components. If a compound word includes a noun combined with an *adjective* or *preposition*, the principal noun is made plural. (Here's where it is important to learn the names of the players in the Grammar Game! An *adjective* describes a noun or pronoun, and a *preposition* introduces a phrase that describes the noun or pronoun.)

More than one *father-in-law* becomes *fathers-in-law*; more than one *heir-apparent* becomes *heirs-apparent*; more than one *looker-on* becomes *lookers-on*.

If no part of the hyphenated compound word is a noun, the plural is added at the end. Thus, *follow-up* becomes *follow-ups*; *strike-over* becomes *strike-overs*; *trade-in* becomes *trade-ins*; and *write-up* becomes *write-ups*.

Likewise, if a compound noun is written without the hyphen, the plural is added at the end: *businessmen, cupfuls, letterheads, stepchildren*.

You'll find that many compound nouns using hyphens morph into single words after extensive usage.

Latin Nouns Et Al

We're talking Roman Latin here, not Spanish Latin. Because so many of the words used in U.S. language evolved from Latin, there is disagreement about whether or not to retain the original spelling. And disagreement, mostly among academics, indicates lack of "rules" which indicates an opportunity to choose your own.

U.S. language is full of words brought from other countries. It is estimated that as many as 150 languages from around the world contribute to today's U.S. language. Many of the words stick to the rules of their own, especially Latin and Greek words. Latin and Greek form the roots of many U.S. words and are handy to know.

Some of these Latin and Greek words that end in *is* are made plural by changing to *es*: *analysis / analyses, basis / bases, diagnosis / diagnoses*. [This has resulted in similar-sounding words treated in a similar way, like the ludicrous pronunciation sometimes given the plural for *process*. Although it is pluralized with a simple *es*, one often hears the plural mispronounced *process-eez* rather than *process-ez*. Puleeze!]

In a perverse way, many Latin words end with a plural *a*, which can be made singular by changing the *a* to *um*: *addenda / addendum, curricula / curriculum, data / datum, media / medium*. Because the plurals end in *a*, we're tempted to consider them as singular and we want desperately to add an *s* to make them plural.

Constant use of plural words like *data* and *media* are resulting in the U.S.-ization of the words; that is, they are regularly being used both as singular and plural in their original form, or as singular words utilizing the simple *s* "rule": *datas* and *medias*.

> ### News or ESP?
> *Note that media include newspapers, radio, and television, while mediums are people with ESP powers. Maybe they're not so different after all.*

As the Latin plural rules are becoming lost in common usage in the U.S., some of the nuances of the English language are getting lost too. Until they are completely erased, those wanting to appear well-educated, pompous, or self-important, may appreciate some guidelines.

Here they are:

Latin words ending in *us* (masculine) are made plural by changing the *us* to *i*: *alumnus / alumni, nucleus / nuclei, stimulus / stimuli*.

Words ending in *a* (feminine) are made plural by changing to *ae*: *alumna / alumnae, formula / formulae, vertebra / vertebrae*. Sure, some grammar books and dictionaries are acknowledging such plurals as *nucleuses, formulas, vertebras*. Still that subtle use of the masculine plural (*alumni*) that is meant to include both women and men indicates a return to recognizing the sexist discrimination in words. (*Man* does not include *women*; nor does *alumni* include *alumnae*.)

More Latin. Words ending in *ex* or *ix* have, until now, been made plural by changing to *ices*, as in *appendix / appendices, index / indices*. Thankfully, that too is changing to allow us to make the words plural by adding *es* (*appendixes, indexes*).

We're also loosening up on words ending with *on*, but in different ways. The singular words *criterion* and *phenomenon*, made plural in Latin by changing the *on* to *a* (*criteria* and *phenomena*) are finding acceptance today in U.S. English as *criterias* and *phenomenons*.

The French, a language based on Latin, gave us the *eau* words, made plural by adding *x* (*bureau / bureaux, chateau / chateax*). Now, many use the simple *s* ending to form the U.S. plurals: *bureau / bureaus, trousseau / trousseaus, chateau / chateaus*.

Possessive Nouns

When one thing belongs to another, U.S. language uses what is called a *possessive* form to express it. An effective anarchist knows how to express possession. A possessive is formed by adding an apostrophe-*s* ('*s*) or a lone apostrophe (') to the noun (*the manager's meeting* or *the managers' meeting*), depending on whether the noun is singular or plural. See how one little mark can pass along information? Of course this may cause considerable confusion encompassing the use of the possessive — mostly because of the placement of the apostrophe. Here is a simple four-step guideline.

Step 1: Make certain that the possessive case is needed, that you aren't using a plural (they sometimes sound the same since they both can end in *s*).

The *managers* will meet today. (plural, not possessive)

The *manager's* report is expected. (singular, possessive)

Step 2: Determine whether the noun is singular or plural.

The *manager's* report is due today. (singular possessive— one manager)

If singular, continue to Step 3.

If plural, go to Step 4.

Step 3: If singular, add an apostrophe-*s*.

The *teller's* hair is red. (singular possessive — one teller)

The *woman's* timing is excellent. (singular possessive — one woman)

Step 4: If plural (and if it ends in *s*, add an apostrophe only.)

The *managers'* reports are due today. (plural possessive)

If the noun ends in any other letter, add apostrophe-*s* ('*s*)

The *men's* schedule is grueling. (plural possessive — more than one man)

The *carpenters'* schedule eliminates Sundays. (plural carpenters, one schedule)

Example: If you wish to refer to *the hat belonging to the dude*...

Step 1: *Belonging* says it is possessive.

Step 2: Since there is only one dude, the noun is singular.

Step 3: Add an apostrophe-*s* (*dude's hat*).

Example: If you wish to form the possessive *for hats belonging to all the dudes*...

Step 1: *Belonging* says it is possessive.

Step 2: Now there are several dudes (plural). Skip to Step 4.

Step 4: Since *dudes* ends in *s*, add an apostrophe (*dudes'* hats). If the hats belonged to *women*, you would add an apostrophe-*s* (*women's* hats).

Easy as 1-2-3-4! Conversely, when you see a possessive written, you can easily discern whether or not a single noun or a plural noun possesses the whatever. The *witnesses' testimony* tells us immediately that more than one witness was testifying, and they agreed upon a single testimony. The *witness's testimonies* indicates one witness and several testimonies. *The witnesses' testimonies* shows multiple witnesses with multiple testimonies. What a trial that was!

> **Possessive Nouns**
> **1-2-3-4**
>
> Step 1: Determine the noun is possessive.
>
> Step 2: Is the Thing singular or plural?
>
> Step 3: If singular, add apostrophe-s.
>
> Step 4: If plural and ends in s, add an apostrophe.
>
> If plural and ends in anything else, add apostrophe-s.

Verbal Nouns

Did you know that words other than nouns can behave as nouns? These words are called *verbal nouns*, and there are three of them. *Gerund. Infinitive. Participle.* If you want to impress friends, use any of these words — but first, know what they mean.

Verbals are Action Words (verbs) impersonating other parts of speech. Something called a *gerund* is actually "a verb posing as a noun" and must be treated as a noun. Here's how it works: *speak* is a verb. But when we use the gerund form *speaking*, it impersonates a noun. (*Speaking exposes our thoughts.*)

The infinitive verbal involves the infinitive form of the verb (*to do something*), and also behaves like a noun. (*To speak honestly exposes thoughts.*)

Know also there is a verbal called *participle*, which is a verb posing as an adjective modifier. As in: *Spoken loudly, the words sounded harsh.* Or: *Speaking loudly, she poured out her thoughts.* Both *spoken* and *speaking* are participles. You can identify them as verbs by their base forms (to speak). Verbals are discussed as Action Words, coming up, since they involve verbs, and also in the Modifier Section because some verbals function as modifiers.

Proceed slowly and enjoy the review. Writers rely heavily on verbals, sometimes too heavily. Still, a well-placed verbal transmits a world of ideas. (*Revolting feels good.*)

GERUNDS

Gerunds are the verbs that impersonate nouns; they are identified by their "ing" endings. You notice it when the "ing" word is the thing being talked about.

Dressing up is what Marji loved to do.
Screaming and *shouting* are ways Algernon gets noticed.
Marrying a chatter-box is a big mistake.

INFINITIVES

Equally easy to recognize as noun verbals are the Infinitives, the verbs that play the part of nouns. You notice them by the "to do" form of the Action Word.

To reconcile means making a commitment.
To commit takes a lot of courage.
To find the courage may require therapy.

Noun and Verb Agreement

Nouns must agree with the Action Words (verbs) that tell what's happening.

When singular nouns are used, the singular verb form is also used. (*The building sways in heavy winds. The wind blows incessantly.*)

When plural nouns are used, the plural verb form is used. (*The buildings sway in heavy winds. The winds blow incessantly.*)

One S to a Noun / Verb

Ironically, plural *nouns* usually end in s (*members, kids, cars*) and singular *verbs* often end in *s* (*has, jumps, turns*). One guideline that helps people struggling with this weird language is this: Imagine a shortage of the letter *s*. The *s* must be rationed out — one to a noun-verb combination. Either the noun or the verb gets it, not both.

> **One "S" to a Noun/Verb Combo**
>
> Imagine a shortage of the letter "s" when deciding on the numbers in the noun-verb combination. Either the noun or the verb gets it. Not both.
> *The word appears weird.* (Singular noun, put the "s" on the verb.)
> *The words appear weird.* (Plural noun, give the "s" to the noun, not the verb.)

The *members have...*, but the *member has....* In the same way, the *kids jump...* or *the kid jumps...*, and *the car turns...* or the *cars turn....*

Beware! As with most parts of this crazy language, this isn't a hard and fast "rule", just an Anarchist's Guideline.

Subjects Connected With "and"

When a subject is comprised of two or more things connected by *and*, treat them as a plural noun, whether or not they contain an *s*. That is, use the plural verb (without the *s*). Consider subjects connected with *and* as plural. (*The zebra and elephant live in the wilds of Africa. The guitarist and the pianist play in unison.*)

> ***Warning:*** When both nouns connected by *and* refer to the same thing (or person), use the singular verb (with the *s*). *The guitarist and pianist misses her cues regularly.* The singular pronoun offers a clue that one person is both a guitarist and pianist. You have been warned.

Subjects Connected With "or"

When the connector of two nouns is *or*, you have a choice. Usually two singular subjects connected with *or* are treated as a singular noun and take a singular verb (with an *"s"*). (*The artist or the writer receives a grant. The abstract or the cover letter, whichever is sent, contains its own data. An apple or an orange makes a good snack.*)

That sounds easy enough. Two clues verify what is going on: the number of the verbs (*receives, contains, makes*) and the number of the possessive pronoun (*its*). So we'll throw in a what-if! What if one of the noun words is singular and one is plural and they're connected with *or*? Maybe this is easy too, once you remember what Teacher told you. Aha! You forgot. Here's the reminder: "If you are faced with two subjects connected with *or* and one of them is singular and one is plural, *consider the noun closest to the verb when determining its number* and, therefore, when deciding which verb and which pronoun to use. If one or the other sounds awkward, simply change the order of the subjects." Now you remember!

> An artist's rendering or *the schematics are* sufficient to provide proof.
> The schematics or *the artist's rendering is* sufficient to provide proof.
> The hair or the *eyebrows grow* out with dark roots.
> The photographer or the *makeup artists decide* the resulting appearance.

Finding the Noun / Verb

Just like in a mystery story, in order to make sure the noun and verb agree, first you have to find the culprits. In long sentences the clues are not always apparent. Phrases and clauses often mess things up, making it difficult to separate the noun subject from the verb. Well duh! Eliminate the phrases and clauses when searching for the verb and its agreeable subject. Only the first two sentences that follow are correct.

The *board* of directors, which meets on Tuesday of every other week and Thursdays in the summer months, *is* made up of 12 people. (*Correct!* Notice that the verb "meets" is part of the modifying clause.) The *board*... *is* made up of 12 people.

The *board* of directors *meets* regularly for a round of golf. (*Correct* again!)

The *board* of directors, which meets on Tuesdays and includes nine men and three women, *are* dealing with the new budget. (*Incorrect!* The verb should be *is* since it represents a single collection.) The board... is dealing.

The subject of all three sentences is "the board" which will take a singular verb (one that ends in *s*).

PRONOUNS

One reminder that astonishes grownups is that pronouns represent nouns. Somewhere in what you're writing (or reading) is a noun that is being referred to by a pronoun, and it tends to be overlooked. A few pronouns may be exempt grammatically from that reminder (like the anonymous *somebody* and *anyone)*, but too often pronouns are used without regard to what they replace. The pronouns *they* and *it* are the big offenders.

QUICK PRONOUN MENU

A Quick Pronoun Menu is part of this section and just may change your life. Oh, you'll still feel the rebellious urges, but you'll know how to handle them. The Pronoun Menu provides a hands-on review of pronouns in order to recall easily the use of each. *Subjects* are found in Column A, *Objects* in Column B, and *Possessives* in Column C — a reminder that clears up a few questions.

Compound pronouns, reflexive pronouns, and the agreement of pronoun and verb are discussed here. A look at *pronouns after comparisons* and pronouns that follow *to be* are added, along with a few words about collective pronouns. Once and for all, the *who / whom* question will be settled, or will it?

Once more: Pronouns substitute for nouns. They are the stooges that sit in where the noun is not repeated. Occasionally, carelessness hides the actual noun being replaced. Having a good sense of pronouns makes writing clearer and more direct.

Grownups may have been foggy about just how many pronouns there are and what they do. Somehow you know that *I, me*, and *my* are pronouns, but where do they fit in the scheme of the universe?

Be foggy no more! Here is a Quick Pronoun Menu to clear things up for you. Fill in the spaces before you look at the finished guide at the end of the chapter. You probably already know this stuff.

Quick Pronoun Menu

	Column A Nominative The Do-er	Column B Objective The Do-ee	Column C Possessive The Owner
1st Person (S)	_____	_____	_____
1st Person (P)	_____	_____	_____
2nd Person (S)	_____	_____	_____
2nd Person (P)	_____	_____	_____
3rd Person (S)	_____	_____	_____
3rd Person (P)	_____	_____	_____

To begin, place all the first person pronouns in the first two rows across. *First person* means any pronoun relating to the person speaking, both singular (S): *I, me; my, mine;* and plural (P): *we, us; our, ours.*

Next, fill in the second person rows, that is, pronouns relating to the person being spoken to, singular (S): *you, you, your/yours; you, you,* and plural (P): *your/yours.* (Second person is the easy one. Please do not include *you-all, youse, yourn,* or *yez,* even if your friends tell you that *youse* is singular and *yez* is plural!)

Finally, fill in the third person rows with pronouns relating to someone or something else. Singular (S): *she, he, it; her, him, it; her, hers, his, its,* and Plural (P): *they, them, their; theirs.*

The pronoun is an independent kind of word. When you learned how to make a possessive noun, your instruction was to add an *apostrophe-s.* Well, the anarchic, feisty little pronoun is determined to show possession without the apostrophe. Notice in Column C (*mine, ours, yours, yours, hers, his, its, theirs*) the absence of the apostrophe.

And there you have it. To be certain you have the right pronoun in the right place, you can now refer to the completed Quick Pronoun Menu at the end of this chapter. When subjects and objects are discussed (later on in the Sentences Section), you'll be well prepared.

Hold on! Don't think those are the only pronouns. There are more than just those on the chart. Pronouns come in a variety of all-purpose styles, each with its own label. You may even be surprised to realize that you already know them. You just don't often think of them as pronouns. But they are.

Let's differentiate right off the bat. There are personal and possessive pronouns (the ones on the menu), singular pronouns (*each, each other, all, some, anyone, who, nothing, either / neither, everything, much*), a few plural pronouns (*many, few, both, several, others*), reflexive pronouns (personal pronouns with the word *self* or *selves* added), relative pronouns (*who, which, that*), and demonstrative pronouns (*this, that, those,* and *these*). Using the labels in this paragraph, let's look separately at each set.

SUBJECT PRONOUNS (COLUMN A)

Personal pronouns are those listed in the Quick Pronoun Menu. Anyone can see they are divided into three sets. Under Column A are the subject pronouns. These are the Do-er pronouns, the subject of the sentence or clause, the one that must agree with the verb. The personal subject (Do-er) pronouns include *I, we, you* (both singular and plural), *he, she, it,* and *they.*

Whenever using a Do-er pronoun, choose from Column A. These are the pronouns to look for in those up-until-now terrible instances when you need to answer the question: Who is it?

Now at last you can respond confidently: *It is I (you, he, she, it).*

Use Column A pronouns that follow the words *than* or *as* where another verb is implied.

No one is better qualified than she (is).
Both sons are taller than I (am).

Choose from Column A when the pronoun defines the subject and is set off with commas. This use is called an *appositive* since it makes positive that you know what you're talking about. Perhaps they should be called "repeaters", since they repeat the subject in one form or another in order to clarify it.

Two managers, *Kiona and I*, will lead the session. (*Kiona and I* are appositives of *two managers.*)

The highest producers are the two district leaders, *you and she.* (*You and she* are appositives of *two district leaders.*)

OBJECT PRONOUNS (COLUMN B)

The pronouns in Column B are the Do-ee pronouns, or objects. They are the ones used when you want to show who receives the verb from the subject. There are two ways this can be done — directly or indirectly.

Directly: *They trained me for the job.* (Who did they train? *Me.*)
Indirectly: *He gives the willies to me.* The *willies* are what is given (the direct object), and the recipient is *me* (the indirect object). One test of the indirect object is to ask if something has been done *to* or *for* someone; then that's the pronoun required (from Column B). You could also write: *He gives (to) me the willies*, but then the purists would complain that what is given is *me*, not *the willies*.

Objects also appear in prepositional phrases. Remember Teacher calling it "the object of the preposition"? *Give the credit to him. To him* is the prepositional phrase (*to* is the preposition; *him* is the object of that preposition). When you see one of those pronoun objects of prepositional phrases, immediately go to Column B.

Perhaps this will forever remove the doubt from your mind about the words that follow the preposition *between*. Because *between* is a preposition, look for the object in Column B (*me, us, you, her, him, it*). At last you know! There is no *between you and I*; there is no *between I and she!* Remember Teacher's warning: Don't use it only because "it sounds right". All the following fit the guidelines:

Between you and me   *Between you and him*
Between you and her   *Between her and him*
Between him and me   *Between her and me*
Between them and us   *Between them and me*

By the way, *between* indicates just two pronouns. If there are more than two things involved, use the preposition *among*.

Courtesy suggests that first person pronouns are placed at the end of the pronoun string, whether two or twenty (*between her and me, him and me, you and me. Among her, him, you, and me.*)

Just like the appositive, or repeater, used in Column A, there is a Column B appositive, or repeater.

The best sales territory was given to them, Margot and him.
They never thanked their bosses, Jackson and me.

Perhaps now you too will wince when you hear "Me and June went to the movies." The subjects should come from Column A with the first-person placed last — *June and I*. Now that's playing nice!

POSSESSIVE PRONOUNS (COLUMN C)

Column C deserves a section all its own, since these pronouns are neither subject nor object. Rather, they are closer to adjectives (modifiers). Possessive pronouns show

> **No Apostrophes!**
>
> *Remember that the feisty pronoun possessives do not need apostrophes, do not want apostrophes, and do not use apostrophes!*

ownership. This can be done in one of two ways. Either use the pronoun with the object owned (*my book*) or use the possessive pronoun (*mine*).

We can refer to my schedule as mine.
His opportunity was his alone.
Ramona looked at her desk calendar and knew that today was hers.
When Arthur forgot his appointment, he knew the blame was his.

BEWARE THE CONTRACTION

A puppy wags its tail. It's cute! (The apostrophe is used only for the contraction *it is*, and never, never for the possessive *its*.)

Theirs is not to wonder why. It's no wonder why; that's its way.
The car is his; it's his car. (It is his car.) *He loves its speed.*

SINGULAR PRONOUNS

You may not have recognized some other pronouns in the past. However, if they substitute for nouns, they are pronouns. When the singular pronouns function as sentence subjects, they use the singular verb.

Some of the singular pronouns: *anybody, anyone, anything, everybody, everyone, everything, somebody, someone, one, nobody, nothing, something, each, either, neither, much.* Use them carefully. Often the subject pronoun falls far from the verb.

> *Each* of the people in the accounting department on the third floor *has* a parking space.
> *Somebody* within the sound of my voice *is* about to be honored.
> *Either* of the desks near the window *looks* out over the lake.

PLURAL PRONOUNS

A few slightly disguised pronouns are plural and take plural verbs. Some of the plural pronouns: *both, few, several, others, many, most.*

> *Many* of the shopkeepers *rally* to stock the new persimmons.
> *Few are* unwilling to unpack them.
> *Several decide* to pass on persimmons this year.

SINGULAR OR PLURAL PRONOUNS

No, this isn't as confusing as it appears — nor as difficult. Stay with it.

Some pronouns can be either singular or plural, according to the meaning intended: *all, none, any, more, most, some.* The key is to look at the prepositional phrase (if there is one, and there usually is) that follows the pronoun in question. By reading the clues, you can determine whether or not the required verb should be singular or plural. This is one of those tight places where exact meaning can be transmitted by carefully choosing your words. The work of a careful writer provides the clues to tell readers how many are being discussed.

> *Most of the good movies are disappearing.* (*They* are disappearing.)
> *Most of the movie has concluded now.* (*It* has concluded.)
> *All of the criticisms were unfounded.* (*They* were unfounded.)
> *All of the criticism reduces the normal weekend audience.* (*It* reduces the audience.)
> *None of the audience care if the lights are low.* (*They* don't care about lights.)
> *None of the audience cares about salted popcorn.* (*It* cares about Milk Duds.)

The pronouns *all* and *none* are up for grabs with some grammarians. (Since the experts can't agree, Teacher may just have skipped this part in the lesson plans.) It's really very simple. If the word clearly is meant as singular, use a singular verb; and do the same for plurals. This is where the fun comes in. You, as writer or speaker, have the option to choose how many you're talking about and to say it that way.

> *None of the children is expected to leave the room during the movie.*
> *All of the children are expected to be in their seats at four o'clock.*
> *None are coming to see the newsreel.*
> *All is not well in the mezzanine.*

REFLEXIVE PRONOUNS

Nowhere in the Quick Pronoun Menu is the word *self*. All the *self* words are called reflexives or emphatic pronouns: *myself, herself, himself* (never *hisself*), *yourself, itself, themselves* (never *theirselves*). There's a reason they are not included in the Menu: their main purpose in our language is to add emphasis. You could omit them if you wish and the sentence will stand.

> *I myself want to do the work.*
> *I want to do the work myself.*
> *You should have tried it yourself.*

A secondary purpose is to act as an object of a verb or the object of a preposition.

> *He tells himself jokes to pass the time.*
> *She tries to give herself reasons to smile.*
> *Juan and Magenta find strength in themselves.*

Notice that most of the *self* words in the first and second person come from the possessive Column C (*myself, ourselves*). The third person words come from Column B (*themselves, herself*). Wouldn't you like to get your hands on the person who decided to switch to objects to cover *her, him, it,* and *them*? There is absolutely no rhyme nor reason, no precedent, no logic. This is one you'll just have to remember.

Don't overdo the *self* pronouns. The simple pronoun usually is enough without the self.

> *This company is operated by my children and myself.*
> *This company is operated by my children and me.* (Better)
> *I would believe a trusting person like yourself.*
> *I would believe a trusting person like you.* (Better)

Other Pronouns Concerns

WHO / WHOM

You knew you'd have to face it sometime. Probably the most nagging language problem rises from the choice between *who* and *whom*. The news is good: current usage is moving away from the *whom*. Yes, we're dropping it from the language, much like we dropped *thee* and *thou*. Teachers probably won't mind either, since it is difficult to teach.

> ### Who or Whom?
>
> *The old question of who or whom is solved easily by placing in the Quick Pronoun Menu the word **who** in Column A (the DO-er) and **whom** in Column B (the DO-ee). Notice that **whom** contains an m, just like **him** (also in Column B).*

There is, however, a simple guideline that might help those who want to have the grammatical edge — and you're welcome to use it, if you must.

Place *who* in Column A of the Quick Pronoun Menu, and *whom* in Column B (with *him* which also ends in *m*).

To test the choice when faced with the who/whom decision, look at the words that follow. Remove the *who / whom* and replace with either *he / she* (Column A) or *him / her* (Column B), whichever makes sense. If *he / she* would make sense, you'll be correct to use *who* (the Do-er from Column A). If *him / her* makes sense, use *whom* (the do-ee from Column B).

Now that you know the grammatical, use it when writing formally, or when you want to impress "Jeopardy!" watchers that you understand the *who / whom* dilemma.

More often, however, you may opt for clear communication that doesn't sound affected or awkward. A simple solution might be to use *whom* only when preceded by the words *to* or *for*. The rest of the time, use *who*.

> *The school honored the family for whom it is named.*
> *The head of the family, to whom they gave the award, spoke briefly.*

Or (informally):

> *The school honored the family who it is named for.*
> *The head of the family, who they gave the award to, spoke briefly.*

WHO, WHICH, THAT, AND *WHAT*

Here's one more admonition: be attentive about using *who* (in any of its forms) only when referring to people. Save *that* to refer to things, animals, and sometimes people (if referring to people as a type or group). Use *which* when referring to things or animals. *What* refers to an undefined noun.

> The leading actor was the one *who* was chased from the set.
> The director *whose* job was on the line called a halt to filming.
> The bull *that* is looking for trouble turned out to be the chaser.
> It was the red cape *that* irritated the bull; it knew *who* to go after.
> The photographer blurted out *that* the problem *which* arose was the fault of no one.
> The actors all quit, *which* ended the movie for the time being.
> Say *what* you will, it was a bad day.
> Onlookers will say *what* they want about the situation.

DEMONSTRATIVE PRONOUNS

If you can get a handle on *who* and *whom*, you will have no trouble extending the process to reach the right decision about *whoever* (subject) and *whomever* (object).

> *Whoever* is shouting must leave the set.
> You can ask *whomever* you wish to watch the day's shooting.

Related to the *who / whom* controversy, but not half as complex, is the use of *whose*. This word belongs in Column C since *whose* is the possessive form.

> *Whose* name do you want on the credits?
> Please give the script to Penelope, *whose* desk is next to the door.

Warning! Warning! Do not use *whose* when you mean *who's* (who is). There often is a mix-up between *whose* (possessive) and *who's* (the contraction for *who is*). (*Who's the fellow whose left hand twitches during love scenes? Jim's the fellow whose hand twitches.*)

PRONOUN AND VERB COMPATIBILITY

Since you already know that verbs must agree in number with their subjects, and you know that pronouns sometimes are the subjects, here are a few tricks to make sure that verbs agree with pronouns that refer to specific nouns.

One business is... Two businesses are... One company is... Two companies are.... That's easy.

The problem rises when you try to replace singular nouns with pronouns that are plural. A company or a business is often considered as a group of people. The words, however, are singular. When referring to a company or a business, use the pronoun *it*, not *them*. (Yes, *them* sounds cozy and familiar when advertising for customers, but grammatically... no.)

The company holds its annual celebration on Saturday.
The business celebrated 35 years in the same building. It held an open house.

In the same way, be sure to treat proper company names as singular. (*The ABC Company is open for business. The Mainline Brothers is celebrating its centennial. Girl Scouts is a strong nonprofit organization.*) Don't be thrown by the plural-sounding names. The outfit is still one organization.

Similarly, just as collective nouns are generally treated as singular (*group, jury, audience, committee, council*), collective pronouns require the same attention: *The jury reaches its decision; the team plays its last game; the committee sits on its hands; the council ends its meeting.* And, you knew this was coming, there will be times that those collectives will appear as plural to reflect the individual members:

The jury reached their decisions.
The team plays their last game as seniors.
The committee sits on their hands.
The council ends their meeting unanimously.

If you want to be more precise in order to get across the idea of a group functioning as individuals, use a word like *number* or *member*. These words require plural verbs and leave no doubt about your meaning.

Members of the jury deliver their verdict.
A number of the team play their final game.

Note: When using the collective noun *number*, you can indicate the singular by using *the number* and the plural by using *a number*.

The number of members leaving the gang is minimal.
A number of members are leaving the gang.

Is this a wonderfully flexible language or what? You have the option of making a precise point by using specific endings, sometimes just a single letter. You can indicate diversity among members of a group or you can show cooperation with this simple choice.

COMPOUND PRONOUN SUBJECTS

Pronouns follow the same guidelines as nouns when dealing with compounds. If two or more pronouns are connected with *and*, use a plural verb. If they're connected with *or*, follow the guidelines described for nouns.

GENDER PRONOUNS

Look again at the Quick Pronoun Menu. You'll notice that the only place where gender rears its head is in the third person singular. Not first or second, not third person plural — just third person singular. Does that give you a clue in eliminating sexist language from your messages, especially business messages?

Cast your pronouns in the first person (*I, me, my*) or the second person (*you, you, you*), or in third person plural (*they, them*). Choose a clause to replace a descriptive sexist pronoun. Eliminate the pronoun altogether (we over-use these little words).

Stay away from the third person singular pronoun unless you can identify the gender of the replaced noun. You'll find more easy guidelines to avoid sexist language in the section on Unbiased Language. And please, in the name of good usage, avoid the awkward *he / she* or *him / her* or the overuse of the word *person*.

PRONOUNS FOLLOWING *BE*

Totally confusing in this language is the use of the correct pronoun following the verb *to be*. Affected writers try to sound more erudite by using words like "be it useful or not", or "be it here or there". What case is used when a pronoun follows the verb *to be* or any of its forms (*am, are, is, was, were, been, being*)? This is an easy one. Use the pronouns in Column A — the subject form, the Do-er.

> *At the conference, the speakers were Martin and I.*
> *We discovered the thief to be she.*
> *If we had wanted a scapegoat, it could have been he.*
> *The next president of the company will be she.*
> *The most surprised people at the party were he and I.*

While these may sound uncomfortable, there's a simple way to decide if you're using the right case. Reverse the sentence.

> *Martin and I were the speakers at the conference.*
> *She was discovered to be the thief.*
> *If we wanted a scapegoat, he could have been it.*
> *She will be the next president of the company.*
> *He and I were the most surprised people at the party.*

After all, that's what was done with such awkward sentences in the first place; they were put together backwards.

CAREFUL!

A pronoun usually is supposed to refer to a definite noun (person, place or thing). Take care to clearly transmit that connection.

> *The doctor and the patient entered her room.* (Whose room did they enter?)
> *Ms. Goo and her agent, Ms. Adams, met with the director, but after an hour's discussion she couldn't reach a decision.* (Who was undecided? Remember that the director could also be a woman.)

After a session with the bookkeeper, the manager reported he didn't understand the regulation. (Who should be studying the regs?)

Hints for Writers

With pronouns, remember to treat them as you would nouns. They are either subjects (Column A) or objects (Column B), or possessives (Column C). Therefore, the guidelines for verb and number agreement are the same. Not only will this keep you on the grammatical straight-and-narrow, you'll find it easier to say exactly what you mean.

If you want to be clearly understood, be careful about the little two-letter pronoun *it*. Notice how much you use this word. The search keys on the computer will tell you quickly how often you use it. Ask yourself if you are replacing a specific noun in each case, or are you purposely avoiding a noun. Do you know what you're trying to say?

> *It occurred to me.*
> *Some people like it.*
> *It often happens that meetings run long.*
> *It was a cold, dark stormy night.*

Use your word skills to describe or define "it" to provide more information for your readers.

> *The idea that occurred to me was alarming.*
> *Some people like eating out.*
> *What happens when meetings run long? (Or: Meetings run long.)*
> *On a cold, dark stormy night...* (Better yet: *The heavy wind blew mercilessly against the windows, revealing a darkness that chilled as much as it concealed.*)

Another pronoun to avoid over-using without reason is *they*. Always know who you mean when you talk about *they*.

Instead of:

> *They say the earth is cooling off.*
> *After trying the soup, they said it burned their tongues.*
> *On television newscasts they promote their news specials.*

Try something like:

> *Scientists agree the earth is cooling off.*
> *After trying the soup, the customers said it burned their tongues.*
> *Television newscasters promote their news specials.*
> Or: *On television newscasts, networks promote their news* specials.

Love your pronouns. Treat pronouns with respect; don't overuse them.

Quick Pronoun Menu

	Column A Nominative The Do-er	Column B Objective The Do-ee	Column C Possessive The Owner
1st Person (S)	I	me	my, mine
1st Person (P)	we	us	our, ours
2nd Person (S)	you	you	your, yours
2nd Person (P)	you	you	your, yours
3rd Person (S)	he, she, it	him, her, it	his, her/hers, its
3rd Person (P)	they	them	their, theirs

VERBS

(Action and Stop-action Words)

Anarchists thrive in the land of verbs. The reason is clear: anarchists act, and that is exactly what verbs do. However, because verbs, like anarchists, come from all around the world, this is very dangerous territory.

Verbs hold the key to the complex puzzle of U.S. grammar. They carry the purpose of the sentence; they tell what is going on with the things and balance the other parts of speech. Some verbs "do" and some verbs simply "be", hence the temptation to call them Do-Be's.

Over time, pundits have tried to make grammar confusing by labeling (or attempting to label) functions of the parts of speech. What has resulted is a plethora of labels that confuse the heck out of anyone learning the fine points of U.S. language.

> **DO NOT ATTEMPT TO MEMORIZE**
> *these terms. You have been warned!*

Glance at the rest of this paragraph. Here are some fancy names for verbs, if you want to look them up. Define, if you can: *present, past,* and *future tense; regular* and *irregular; transitive* and *intransitive; subjunctive; linking; copula; progressive; preterit; perfect* and *pluperfect; passive; participial; imperative; infinitive; modal auxiliary*; and the ever popular *present progressive.* Whew!

As you progress through this chapter, you'll quickly learn ways to use verbs that are reflected in those confusing words. But know this: it's not the fancy labels that matter; it's their function.
What do verbs do? How can you figure out how to use them? Why are verbs considered important enough to garner all this attention?

The answer to that last question is that verbs provide the anarchy stimulus that dares you to overthrow the traditional "rules" and direct your attention to the uses of verbs in sentences. Nevermind what they're called.

The easiest description of verb activity involves the difference between *Action Verbs* and *Stop-action Verbs*. *Action Verbs* show what things "do"; *Stop-action Verbs* show how things "are" (using forms of the verb "to be").

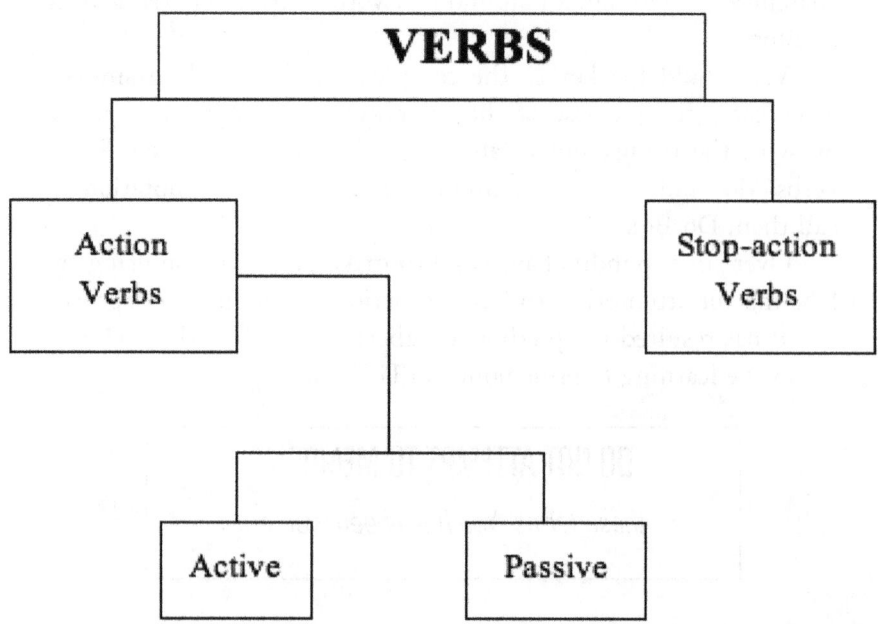

ACTION VS. STOP-ACTION AND ACTIVE VS. PASSIVE

Note the difference between the words "action" and "active". An action verb shows that something is happening and comes in two flavors, *active* and *passive*. An Active verb indicates the subject is doing something:
Subject + Verb = Active:

Cinderella cried.
The step-sisters laughed.

When that action is done *with, to, at,* or *for* (prepositions) something or someone, add an object.
Subject + Verb + Object = Active:

Cinderella cried tears.
The step-sisters laughed at Cindy.

Opposite the active verb is the passive verb, showing the object being done to.
Passive:

Tears were shed.
Cindy was laughed at.

In both instances, *cried* and *laughed* are Action Verbs. In the first example, with *active* verbs, you know who *cried* (Cinderella) and who *laughed* (the stepsisters). In the second example, with *passive* verbs, you know what was done, but not who did it. Until you add the object:

Tears were shed by Cinderella.
Cindy was laughed at by the step-sisters.

STOP-ACTION VERBS

The Stop-action verb simply shows the status quo, the *being*; nothing happens. (With Active verbs, a subject *does*; with Passive, the subject is *done to*!) You could use words like *transitive* and *intransitive* to describe the

Stop-action, but let's not. Hence, the *Do* (action) verbs and the *Be* (stop-action) verbs. With both of the following sentences, you could stop after the verb.

> *The king looked (.) at the bird pie.*
> *The queen ate (.) her bread and honey.*

Any use of the verb "to be" (*am, is, are, was, were, will be*) shows a situation, a status. Other stop-action verbs involve the senses: *feel, seem, appear, look, sound, taste, smell*. It isn't necessary to show what the noun is doing or what the noun senses:

> *The king is very tall.*
> *The elves are very small.*
> *The princess seems irritated.*
> *The prince looked ugly.*
> *The pie tasted delicious.*

The conscientious writer takes a long look at these Stop-action verbs to discover more active ways to describe the situation. During the rewriting phase, the sentences above may be changed like this:

> *The king stands very tall (or over six feet tall).*
> *The elves lack his height (or stand just three feet two).*
> *The princess scowls her irritation.*
> *The prince frowns, his dark eyes glaring.*
> *The pie melts in the mouth.*

Grab the writing reins and throw some punch into your writing. Don't settle for the passive! Or the over-use of Stop-action.

OTHER KINDS OF VERBS

Verbs must **agree in number** with subjects, whether the verb voice is *active* or *passive*. Here is a quick indication of the impact, and hence the importance, of verbs. An overview:

All verbs come with a full suitcase of **tenses**. The primary ones are: *present, past, future,* and *perfect* (there are more). Now add the *simple, progressive,* and *emphatic* (which is easier to recognize than to explain).

Verbs also have **moods** which reflect *indicative, imperative, subjective,* knowledge of which may or may not change your life, but may provide some nuances to your writing.

Verbs are the mainstay of good writing and deserve all the attention they get. You'll find all kinds of suggestions and guidelines in this chapter. To put them to work, see the Sentences Section.

Verbs are the ammunition of a sentence; learning how to handle them well is part of the anarchy of grammar. Yes, whole books have been written about verbs; there is much to know — whether you are a grammar teacher or a grammar masochist. Imagine for a moment, if you can: a present participle subjective intransitive common copulative verb. It might look like this: *The instrument of torture would seem to have been causing intense pain.* Intense pain. Right! But hold tight and you'll be able to untangle that puzzle shortly.

A grammar geek would have a cow at the idea that follows, but verb usage is simplified and made understandable without mention of all those nasty words, like *aoristic, pluperfect, reflexive, intransitive, conjugation, and copulative* — not unless forced.

One of the problems in today's grammar is that each of us learned grammar in different parts of the country, from different teachers, in different schools. The many, many labels applied to verbs are irrelevant (many have similar meanings while others are attached for no good reason except to muddy up the linguistic waters). What follows provides a skeletal picture of verbs and their usage. By knowing this stuff, you'll better understand what you read, you'll control the intent of your own writing, and you could win big prizes on TV game shows. How's that for an anarchist's payoff!

Soon you will call verbs as you see them, doing what they do best at the appropriate time. You can always look up your old grammar purist if you want the fancy words. You probably won't have to, once you see how important verbs are and what they are supposed to do. You already know that important things tend to be simple.

Important? In most languages, the verb is the chief requirement to form a sentence. Something has to happen, even if it is only to exist. That gives us the first clue to verbs. There are two primary kinds of verbs: *Action* (the *do* words — something is happening) and *Stop-action* (the *be* words — inactive, nothing going on, something just *is*).

INFINITIVES

To begin, here's a simple concept. All verbs are put forth (in dictionaries and linguistic discussions) in the *infinitive* form. The basic verb form: *to drive, to think, to be* (or not *to be*). The infinitive is the *to* verb that can behave like a noun. That's it! All of it: *"To be* or *not to be,* that is the question. *To be* and *not to be* are infinitive verbs acting as nouns. In the sentence part that Shakespeare wrote next, "that is the question", the word *that* is a pronoun replacing the verbal nouns *to be* and *not to be.* (Pardon the review of the Things section.) The same applies to any verbs that function as nouns, whether they are the subjects of sentences or objects. (For more about verbals, go back to Things — Nouns — Section.)

To sing well would be a thrill. (Subject)
I've always wanted *to sing* well. (Object)

SPLIT INFINITIVES

Lest you be accused of the crime of splitting infinitives, make sure there is no intervening word, usually a modifier, between the "to" and the "verb". Not that there's anything wrong about that, but if you are writing formally, you'll want to avoid it. If you're using an adverb to modify, put it ahead or behind the entire "to do" verb (as in the word "not" when modifying "to be").

Everyone tries *to put* their best foot forward. (Infinitive)
Everyone tries *to* not *put* their foot in their mouth. (Splitsville!)
Everyone tries *not to put* their foot in their mouth. (Okay)

Space ships have been "known *to sometimes go* where others have not gone before", but the grammar world prefers that they are "known sometimes to go ..." or "are known to go sometimes...." More about infinitive modifiers later in this section.

ACTION VERBS

Action verbs take the infinitive, knock off the "to be" verb, and show movement of the subject with the rest of it: *jump, run, wave, immerse, drive, hear, throb*. These are Do verbs. Consider this sentence and its verbs:

> Tom Sawyer *jumps* the fence, *searches* the woods to *find* the place where two streams *flow* in order to *immerse* his body, hot from *driving* a tractor all day and *listening* to the engine that *throbs*.

Certainly, you can have more than one verb in a sentence. Tom (subject) is doing only two of these verbs (*jumps* and *searches*); the other verbs are part of the clauses that modify the search (*to find* is why he's searching; the streams *flow*; he wants *to immerse* his body, which has been *driving* and *listening* to an engine that *throbs*).

Action verbs show something happening: Tom *jumps* and *searches*. The stop-action verbs show something just being: the streams *flow*; the engine *throbs*. This could have been written in Stop-action: *Tom Sawyer is hot; the stream is there; they seem to belong together*. Nothing happens; they just *are*.

Action verbs (doing) often require both a subject (do-er) and an object (do-ee): Tom Sawyer jumped *the fence*, (he) searched *the woods*; (the boy) immersed *his body*, drove *a tractor*, and heard *the engine*. (The emphasized words are the objects.) Or not! Action verbs written without objects would look like this: Tom jumps *down*, searches *diligently*, drives *all day*. (The emphasized words are not objects, but modifiers which tell something about the verb.) These verbs do not require objects; they speak the action for themselves. And that is powerful writing.

ACTION VERBS CAN BE ACTIVE OR PASSIVE

Active and *passive* are the voices of the verb. That's all Teacher was talking about when mentioning *voices* of verbs. The verb speaks either loudly or softly by this choice. Both Action and Stop-action verbs can be either active or passive.

> Mama Turtle *raises* her voice to call her babies. (Action / Active)

The voice of Mama Turtle is *raised* to call her babies. (Action / Passive)
The babies *hear* the voice of their mother. (Stop-action / Active)
The voice of the turtle *is heard* in the land. (Stop-action / Passive)

The active voice makes the subject of the sentence the do-er. The passive voice makes the subject the do-ee. It's that simple. When you want a strong, direct sentence, use the active verb and tell who or what is doing it. When you want to avoid the responsibility for who-dun-it, use the passive.

The emperor opened the meeting. (Active — tells who did it.)
The meeting was opened by the emperor. (Passive — turns the object *meeting* into a subject and the subject *emperor* into the object.)
The meeting was opened. (Even more passive — avoids telling who did the opening.)

PASSIVE: GOOD OR BAD?

Some people thrive on direct confrontation and seldom slip into the passive. Some people use the passive all the time and find difficulty in writing a direct sentence. What does that tell you?

Don't misunderstand: passive is not bad. There are times when you won't want to identify the do-er, purposefully, and out of leniency.

A car is parked in my parking space. (Passive)
Some jerk parked a car in my parking space. (Active, in fact, aggressive!)

STOP-ACTION VERBS

Grammarians offer a variety of names for stop-action verbs: *linking, intransitive, copulative, attribute complement*. They all mean about the same thing. Instead of *doing*, these verbs just *are*. These are the *be* verbs.

> **Lazy Stop-action**
>
> Stop-action (or linking) verbs usually refer to the senses or the state of being. They don't do anything.

The most common name for Stop-action verbs is *linking*, and most linking verbs are related to forms of the verb *to be: am, is, are, was, were, being, been*. Think of these verbs as linking together the subject and the predicate. They don't do anything to the predicate, except to link it.

> The Big Bad Wolf *looks* angry.
> Granny doesn't *hear* well.
> Wolf *smells*. (It needs a bath.) (linking)
> Little Red *seems* distracted.

You may not recognize many of the following as linking verbs. They relate to the status or to the senses: *appear, seem, look, smell, feel, taste, listen, sound, tend, grow, become, state, end* — all linking verbs.

Some of the sense-ible words can also be Action verbs when you add an object. Change those same Stop-action verbs into Action verbs to notice the difference.

> The Big Bad Wolf looks *at the lone cottage in the woods.*
> Granny doesn't hear *the wolf at her door.*
> Wolf smells *dinner inside the cottage.*
> Little Red seems *to wander about the woods too much.*

Notice the objects of the verb in these sentences — thus changing them into Action verbs. Something is happening. A Stop-action verb *requires* no object. Simple guideline: Look at the words following the verb. Do they modify the verb (tell more about it) or do they just relate, describe, or replace, the subject?

VERB MODIFIERS (ADVERBS)

The word or words describing a Stop-action verb are called *adverbs*. (The *ly* usually gives them away.)

>The pounding ended *quickly*.
>Granny listened *intently*.
>The wolf *finally* cooperated. (Look! The *ly* adverb preceded the verb. Can it do that? Yes!)
>Little Red rose up *defiantly* and cheered *loudly*. (Two verbs! How about that! *Defiantly* shows how the little girl *rose up*, and *loudly* describes the way she *cheered*.)

SUBJECT DESCRIPTION (ADJECTIVE)

Don't make this difficult by using the technical term (appositive), unless you want to show off. An *appositive* is an adjective that links the subject with a Stop-action (or linking) verb. *Sam* (subject) *seems* (verb) *happy* (appositive — or adjective describing Sam — happy Sam).

>The doctors are *tired*. (Stop-action; *tired* describes the *doctors*)
>The patients were *cured*. (Stop-action; *cured* describes the *patients*)
>The interns are Mary Dawn, David James, Richard Harris, and Margy Gale. (All these people modify the interns, thus clarifying the subject. Think of it as making an ap-positive identification).

SUBJECT EXCHANGE

True linking verbs are Stop-action verbs that are interchangeable with the subject. Picture the linking verbs as an equal sign in a mathematical equation. Because they link what comes before and after the verb, the sentences usually are reversible, equal.

> *Tired* are the *doctors*. (Tired = doctors)
> *Cured* are the *patients*. (Cured = patients)
> *The interns*, Mary Dawn, David James, Richard Harris, and Margy Gale, are the *doctors*. (Interns = doctors)

Knowing the proper pronoun to use comes in handy in choosing the appropriate modifiers and appositives. When in doubt, check your dictionary and look for the verb's identification. Following the verb, you will find either v.t. (meaning *verb transitive*, or Action) or v.i. (*verb intransitive*, or Stop-action).

> Eleanor *decided*. (no object required)
> Eleanor *decided* immediately. (still no object required; *immediately* is the adverb that modifies *decided*)
> Eleanor *was* decisive. (an appositive that positively tells who or what Eleanor is)
> Eleanor *is* beautiful. (an appositive that describes her perfectly)
> Eleanor *decided* the issue. (Action verb with an object, *the issue*)

The first four sentences are Stop-action; the last is Action.

SOMETHING *IS* OR IT *IS*!

The little verb *is* (or any form of the verb *to be*) raises two options. In many languages other than English, two different words are used to distinguish between the two separate meanings. US-ers make do with just one — *to be*, which usually takes the form *is*, but also includes *am, are, was, were, be, been*.

The distinction has to do with forever. In one of those other languages, the speaker must first decide whether something is forever, or just a passing fancy, temporary. Then the appropriate verb can be chosen. In U.S. language, the *is* just *is*.

> *Clara is a typist.* (for today or for this year, but not forever)
> *Clara is a woman.* (for today and forever, one hopes these days)
> *She is happy.* (back to now, the moment, a temporary condition)

Even though the distinction between the two forms is not made in U.S. grammar, it helps to be aware of differences. Also notice the use and overuse of the verb *to be*. It's the easy way to write quickly. One writer, a psychiatrist, managed to write a complete book on the subject without using the verb (*to be*). The author avoided labeling the subject for all time with the *forever* meaning, and also avoided making judgments with the temporary meaning. Is the patient distressed at the moment or forever? Or psychotic? Or misguided? Or depressed? Apparently, the shrink's theory refused to lay the forever trip on the patient when the condition could be temporary and alleviated.

Check your *is*es (the plural of *is*) from time to time to see if you're overusing the word in one context or another. But please don't worry about this overuse in the first draft. Do the checking during the re-writes. Straining to avoid "is" during the creative process may result in permanent damage to your novel.

Here's another warning: when using the past tense — describing a trip, for instance — be careful about putting the temporary meaning in the past tense.

Vienna *was* beautiful in winter. (Perhaps you were there in winter and Vienna seemed beautiful to you, but Vienna *is* beautiful every winter, whether or not you're there.)

The Grand Canyon *was* more than a mile deep. (It still *is*!)

VERBS THAT DON'T START THAT WAY

Here is a sentence to contemplate:

Using a stronger action verb than is will power up your writing.

In this sentence, the verb becomes *will power up*. The first seven words form the noun / subject / thing. Perhaps a better verb would be *empower*. In today's language, thanks to the computer industry and its technical terminology, one might be tempted to concoct a verb such as *uppower*.

Golly, this is a touchy subject. Teacher would faint at concocted verbs in common usage today: *upload, onload, offload, onturn, input, throughput, oversend, outgo, intake,* even *upchuck*. But listen to the speaking and writing world; these words are becoming more and more common as verbs — weird but common.

Segments of the business world (and other technical language units, such as the military and the medical worlds) love to coin words. While many of them can be shaped into many forms, one faulty conclusion is that any word can be similarly reshaped. This is a long way to explain how *prioritize* came into being. While the anarchist hates that word, it's a verb that grew out of a noun and now is included in most dictionaries.

> Managers need to *set priorities* for their work on Monday mornings.
> Managers need to *prioritize* their work on Monday mornings.

A couple other business verbs have been created from their noun sources. Office staffs now use *growing* as a verb to indicate the process of business development, or use *sourcing* as a verb to indicate the process of searching for a source. In addition, the verb *outsourcing* has become part of the language. Military, police, and medical people seem to have started this trend with their need for speed. Why ask for a committee meeting when you can ask for a *com-meet*? Why ask for a toxicology screen report when you can ask for a *tox-screen*, or a chart for dosage when you can ask for *dosing*? Or ask for an image reproduction when you can ask for *imaging*? Imaging on an electronic instrument has been reduced even further, to *IMing*.

Other noun-made-verb words that are part of U.S. usage are *mirandize*, *blindside*, and *gaslight*. Yes! These are fairly understandable verbs. *Mirandize* means "to read the Miranda Act apprising criminals of their rights"; *blindside* means "to hit someone unexpectedly on their blind side"; *gaslight* means "to play with someone's head", as Charles Boyer did with Ingrid Bergman in the psycho-drama "Gaslight".

> The officer *mirandized* the car thief.
> The thief tried to *blindside* the jewelry store clerk.
> She claimed he had *gaslighted* her by expressing interest in her appearance.

Perhaps the best advice is to use words of this nature as you would technical language — carefully and appropriately. If you know that your audience will understand what you're saying, go ahead. [Do you actually remember Boyer and Bergman?]

SUBJECT-VERB AGREEMENT (THE *S* RATION)

In a sentence, the subject and verb must agree in number. That's the only way the reader can be sure of who's doing what.

If one person or thing is the do-er, then the verb must reflect the singular state. The same goes for plurals. The hint (in the Things Section) about rationing the use of *s* applies equally to verbs. Subjects and verbs need to agree in number, and checking on this during the editing, rewriting process, need not be difficult.

You may want to review *s*-rationing? Imagine there is a shortage of the letter *s*. You may use only one *s* in the subject-verb twosome. If you use it on the subject, leave it out of the verb, and vice versa.

> The proposal state<u>s</u> the purpose clearly
> The proposal<u>s</u> state the purpose clearly.

It's a simple test that won't apply all the time, but it applies more often than you may have noticed, with some very unlikely verbs.

> The *rings match* your dress beautifully.
> The *ring matches* your dress beautifully.
> The *chairs are* out of place.
> The *chair is* out of place.
> The *coffee machine was* working yesterday.
> The *coffee machines were* working yesterday.
> Whenever the *boss goes* out of town, *they* play. (Note the plural "they". You know who is playing!)
> Whenever the bosses go out of town, he plays. (You can deduce who is playing here as well!)

DOUBLE VERBING

Double verbing is the tendency to use two or three verbs to say what you want. You may try to imagine, instead of imagine; or you may make a decision rather than decide. Double verbing uses too many verbs. Save our sentences! Cut down on verb usage!

Today I thought I would sit down and begin to start to write to tell you the decisions I have *made*. (Look at all those verbs: seven! Count them!)

Try instead: *I'm writing to give you my decision.*

The reason I *want* to *tell* you what I *have decided are* many. (Too much!) *I have many reasons for telling you my decision.*

If you want to become identified with good clean writing, take a look at the number of verbs you use in a single sentence. Are you putting a strain on the verb pool? Are you using more than you need? Why is *making a promise* easier to write than *promising*? Be concerned about future global verb shortages!

Over-verbing	Better
Set up a schedule	schedule
Start to print	print
Begin to think	think
Organize a plan	organize (or plan)
Try an experiment	try (or experiment)
Risk a change	risk (or change)

Over-writing with double verbs is one reason for long-winded reports. Double verbing indicates a lack of clarity, indecision. Don't fall into this trap.

WIMPY VERBING

Another trap to avoid is using wimpy verbs. While you have a rich language with more than a million words, the public sticks to using only a couple thousand of them. This means two things: you are not very creative with your language, and you apply multiple meanings to a few words. Some U.S. English words carry as many as 100 or more meanings.

Consider the multiple meanings of the following verbs: *get, take, put, make, do, have, go, come,* and the ever-popular *be.* Look them up in the dictionary. Some of these words require pages to define (depending on the size of your dictionary). When a word carries so many meanings, it is difficult for the reader to know which one the writer has chosen.

The cure? Simple. Find exactly the meaning you wish, and find a better verb that carries your meaning. A good thesaurus provides enough alternatives for a lifetime. Make sure you have an updated copy of your own. Here are some suggestions:

Put: *place, drop, select, plunk down, prop up, file, locate, stick, lower...*
Take: *secure, acquire, grab, pull, receive, accept, steal, apprehend...*

VERB TENSE

The simple tenses for verbs are *present*, *past*, and *future*. Getting a handle on just these three will provide a fair amount of control over verbs.

But there are more tenses that will fine-tune the timing of verbs — when something happens. Some of these tenses (and no, you won't be thrown a mess of them) include *progressive, emphatic*, and *auxiliary* verbs. Some of these labels are enough to drive a non-linguistics professor to drink (and probably a few of them too).

Verbs tell not only *what* happened, but *when*. The word tense refers to the *when*. It's the *when* that is under scrutiny now. You have three choices in time: *past, present, and future*. To achieve this difficult feat, enter the contest with a clear head, keen eye, sense of humor, and sometimes engage the assistance of auxiliary verbs (such as *have, be, can, will*).

In some Eastern languages, there is just one verb. To make it past tense, words are added to indicate when it happened; to make it future, other words are added to indicate when it will happen. Don't you wish you spoke Chinese?

Verb: to wave. *I wave yesterday; I wave today; I wave tomorrow*. Simple enough.

Some Native American tribes had a better idea. They used the verb they wanted and pointed over their shoulder for past tense, to the ground for present, and to the horizon for future.

PRESENT TENSE
Here in the good ole U.S. of A., the present tense shows something happening at this time. The tense can take the form of *simple, ongoing*, or *emphatic*.

Don't panic! We're not going to get into complicated labels. This will be as painless as possible. But because verbs are the meat of the language discussion and may be all that you carried away from grade school grammar, forge ahead. The *simple, ongoing*, and *emphatic* indicate varying degrees of the present tense.

Simple: *I shout.*
Progressive: *I am shouting* (ongoing action).
Emphatic: *I do shout* (you bet your life I do!).

By adding auxiliary verbs, you can form the perfect or complete tense.

I have shouted. (And now I'm finished.)
I have been shouting. (That's why my throat hurts.)

Stick with it, there's a bit more. The following sentences are simple, present tense sentences.

You do your best.
She catches your cold.
He takes two hours for lunch.

PAST TENSE

The simple past indicates action that happened before the present time and may be formed by either regular or irregular verbs. The way to show the past tense of regular verbs is to add *ed* (*Mom cooked dinner; Dad fixed the door; I played for hours.*) You should have no trouble with simple past tense.

However, those danged irregular verbs can mess up the guidelines. Simply put, there aren't any guidelines. Good anarchists make up their own! The irregulars have to be remembered (more about them later). For now, look at the past tense of a few irregular verbs: *do, catch, take*. The past tense: *did, caught, took.*)

You did your best.
She caught your cold.
He took two hours for lunch.

Past complete requires an auxiliary verb (*had, had been*). This tense indicates an action that occurred before a past time or prior to another past action. The implication may be in the verb or it may be spelled out.

> *You had done your best. You had done your best, but she did better.*
> *She had caught your cold. She had caught your cold before you kissed her.*
> *He had taken two hours for lunch. He had taken two hours for lunch before anyone noticed.*

FUTURE TENSE

The future tense is the easy one. It is formed by adding the auxiliary *will* to the present tense.

> *You will do your best.*
> *She will catch your cold.*
> *He will take two hours for lunch.*

The future complete tense uses the auxiliaries *will have* and *will have been* to indicate an action completed by a specified future moment or prior to another future action.

> *You will have done your best* (by completing the training program).
> *She will have caught your cold* (after another long kiss).
> *He will have taken two hours for lunch* (if he's not back in another half hour).

PROGRESSIVE TENSE

The progressive tense indicates action that is ongoing, progressing nicely, thank you. It is formed by adding the corresponding time tense of the auxiliary verb *to be*.

Present progressive:	*You are doing your best.*
Past progressive:	*She was catching your cold.*
Future progressive:	*He will be taking two hours for lunch.*

Sometimes called *present ongoing*, this form is a *participle* (a scary word that will be dealt with a bit later). Sometimes the way to recognize this verb is the use of *ing* or *en* with an auxiliary verb in front.

> *You are doing your best.*
> *She is catching your cold.*
> *He has taken two hours for lunch.*

COMPLETE (PERFECT) TENSE

To make a verb action *complete* (some call it *perfect*), use the present tense with one of the auxiliary verbs *has, has been, have, have been*. This tense shows that something has been completed, that some action begun in the past may continue into the future, and that past actions may happen again.

> *You have been doing your best. You have done your best.*
> *She has been catching your cold for the past few days. She has caught your cold and will suffer for weeks.*
> *He has taken two hours for lunch since he started to work here. He has been taking two hours for lunch and doesn't think a thing of it.*

INFINITIVE MODIFIERS

An infinitive is the basic form of a verb, used with the word *to* (*to do, to have, to wave, to catch, to take*). When using auxiliary verbs or two-part verbs, the natural inclination is to toss a modifier (adverb) in the middle. Go ahead. Dare the language forces to come down on you! Sometimes the modifier works better in the middle of the infinitive.

> *He wants to always choose the restaurant.*
> *We chose to quietly take turns.*

Just make sure the modifier is actually where you want it. Many feel the adverb should be placed before or after the entire verb.

> He always wants *to choose* the restaurant.
> We quietly chose *to take* turns.

Watch out when using infinitives; they can be awkward with that tendency to split.

> *She wanted not to ever see him again.* (Awkward)
> *She wanted not ever to see him again.* (Better)

In general, try to keep the verbs together, especially when too many intervening words could mess up the sentence. Those modifiers need to be placed as close as possible to the words they modify.

She too could have gone.
She could too have gone.
She could have gone too.

He wants to loudly proclaim his love.
He wants loudly to proclaim his love.
He wants to proclaim loudly his love.
He wants to proclaim his love loudly.

The verbs are *could have gone* and *to proclaim*. Notice how the meanings change when a verb is split up (*split up* is the entire verb!). To sometimes split a verb is not as bad as to often or with many words and clauses in the intervening space like this split an infinitive.

Enough said.

REGULAR AND IRREGULAR VERBS

Remember the long lists of verbs that you had to memorize in school?

Irregulars are the verbs that don't follow the simple way to make verbs past tense (*ed*) or past participle (*ing* or *ed*). You could call them anarchist verbs. There is neither rhyme nor reason for the variance, just a list of renegades to be memorized. The alternative is to carry around a dictionary that identifies these three verb parts in front of the definition.

School kids giggle at *drink-drank-drunk*. And they've never been sure about *swim, swam, swum*. The list may look something like the following — although Teacher may have produced a much longer one.

Present	*Past*	*Past Participle*
catch	caught	caught
do	did	done
drive	drove	driven
go	went	gone
lead	led	led
ride	rode	ridden
swim	swam	swum
take	took	taken
give	gave	given

What you notice is that none of the past tense verbs end in *ed*. That's because none of these anarchists are *regular* verbs that know how to follow "rules". *Regular* verbs form the past tense with *ed*; *irregular* verbs don't.

Verbs that show up on the irregular verbs list have to be memorized, verb for verb, or looked up in the dictionary every time you use one of them. Sorry, irregulars don't conform to guidelines.

One more hint: words in that third column of past participles need auxiliary verbs — some form of *to have* or *to be*.

> *I catch a cold today. I caught a cold yesterday. I have caught many colds in the last year.* (I must see a doctor!)
> *I go to the doctor. I went to the doctor. I have gone to the doctor.* (Now I'm better.)
> *I swim at the community pool. I swam at that pool during the past year. I have swum there so much I caught a cold.* (Got it?)

DO-BE MOODS

Verbs come not only in tenses and voices, but they have *moods*. These correspond to the way you feel, similar to the emotional emphasis you use when you speak. Generally, the three recognizable moods are: Plain, Demanding, and the Fairy Tale Syndrome.

PLAIN MOOD

Teachers might call it the "indicative mood", but you can ignore that and call it a plain old "mood". This is the usual mood used for a normal kind of sentence, even though Teacher loves to call it *indicative* (it indicates... what?).

> *The radio personality injects humor into each program.*
> *Humor offers listeners the light touch to serious subjects.*

DEMANDING MOOD

The demanding mood is the one to use when giving orders. (Teachers often call it the *imperative* because it makes them feel in charge.) People giving orders remove the personal aspect by eliminating the subject (usually "you"). To make it even more imperative, add an exclamation mark.

> *Put some humor into your presentation!*
> *Lighten up!*
> *Do it now!*
> *Please see me in my office after class.*

THE FAIRY TALE SYNDROME

Okay, this one is made up. Teachers call it by a most formidable word — *subjunctive* — meaning "lacking in reality". What it refers to could realistically be called "The Fairy Tale Syndrome", and it uses a form of "to be" (usually *was* or *were*) to indicate whether the statement is *what-if* or *make-believe*. The *what-if* indicates there is a possibility of the statement being real; the *make-believe*, however, removes any doubt about something actually happening. The *make-believe* is utterly impossible.

> What-if: *If I was to walk to the mall...* (it could happen).
> Make-believe: *If I were to walk to the moon...* (not possible, yet).

The old *subjunctive* mood is disappearing as language morphs into simpler usage. Current business usage recognizes the difference between "was" and "were" only as a wish mode — a fairy tale.

> *If he were a woman, he'd never get the job.* (He can't be a woman, at least not grammatically.)
> *If they were here now, the trustees would agree.* (They aren't here.)

What makes this worthy of discussion is the use of *were* in what amounts to the present tense. The present tense is usually *is* or *are*. Using the present tense may alter the entire meaning of the sentence.

> *If he is a woman, no one would ever know.* (He might be covering up something.)
> *If they are here now, the trustees can take a vote.* (They have just arrived.)

Both of the above sentences don't imply the absence of fact. But look what happens when the actual past tense is used: *If they were here yesterday...* a whole new ball game. To indicate the past tense in the Fairy Tale mood, throw in the auxiliary verbs (*would have been*). *If they would have been here yesterday, the trustees could have taken a vote.* (But they weren't, were they? You can't do-over yesterday.)

> **Fairy Tale Syndrome**
>
> *When something you're saying is doubtful, use "was" to indicate that it's a possibility, and "were" if there isn't a chance in hell.*

Another use of the FTS is the future tense, something that you are hoping, suggesting, requesting, or demanding to happen. This requires the use of the verb "be".

I will recommend that person be given a cushy job.
The trustees obeyed the request that everyone be on time.
Perhaps this will be their lucky decision.
They demand the troublemaker be removed from the company.

While the above sentences are appropriate, that verb "to be" gets overworked in business. If is often used when a simple-tense verb would do.

If that person be *expecting the job, there is trouble.* (ugh!)
If that person is expecting the job, there is trouble. (better)

Whether the trustees *be* challenging tradition or not, they enjoy the power. (uh-uh)
Whether the trustees *are* challenging tradition or not, they enjoy the power. (better)

SHALL OR *WILL*

There was a time, back in the days of "thee" and "thou", when the distinction between the words "shall" and "will" were clearly drawn, driving most school children wild.

Today you can relax. The shadowy nuances have been dropped in all but the distinctly legal and legal-like forms of usage. Use *will* to your heart's content, and leave *shall* to walk softly into the night.

Once in a while, when you get serious and want to startle someone into complying with your request, toss in the *shall*... and duck. This serves as a warning or admonition that you mean business.

There shall be no smoking in this office.
All smokers shall use the back door when leaving to have a cigaret.

The ironic part of this guideline is that the message probably would get across without the "shall". When the message comes from the top or is delivered in a terse memo in a plain brown envelope, it tends to be taken seriously.

There will be no smoking in this office.
All smokers will use the back door when leaving to have a cigaret.

Treat your verbs as you treat your friends, with respect and care. These are the workhorses of writing, the movers and shakers, the words that make things happen and show what things are like.

To understand the power of verbs on things, look again at the Nouns and Pronouns Section, then trim both Things and Verbs with the Bling of the following section.

MODIFIERS (Bling)

(Adjectives, Adverbs, Clauses, Phrases)

Modifiers are the bling that dress up grammar, the enhancing words that come in a variety of forms — single words, phrases, and clauses, all of which are reviewed in this section. Any anarchist worth their mettle would know that too much bling calls attention to the activity and its purpose. Too much bling in a sentence obscures the meaning of the sentence with its preponderance.

Did you know that infinitives (usually connected with verbs) can also serve as modifiers? As can participles, those dreaded things that nobody has defined for you (until now).

As helpful as modifiers are in clarifying and enhancing written work, anarchists warn against depending on grammatical bling too much. You won't find many anarchists wearing more than three pieces of gold jewelry; nor do they use more than three pieces of grammatical bling. Just saying!

Adjectives modify Things, the nouns and pronouns. Like bling, Adjectives dress up or dress down the things that are being discussed. If you're looking at a bird, you may want to know whether it is a *predator* bird or a *song* bird. *Predator* and *song* are Adjectives, providing the bling for noun, "bird", definitely a Thing.

The main job of Adverbs is to modify verbs, the Do-Be's. Were you looking *longingly* at the bird? And did you look *often*? *Longingly* and *often* are adverbs that describe the Do-verb (*look*).

Hold on! Adverbs also modify adjectives, and other adverbs. Betcha didn't remember that. That bird may have been a *dark* blue, or it sang an *exceedingly* sad song. *Dark* and *exceedingly* are both adverbs. Also, you may have looked *very* longingly or *too* often. *Very* and *too* also are Adverbs. These modifiers add clues about the why, how, and how much of Things.

Both Adjectives and Adverbs enhance writing, much like bling dresses up or down. When overdone, however, Adjectives and Adverbs detract from writing as much as overdone bling does to personal appearance. Too much bling can scuttle a sentence. Too little can dull it down.

In this section, you'll discover the impact of specific vs. non-specific Adjectives. And you'll chuckle at the misplaced Adjectives that twist the meaning of an otherwise perfectly good sentence. Did you see the "lady with the horse's hat?" or "the lady's hat with the horse?" (Always put the modifier close to the modified word.)

Did you realize that the Articles *a, an,* and *the* are types of adjectives? Special attention is given to words such as *only, almost,* and *all,* while clearing up the usage of *almost* or *nearly? continual* or *continuous? likely, liable,* or *apt? a lot* or *lots?* And whatever could be wrong with a nice modifier like *nice?*

Here are guidelines to assist with the maddening comparative bling. Is it *fun, funner, funnest*? Under discussion will be the Adverbs as they are associated with those Stop-action verbs. Did the squirrel smell *bad* (adjective) or did it smell *badly* (adverb)?

Most adverbs are easily identified by the *ly* at the end (*excitedly, slowly, quickly*). Some adverbs are confused with similar adjectives (*bad, badly; good, well*). Different problems arise, however, with adverbs such as *scarcely, hardly, barely, sure, smooth, very,* and the ever-popular *really*. The misuse of *hopefully* is vigorously attacked.

The differences between phrases and clauses — and their functions — are included in this section. You may already know that a bling phrase is a group of words that modify a Thing (noun), often in the form of a prepositional phrase. What sets off a clause as a distinctive kind of bling is the presence of a verb in one form or another. *She spotted the red sports car on the side of the road.* (Phrase. The car was seen *on the side of the road.*) *She spotted the red sports car sitting on the side of the road.* (Clause. The car was *sitting on the side of the road.*) But look at what happens when the sentence begins with the clause: *Sitting on the side of the road, she spotted the red sports car.* Now we know where *she was* when she spotted the red sports car. Pay attention, and you'll never again misplace another modifying clause or phrase.

ADJECTIVES

Let's start with the easy ones — Adjectives. Adjectives modify Things — nouns and pronouns — and may show up as a single word. Adjectives may assume the form of a phrase or clause. Adjectives show you how pretty or how ugly a creature may be, how that creature appears, what color are the eyes, what shape is the nose. Adjectives also provide the length of a report, the importance of an omen, the value or lack of worth of a rock. Adjectives work both ways, adding to beauty or detracting from it — just as bling can enhance appearance or detract from it.

Adjectives (words, phrases, clauses) modify (describe, limit or restrict) Things (nouns and pronouns). They generally answer the questions: what kind? how many? which one? They paint pictures with descriptive words that give writing greater depth and meaning.

The strongest, ugliest, weakest words are adjectives. They're the words that dress up (or down) the nouns. Look into her *clear, blue* eyes. Run your *eager* fingers through his *curly brown* hair. You can use adjectives sparingly, one or two at a time, or you can use whole strings of them. *The gentle, straightforward, whispered, resonant* voice had its *lethargic, somnolent* effect on the *disorderly, confused, riotous, deranged* crowd. (Even an anarchist would consider this too much!)

When using more than one adjective, you may want to place commas between adjectives that express the same trait (*lethargic, somnolent*). But notice the difference between *clear, blue eyes* and *clear blue eyes*. In the first, the eyes were both *clear* and *blue* (two different traits) as shown by the comma. In the second, *clear* modifies the shade of *blue* and thus becomes an adverb, without a comma. More later about how adverbs modify adjectives.

Generally, adjectives are found in front of nouns. But when you want to emphasize the bling, place it after the noun.

The gentle and resonant voice calmed the disorderly and riotous crowd.
The voice, gentle and resonant, calmed the crowd, disorderly and riotous.

Another place to look for adjectives is following a Stop-action (linking) verb, especially that little *is* word. *Monica is tall; Monica is happy; Monica is wild and crazy.* Yup! *Tall, happy, wild and crazy Monica.* That pretty well describes her. To mollify the label seekers, adjectives used in this way are called *subject complements*. They complement (describe) the subject.

Adjectives bring you closer to people through your words, help you notice and feel more of what you're talking about. For instance, you have a *briefcase, hair,* and a *jacket*. Add an adjective, say *red*, to each and you have a *red briefcase, red hair,* and a *red jacket*. Now the things become visible (as do you with your anarchistic tendency towards red). There is more to notice.

To move even closer, form the adjectives into judgments. Try inserting one of these adjectives: *gorgeous, large, baggy, sleazy, sexy*. Get the idea? Now you're getting personal!

Advertising copywriters, business executives and sales people use adjectives to sell products and services. Some use them to describe accurately; others overuse them; still others abuse them. Notice how skillfully adjectives shape ideas, opinions, even appetites. What appeals to you more: *a piece of pie* or *a scrumptious, lemony, tart, and creamy lemon pie*? For a lesson on adjectives, read the menu in a good restaurant.

Notice how certain adjectives appear all over the place, especially in advertising, as if on cue: *lite, new, recycled, free, low-calorie, low-fat, green, discounted, luxury.*

POSSESSIVE ADJECTIVES

Notice how possessive the world around you has become: *my* house, *my* car, *my* cell phone, *my* country, *my* office, *my* favorites — as if it were possible not only to claim all these things, but to actually own them. The same applies to others: *her* desk, *their* office, *his* golf clubs, *her* book club. These are called *possessive adjectives* and combine the elements of Column C of the Quick Pronoun Menu. They are pronouns which act as modifiers.

Nouns can be used as possessive adjectives. *The family's house, David's car, Georgia's cell phone, an American's country, the lawyer's office, Mom's favorites*. All these people — the family, David, Georgia, an American, even the lawyer and Mom — have become adjectives. The same applies to other things: *the car's owner, the team's record, the house's color*. Try to stay away from inanimate things owning other inanimate things. Better to change the previous possession to *the owner of the car, the record of the team, the color of the house.*

> ### Who Owns What?
> *Generally, people own things, rather than things own things. But who owns people?*

Consider actual ownership when using the possessive adjectives. Also consider which is more important, the ownership or the owner. Then read it aloud and listen to the sounds of the words. Generally, people own things, rather than things own things.

A philosophical note: choose very carefully when referring to your relatives. Is she honestly "your" wife? Is he actually "your" husband? Are they "your" children? Can one person "possess" another? There are times when words of this kind discriminate. Use them carefully.

LOCATION, LOCATION, LOCATION

The location of the adjective can shift meaning in a sentence. Consider:

Only she had time for me.
She had time for only me.

The insults came from the angry stranger.
The angry insults came from the stranger.

After long hours of waiting, he arrived.
After hours of long waiting, he arrived.

When reviewing a piece of writing, go over it with the express purpose of checking the location of the bling. A misplaced modifier discombobulates an entire idea. It causes havoc in some cases, especially the phrases and clauses.

The man entered the office only claiming to be the patient of Dr. Rogers who was sexually dysfunctional. (Who had the problem?)

The doctor explained to the nurse that she had taken a long lunch and needed to apologize. (Who was about to say "I'm sorry"?)

COMPARATIVE ADJECTIVES

*"GOOD, BETTER, BEST,
NEVER LET IT REST
UNTIL THE GOOD IS BETTER
AND THE BETTER BEST."*

Adjectives make the greatest words for comparisons. Ordinarily, a simple "er" is added to an adjective to produce a *comparative* (of one thing to another).

> ### Short vs. Long Bling
> *Most short adjectives (and adverbs) are compared easily by adding "er" or "est". However, the longer ones work better with a booster (the more elegant, rather than eleganter; the most elegant — rather than elegantest).*

This is better than that.
She is richer than her friend.
The meeting was longer than the faces in the room.

An "est" added to an adjective produces the *superlative* (comparisons of three or more things).

This is the best way to do it.
He had the poorest grades in his class.
The meeting was the longest in memory.

Then some prof threw in a qualifying "rule": the simple "er" and "est" work with short adjectives. With long adjectives, it is necessary to toss in the words *more, most, less, least*. But, that somebody didn't say *how* short or *how* long. An anarchist's decision.

For the most part, the simple "er/est" guideline can be followed. But tread carefully.

Base adjective	*Comparative*	*Superlative*
pretty	prettier	prettiest
sorry	sorrier	sorriest
long	longer	longest
capable	more capable	most capable
detrimental	more detrimental	most detrimental
exhausted	more exhausted	most exhausted

A few adjectives qualify as irregulars:

good	better	best
bad	worse	worst
much	more	most
less	lesser	least

EVEN

Even if you never even write another word for even a brief time, you even have to know that you'll probably never even regret it.

Even is one of those troublesome adjectives that can change the meaning of a sentence by its placement. Re-write that opening sentence without the "evens" and discover a more powerful sentence hiding behind.

If you never write another word for a brief time, you have to know that you'll probably never regret it.

Take great care to place this and every modifier next to the thing it modifies. Sometimes, you'll discover that certain bling can be left out without spoiling the meaning, and often enhancing it. (Put on the earrings, locket, and bracelet, then remove one. Good advice.)

The adjective "even" has several meanings: *flat, smooth, tranquil, uniform, equal in degree*. As an adverb, *even* means: *to a higher degree, at the same time, in spite of, in fact.* All of which points to the need to find the more specific word to express your meaning.

Using these definitions, notice how *even* modifies the meanings of the following sentences:

> Adjective: *Even the quarterback insisted that the linebackers practice more.*
> Adverb: *The quarterback even insisted that the linebackers practice more.*
> Adjective: *The quarterback insisted that even the linebackers practice more.*
> Adverb: *The quarterback insisted that the linebackers practice even more.*

Now take out "even" altogether and rearrange:

> *The quarterback insisted that the linebackers practice more.*

Place your grammar bling as carefully as you do your personal bling. Wearing a bracelet in your ear would change your image completely.

QUANTITY / NUMBERS

Adjectives that indicate quantity or number include: *this, that, those,* and *these.* Note they are pronouns from Column A in the Quick Pronoun Menu and serve as adjectives when modifying specific nouns or other pronouns: *this computer, that decision, those idiots, these words.*

Beware of sneaky nouns that have questionable states of singleness. Use *this sort* or *that type,* and *these sorts, those types* (matching plural pronoun adjectives with plural nouns). *Also this company / these companies; that team / those teams.* And please, oh please, don't snatch from Column B and choose one of *them* as an adjective.

Do NOT ever ever ever choose *them* (Column B) pronouns. Ugh!

Some more words that can be either adjectives (when they modify other words) or pronouns (when they stand alone): *few, many, some, all, any.*

> *Few children love spinach.* (Adjective)
> *Few eat three meals a day.* (Pronoun)
> *Many adults choose to read* Harry Potter. (Adjective)
> *Many prefer* Wuthering Heights. (Pronoun)
> *Any one of the chorus could have soloed.* (Adjective)
> *When could any alto hit a high note in concert?* (Pronoun. Note that *any* is a singular pronoun and takes a singular verb.)

ULTIMATES

An adjective *ultimate* means "the most, the greatest, the highest, the best — and nothing and no one is better". Well, that's a rough meaning, but *ultimate* means "the final answer". There are no degrees, no comparisons, no possibility of being "somewhat pregnant". Either you are or you're not.

The most noticeably mis-used ultimate is the word "unique". Something that is *unique* is "one of a kind", not *somewhat unique* or *rather unique* or *very unique*.

Several words fall into this category, but need to be considered in the context of their use. Take *perfect* for instance. There is no degree of perfection, as *very perfect* or *somewhat perfect*. However, it would seem perfectly all right when talking about seeking perfection to use a modifier like *nearly perfect*.

When Mary Poppins describes herself as "practically perfect", she is not indicating a degree of perfection (as if she had used *nearly*), but she's indicating she is perfect in a practical way. *Practically* is an adverb (the *ly* says so. Ah those Brits!)

Some common ultimate adjectives: *square, round, first, last, best, correct, wrong, dark, light, silent.*

By using modifiers, such as *nearly, almost, very*, or *sort of* with ultimate adjectives, it is possible to indicate the attempt to become the ultimate. Like glycerin, know what you're handling when you try it. There *could* be a state of *being nearly pregnant, very round, almost last, nearly wrong, almost dark, the very best.* A good anarchist pays attention when dabbling with these words. They could bubble, foam, and blow up.

ORDER OF ADJECTIVES

Many grammarians have tried to devise an order to multiple adjectives. And, of course, not too many of them agree. Exhaustive research turned up as many lists of order as there are grammarians. The following seems to be an acceptable order. Decide for yourself and place your list in Your Style Manual.

1. Article (a, an, the)
2. Opinion (beautiful, tattered, horrible, silly)

3. Appearance, i.e. size, shape, condition (large, tiny, round, tilted, rich)
4. Age (new, old, ancient, young)
5. Color (red, shiny, blue, pinkish)
6. Origin (lunar, Asian, Mexican, Cherokee)
7. Material (cotton, leather, woolen, paper)
8. Purpose (often ending in "ing" as: sleeping bag, twinkling stars, flowering plant).

A sample sentence containing this order:
   A *silly, tiny, young, green, Martian, fleshy, invading alien named Charlie stepped out of the previously considered unidentified flying object and greeted us with, "Hello, Friend."*

COMPOUND ADJECTIVES

Sometimes it takes two words to describe an object. When they are attached to each other with a hyphen, they're called compound adjectives. These compounds are treated as single adjectives. The hyphen tells us they are compound; without it, the words revert to other meanings.
   For instance, *a run-on* sentence, *nose-to-the-grindstone* workaholic, *brown-bag* lunch, *I-don't-care* attitude. Adjectives so constructed are excellent tools for describing precisely what a writer chooses to say.
   Without the hyphen, however, *run on* may mean "to talk a lot or run ahead"; *brown bag* becomes "a receptacle with a brown color"; *I don't care* is still "an attitude", but it's expressed as subject-verb.
   Compound adjectives need each other to express certain ideas. You may refer to the area behind your house as the *back yard*, as opposed to the side yard. But if you wished to indicate a special area, it could become a *back-yard* or even a *backyard* (one word), as in *backyard barbecue*. It's not a *back barbecue* or a *yard barbecue* — the two adjectives need each other: *backyard*.
   Most compound adjectives become single words after a long time of usage. That *brown bag* became a compound when someone invited another to a *brown-bag* lunch. There were so many of these lunches that the hyphen soon was dropped to become a *brownbag* lunch.

A favorite problematic combination may occur when compound words are separated, especially if both parts function both as nouns and verbs. Take these two: trouble and shoot. Combine them to form *troubleshooting*. Now separate them and see what happens: *trouble shooting* (as in: *She found trouble shooting her sick dog.*)

The process of developing compound adjectives involves most other parts of the language, sometimes called "borrowed magic". Nouns, adverbs, pronouns, even verbs, are borrowed for the description, magically turning themselves into adjectives. And the magician is the hyphen.

> **Evolution of a Compound Adjective**
>
> 1) *Two words are commonly used together: as* **back yard**.
> 2) *The words are hyphenated:* **back-yard**.
> 3) *Eventually, the hyphen is dropped:* **backyard**.

Notice that hyphenated words usually *precede* the noun being modified. When the words are used *after* the subject noun, the hyphen is not needed.

The all-night party was held at Nancy's house.
The party at Nancy's house lasted all night.

The hard-to-please teacher discouraged his students.
The teacher who was hard to please discouraged his students.

The too-drunk anarchist was told to leave the house.
The anarchist was told to leave the house after becoming too drunk.

Some other compound adjectives always require the hyphen — numbers such as thirty-five, and fractions, such as one-quarter, and other multi-words. They will be discussed in ensuing sections on Hyphens, Spelling, and Numbers.

Here's an inside secret: if you choose to use an adverb as part of your descriptive compound adjective, you won't need the hyphen. Why? Because that adverb will disclose itself with its tell-tale "ly". For instance: wrestle with a *fully packed suitcase* or a *dangerously overloaded computer*. In these cases, the adverb modifies the adjective. More about this in the next section about Adverbs.

Some regularly used combinations of words pass for compound adjectives after considerable usage, and require no hyphen. Here are a few: *first grade teacher, special delivery mail, string bean casserole, strong arm tactics, North Dakota winter, New Deal economics.*

The conundrums begin with words used with compound adjectives that have multiple meanings. Where would you place hyphens in the following sentences?

She wanted to buy three quarter pound steaks. (Three quarter-pound steaks? Or three-quarter-pound steaks?)
Please sell me ballpoint pens. They come in 50 gross boxes. (Do I require one 50-gross box or 50 one-gross boxes?)
The wedding party occupies twenty three room suites. (Did they need 20 three-room suites? Or 23-room suites?)

Adjectives are not plural. If a contract runs for three years, it is a *three-year* contract. If a warranty lasts for ten years, it is a *ten-year* warranty.

TEST: There is a special-meaning test you can apply to this kind of adjective. Determine if either word can be used alone to describe the thing. Is it a *special test* or a *meaning test*? No, it is a *special-meaning* test.

SAY IT SLOWLY: P-A-R-T-I-C-I-P-L-E

The word "participle" strikes terror in grammar classes. Not sure why because most dictionaries actually provide the participle form of a verb. Yes, you heard right, a verb. Why then, you may ask, is the subject coming up in the modifier section?

The answer is simple: because a participle can act as an adjective modifier. The secret is out: the modifying participle is an impersonator. Sometimes listed under the heading "verbal", the participle is a verb impersonating, or acting like, an adjective.

The participle is easily recognized by "ed" or "ing" and usually found at the beginning of a sentence. The present participle ends with "ing":

1. *Smiling* at the rain, Sue began her morning walk.
2. *Hoping* for sunshine, she forgot her umbrella.
3. *Screaming* for attention, Steve stomped from the room.
4. *Texting* on the iPad, he lost control of the car.

The past participle ends in "ed" or "en":

5. *Surprised*, she saw snow begin to fall.
6. *Astonished*, the teachers watched it pile into threatening drifts.
7. *Shaken*, the passengers couldn't move.
8. *Broken* by the heavy snow, the shovel became useless.

Notice too that the thing that follows a participle is what the participle is referring to. *She* was surprised; *The teachers were* astonished; *the passengers* were shaken; *the shovel* was broken. It doesn't make sense (and it's grammatically inappropriate) to write: *Astonished, it piled into threatening drifts.* Snow doesn't usually become astonished.

If these participles were to appear at the end of the sentence, not much would change in the meaning (1-4 below), although it presents an opportunity to clarify the why of the participle (5-8 below).

1. Sue began her morning walk, smiling at the rain.
2. She forgot her umbrella, hoping for sunshine.
3. Steve stomped from the room, screaming for attention.
4. He lost control of the car, texting on the iPad.

5. She saw snow begin to fall, surprised at the size of the flakes.
6. The teachers watched it pile into threatening drifts, astonished at how quickly they formed.
7. The passengers couldn't move, shaken by the suddenness of the storm.
8. The shovel became useless, broken after lifting the heavy snow.

INFINITIVES AS IMPERSONATORS

Another verb that impersonates adjectives is the infinitive form, easily identified by the "to" form of the verb — *to do* or *to be* (or *not to be*, if that is the question).

>This is the time *to begin*. (modifies *time*)
>There are consequences *to consider*. (modifies *consequences*)
>The Internet is a great place *to google*. (modifies *place*, and yes "google" is used as a verb!)
>Check out Twitter when looking for something *to do*. (modifies *something*)

Problem Adjectives

AWFUL / AWESOME
Awful is an emotionally packed word that offers a range of feelings from strange to terrifying to magnificent. It also is used as an intensifier, as in *awful happy*. *Awesome* is the word to use when you mean "full of awe, inspiring, extraordinary".

CONTINUAL / CONTINUOUS
Continual means "without a break, regularly, frequently, steady", as *a continual payment of monthly charges*. *Continuous* means a slightly different sense of ongoingness; it means "uninterrupted in a sequence of time or substance", as *a continuous knocking sound*.

DUE TO / BECAUSE
Due is an adjective meaning "adequate" (*due proof of loss*), "owed or owing" (*due on Friday*), "ascribable" (*due to a few people*), "directly" (*due north*). It does not mean *because*. *Due* should be used only when an adjective modifier is needed, and not when you mean *because*.

Because is the handy-dandy word to use when you wish to show cause and effect. Because something happened, this was the consequence. *Because the weather turned cold, the meeting was canceled.*

EMINENT / IMMINENT
People are *eminent*, that is, reputable, important. Events can be *imminent*, that is, about to happen, impending.

FAMOUS / NOTORIOUS
If someone is *famous*, you know them, no matter how you feel about them. On the other hand, if they are *notorious*, you judge them to be disreputable, out of favor.

FEWER / LESS
Use *fewer* when you can count the something it modifies: *fewer hours were lost by eliminating breaks.* Use *less* when you cannot count it, or when the numbers are obscure: *less attention results in less stress.*

That well-known phrase, "in 25 words or less", is an idiomatic exception to this guideline. The term has been misused in contest rules for such a long time that few notice it is grammatically out of whack. When such misuse occurs long enough, the term *idiom* is applied (to ease the guilt of grammar teachers, no doubt).

GOOD / BAD VS. WELL
Good is a hunky dory adjective; *well* is feeling good (a hunky dory adverb). Another *well* is an adverb describing to what degree something is done. (A third *well* is a place to throw coins while wishing.)

Bad is just bad, unless you use jargon (another term invented to remove guilt from grammar teachers). Then *bad* means "good" and *good* is bad.

"How are you?"
"I'm good."
"Oh, you're behaving at last! I asked if you were well?"
[Blackout scene — you don't want to know.]

HEALTHFUL / HEALTHY
A person has a *healthy* outlook on life, which leads to a *healthful* state of mind. In general, people are healthy; inanimate objects are healthful (as asparagus).

HISTORIC / HISTORICAL
When something happens that is outstanding or spectacular or devastating, it goes down in history and is considered *historic* — referring to that specific occurrence. When referring to things in the past in general, the word is *historical*.

> *Raising the flag on Iwo Jim was a historic event.* (Notice that the "h" in historic is pronounced.)
> *Events of World War II have historical significance.*

LATER / LATTER
Sometimes this is a spelling problem. *Later*, of course, means "at a time yet to come". *Latter*, pronounced to rhyme with *matter*, refers to the second of two mentioned subjects. *Later*, in the Spelling Section, learn to spell *later* and *latter*, the *latter* having two *t*'s.

LIABLE / LIKELY / APT
Shades of meaning separate these words. You can remember which is which by looking at the degrees of impact each has.

> If a friend is *apt* to call you at midnight, there is a strong tendency for this behavior.
> If a friend is *likely* to call you at midnight, count on it; the probability is there.
> If a friend is *liable* to call you at midnight, be prepared for bad news. Liable has strong legal connotations and must be used carefully.

LOTS / A LOT
Grammar teachers for years have tried to drown the word "lots". Unless you deal in real estate (selling lots for homes), check your writing to avoid this word. Verbal usage gets lost too quickly to check, but the overuse of the word indicates a lack of better adjectives — some very apt ones, such as *very, much, many, several,* or *a whole bunch.*

When you have many things, you may refer to your holdings as *a lot*, but not *alot*. Forget *alot*; it's not a word.

MOST / ALMOST
Most has to do with numbers; *almost* has to do with proximity, being slightly short of a goal, nearly. *Most of the golfers were almost finished with the first nine holes.*

NICE
Have a nice day. The dinner was nice. She has a nice disposition. He is nice to his mother. Oh dear! If someone has a good, standard, across-the-board definition for this word, most writers would like to know. *Nice* means something different for each person using it and each person hearing it. So play *nice* and find a more accurate word to describe your day / dinner / disposition.

REAL / REALLY
When you are tempted to use a form of this word, ask yourself if you mean "true, not fake"? *Real* means that you aren't trying to pass off something phony as the real thing. *Real* or *really* also do not mean *very*. Most of the time a speaker tries to avoid the *very* by invoking *really*.

> *This is a real opportunity to perform good works.* (Not *a real good opportunity.*)
> *The shoetree isn't really a tree.*

REOCCURING
Not a word. You want to use *recurring*.

TERRIBLE
Similar to the word *awful*, this word means something nearly the opposite the way it is used. *They played a terrible game of doubles tennis.* Was that game full of terror? Come on! If a game is not played well, it is played awkwardly, tirelessly, badly, or amateurishly. Say so, but stay away from *terrible* unless you mean "evoking terror".

THEIRS / YOURS / OURS
These possessive pronouns (Column C in the Quick Pronoun Menu) do not require apostrophes.

> *The advice is theirs to give, yours to hear, and ours to act upon.*

The possessives without the "s" (their / your / our) form adjective modifiers (*their tempers, your bicycle, our affair*).

VIABLE

This is a very specific word that has a very specific biologic meaning — "able to support life, capable of surviving, existing, developing". It comes from the words *vital* and *vivid*, meaning "to have life", and it is used most often by biologists. Use *viable* in the context of living matter and its ability to survive. In other contexts, consider such words as *plausible, possible,* or *feasible.*

ADVERBS

Where adjectives are the bling that dress up Things, Adverbs are the bling that add meaning to Do-Be's. Additionally, as an extra gemstone adds something to ordinary bling, an adverb can also add something to an adjective — bling on bling, like polish on a pendant.

> **WARNING:** Not all "ly" words are adverbs. Some words ending in "ly" are actually adjectives (lovely, ugly). Look closely at the word being modified.

Adverbs provide the how, why, where, and when to verbs. They also describe or limit other adverbs, adjectives, and whole sentences. Most adverbs are easily recognized by endings in "ly". While there are similarities between adjectives and adverbs, there are also some major differences.

The adverb enhances a verb by telling when something happened, where it happened, how or why it happened, and to what extent it happened. Like the name itself, an *add-verb* "adds something to the verb".

Ah, but these little darlings can do much much more. Adverbs can dress up (modify) adjectives and (yes, there's still more) they can modify other adverbs.

A *high wall* can become an *extremely high wall*; a *long day* can become an *unendingly long day*; a *powerful* punch can become a dangerously *powerful* punch (adverbs modifying adjectives).

Some adjectives (*beautiful, thick, quiet, horrible, fantastic, loud*) can become adverbs by the addition of "ly": *beautifully, thickly, quietly, horribly, fantastically, loudly.*

> *The beautiful dancer executed her leaps beautifully.*
> *The assistant quietly assisted during the quiet meeting.*
> *The loudly played music overwhelmed the loud party-goer.*

Much of what you learn about adjectives will apply to adverbs. There are accurate ones and inaccurate ones. Just as *awful, terrible, horrible* add specific meaning to things, so do adverbs apply similarly specific meaning to verbs.

COMPARATIVE ADVERBS

Much like adjectives, comparative adverbs tend to end with "er" and "est" (*fast / faster / fastest, easy / easier / easiest*). Similarly, some adverbs take kindly to booster modifiers (*more, most, less, least*).

How fast does the jogger run? *Fast, faster, fastest* (the winner!).
How far does the jogger run? *Far, farther, farthest* (still the winner!).
How gracefully did the jogger accept the trophy? *Gracefully, more gracefully* (than the jogger in second place), *most gracefully* (for an oftentimes winner).
How did the jogger retire? *Quietly, more quietly* (than others), *most quietly*.

One guideline lies in the length of the adverb. The shorter ones take *er / est* and the longer ones need the boosters. Your choice!

ADVERBS WITHOUT *LY*

Many adverbs arrive without the "ly". Pay attention to the word being described.

> The *very* quick tempo of the marchers quickly tired them out.
> The flutists often slowed down.
> The drummers kept up an *even*-handed pace.
> In all, the band performed *very well*.

ADVERBS WITH VERBS

Find the verb; look for the bling that describes it.

> *The center snapped the football very quickly.* (snapped/very quickly)
> *The linebackers forcefully plowed through the opposition.* (plowed/forcefully)
> *The running end efficiently caught the short pass.* (caught/efficiently)

ADVERBS WITH ADJECTIVES

Find the subject and its modifier. Now look for the modifier of the modifier (the adverb modifying the adjective).

> *Adeline became devilishly controlling.* (Adeline/devilishly controlling)
> *Her very good friend had become cruel.* (friend/very good)
> *Adeline, naturally upset with the friend, dumped her.* (Adeline/naturally upset)

ADVERBS WITH OTHER ADVERBS

Look first for the adverbs that describe the verb; now find the word that tells more about that adverb.

> *The trees cried very sadly with the endless wind.* (sadly/very)
> *Fir trees groan considerably louder than elms or oaks.* (Louder/considerably)
> *They bend more easily than deciduous trees.* (easily/more)

ADVERBS WITH SENTENCES

These are easy to find. *Usually* (there's one now!), they are found at the beginning of a sentence. But, look for one at the end too.

> The team was aware of its appearance, *understandably*.
> *Casually*, they preened in front of the mirror.
> *Finally*, all of them believed they were unbeatable.
> The team understood the meaning of ego, *surprisingly*,

MISPLACED MODIFIERS

Be careful — very careful — where you place the bling that could change the meaning if it were placed elsewhere. Consider the following "only".

> *He **only** wanted to sing with the band.*
> *He wanted **only** to sing with the band.*

*He wanted to **only** sing with the band.*
*He wanted to sing **only** with the band.*
*He wanted to sing with **only** the band.*
*He wanted to sing with the **only** band.*

Six sentences that have six different meanings — just because of the placement of one word — of *only* one word.

INFINITIVES AS ADVERBS

That impersonating infinitive verbal can portray a verb that has morphed into an adverb. Easily identified as the "to do" or "to be" verb, this kind of bling provides additional information about a verb.

We climbed the tree to see where we were. (*to see* modifies *climbed*)
The neighbors yelled to scare us. (*to scare* modifies *yelled*)

Troublesome Adverbs

HARDLY, SCARCELY, BARELY

These words are negatives and need to be treated like any other negative when complying with the guideline about double negatives: Do not use double negatives. If you use one negative modifier, you don't need to use another.

There's not hardly a reason for this. (Not OK)
There's hardly a reason for this. (OK)
There's not a reason for this. (OK)
She didn't hardly have time to catch her breath. (Not OK)
She hardly had time to catch her breath. (OK)

HOPEFULLY

Here's where grammar anarchy can get rid of a very misused word. If you counted all the times *hopefully* is misused, you'd never get anything done.

Hundreds of times each second, someone uses the word *hopefully* in an ungrammatical way.

> *This problem must be solved hopefully very soon.*
> *Hopefully, we can abolish this problem.*

Hopefully is an adverb. The adjective is *hopeful*. The chances of the differences being observed in daily usage is not very *hopeful*. Just look for the verb that *hopefully* is asked to modify. Does it do its job?

> *The forward held the ball hopefully as she took aim.* (Ok. She held it with hope.)
> *The forward hopefully aimed the basketball at the hoop.* (Did the forward hope it would hit the rim, or are we hoping she is aiming at the hoop?)

IRREGARDLESS
Not a word. Use "regardless".

REALLY
This is a word that could be removed from the U.S. English language and not bother many people — except those who use it constantly as a space filler. The word *real* means "actual, alive, true, not fantasy". This and many other adverbs are often used carelessly. Look closely at what you're saying and you'll probably discover that you really (in reality) mean to use *very* or something more specific. *Really*, like *hopefully, basically, honestly, actually*, and *absolutely*, are often used to fill up space while the speaker thinks of the next words. These words appear less frequently in writing (polished, edited writing). I really mean it!

PRETTY
Ditto — everything above that relates to space fillers. That's pretty much the way it is. (Have you ever seen a "much" that was pretty?)

REAL GOOD
When something is referred to as tasting "real good", it ought to taste *delicious*. Common usage passes *real good* as an idiom (everybody says it). Now you know that everybody can be wrong and still remain in step with

everybody else. When something has been done right, use the adverb *well* and modify it with the more appropriate *very*. *That job was done very well* is preferable to *you did a it real good* (or worse: *you done real good*). Again, have you ever seen a "good" that was real?

RUN SMOOTH

You probably have been warned about using the adjective *smooth* to refer to "the sound of an engine". *Smooth* usually means "without wrinkles". Most dictionaries now include a definition that gives *smooth* a meaning of "functioning without hindrance", including engines. See how some anarchist put up a fight and won that round? However, be sure to use the adverb *smoothly* with verbs.

The project was finished smoothly.
The water flowed smoothly along the new riverbed.

SHORT, SHORTLY

You can see why a grammar anarchist is necessary. Some words just beg to be ruled out. *Short* has a dictionary definition as well as a grammatical function that is different from *shortly*. *Short* is both an adjective (*a short old man*) and an adverb (*the meeting fell short of expectations*). *Short* is an adverb that does not always end in "ly".

1) The *short* board fell two feet *short* of the wall.
2) The carpenter recognized *shortly* the need for a new board.
3) The carpenter spoke *shortly* to the lumberyard owner.

In sentence 1, the first *short* is an adjective modifying *board*; the second is an adverb indicating where the board fell. In sentence 2, the adverb *shortly* modifies the verb *recognized* and means *soon*. In sentence 3, *shortly* is an adverb meaning *curt* or *rudely brief*. (Or does it mean he encountered the owner in a short period of time?) Be specific!

SURELY

Here's another troublesome adverb. Its root word is *sure*, defined as "certain, secure, steady, inevitable, destined". Because it is related so closely to *certain*, it is often equated with *yes*. The words *sure* and *surely* can best be used when the meaning is closer to inevitability than to the simple *yes*. It's also a dandy word to use to indicate steadfastness and reliability. *The trapeze clown surely matched a sure foot with a sure demeanor.*

VERY

Very is a perfectly good adverb that is over-used when a more specific word would better tell the story, and under-used when it needs to show a greater extent. Some grammarians suggest that *very* should not be used to modify a word that has a verb root: *displease, satisfy, dislike, interest, grow*. Avoid: *very displeased, very satisfied, very interested, very grown*. You decide, and add it to Your Style Manual.

WELL / BADLY

The adverbs are *well* and *badly*. (*Good* and *bad* are the adjectives.) When something is done acceptably, it has been done *well*. If that something was not acceptable, the job was done *badly*. Both of these words modify verbs, and they describe *how* something was done.

Notice the different, sometimes twisted, meanings that occur when using the wrong form of the word.

> *The fish smells bad.* (Find the air spray!)
> *The fish smells badly.* (Poor fishy has a cold.)
> *The mugger appeared dangerous.* (The mugger may have looked angry.)
> *The mugger appeared dangerously close.* (The mugger moved right in front of me.)
> *The chicken tastes crisp.* (Ummm, good!)
> *The chicken tastes crisply.* (It's little tongue shot right out there!)

MORE TRICKY ADVERBS — OR ARE THEY?

Already is an adverb meaning "previously". *All ready* means that everyone "is prepared".

Awhile is an adverb meaning "for a short time". Do not confuse it with the prepositional phrase "once in a while". Here, *while* is a noun, the object of that preposition "once".

Formally means to wear a tuxedo or ball gown, or to behave in a formal manner. *Formerly* is an adverb meaning "once upon a time".

Maybe is an adverb meaning "perhaps". *May be* is a verb suggesting "a possibility of being".

Seldom ever doesn't make sense; the words are opposites. *Seldom* means "occasionally"; *ever* is a long time. What may be meant is *seldom if ever*, meaning there's "a long, long wait ahead".

Too is an adverb that means "excessive, extreme", as in: *Six espressos cost too much*. Grammarians call "too" an *intensifier*. Too often *too* becomes confused with the preposition *to* or the adjective number *two*. *Too* also means "also".

Sincerely yours. While we're talking about adverbs, let's take a look at the ones that generally close business letters. A grammar anarchist calls them Terms of Endearment: *sincerely, cordially, truly, warmly, respectfully,* ad nauseam. The good news is that they can be omitted, wiped out, left out, eliminated, deleted, removed, dropped, forgotten. (For more about Terms of Endearment, see the section on A Writing Style of Your Own.)

BLING PHRASES / CLAUSES

Both adjectives and adverbs often take the shape of Phrases and Clauses. Remember the difference between phrases and clauses? Both are made up of more than a single word. A phrase generally begins with a preposition" while "a clause contains a verb of its own".

The child ran to the store. "To the store" is a prepositional phrase that takes the role of adverb modifying the verb *ran*. (Where did the child run?)

The child, who ran to the store, was exhausted. "... who ran to the store" is a clause containing the verb *ran*, and explains what the child did to become exhausted. (When you reach the Comma Section, you'll understand why the commas are important. Without them, *The child who ran to the store...* becomes a long subject with *who ran to the store* as an adjective clause modifying child.)

ADJECTIVE PHRASES / CLAUSES

There are times when one word or two just won't do the job. An entire phrase or clause is needed to get the descriptive point across. An adjective phrase describes a noun or pronoun, exactly as a single-word adjective does.

The daisies with the most sunlight grew taller than the others.

The phrase "with the most sunlight" modifies *daisies*. You can change that into a clause by adding a verb:

The daisies that caught the most sunlight grew taller than the others. (See how that works?)

Here's a reminder to put the modifier where it belongs. What if that sentence read: *The daisies grew taller than the others that caught the most sunlight?* How can daisies grow taller without much sunshine?

That reminder applies to all kinds of modifiers.

Get a load of the woman standing next to the horse's hat.

The placement of commas in a sentence containing an adjective phrase or clause can change the entire meaning.

A man smoking a cigarette set the house on fire.
The man, smoking a cigarette, set the house on fire.

In the first sentence, we know that the arsonist is a guy who was smoking. In the second sentence, we know who that man is and that he set the house on fire while smoking a cigarette. (All that with just a couple of little commas.) More about commas in the Punctuation Section.

ADVERB PHRASES / CLAUSES

Just as adjectives can show up in phrases and clauses, so can adverbs. The only difference is that adverb phrases and clauses modify verbs, adjectives, and other adverbs — just like any responsible adverb word would do. Again, the inclination to look at the placement of these phrases and clauses is important.

> The astronauts geared up *before dawn on the morning of the takeoff.* (Notice three prepositional adverb phrases.)
> The astronauts geared up *after they ate breakfast.* (Clause)
> The astronauts ate *with their fingers* and scattered crumbs *in a very disorderly way around the locker room.* (*with their fingers* is an adverb that modifies the verb "ate"; *in a very disorderly way* and *around the locker room* are adverb clauses that modify "scattered".

The italicized phrases and clauses modify the verbs that precede them. Which brings us (again) to misplaced modifiers.

> *The astronauts ate and scattered crumbs with their fingers in a very disorderly way around the locker room.*

By moving the modifying phrase, *with their fingers*, the meaning in the above sentence shifts to the way they ate and scattered crumbs.

> *The wives agreed to meet with the hungry astronauts in a hesitating manner when they returned from orbit.* (Where does "in a hesitating manner" belong? Near which verb? And look at that pronoun, *they*! Who is returning from orbit?)

The wives agreed in a hesitating manner to meet with the hungry astronauts when they returned from orbit. (Now we know who is hesitating and who is returning from orbit!)

ABSOLUTE PARTICIPIAL PHRASE

A good grammar anarchist would never use a word collection like that — at least in front of others. An absolute participial phrase is one that consists of a noun / pronoun with a participle (complete verb). It modifies the predicate of the sentence (that is, everything that isn't the subject, remember?) and it is awkward. Never mind the labeling, just learn to recognize it:

> Avoid: *Adeline being a bad singer the song was ruined.*
> Instead use: *Because Adeline was a bad singer, the song was ruined.*
> Or: *Adeline, a bad singer, ruined the song.*

> Avoid: *The moon being full, everyone howled like wolves.*
> Instead use: *Because the moon was full, everyone howled like wolves.*
> Or: *The full moon caused everyone to howl like wolves.*

DANGLING VERBALS

Any modifier that is misplaced is said to be one that *dangles*. The cure lies in moving the dangling modifier close to the word it modifies. To make it a true "dangler", the verbal would not be related to any words in the sentence.

When a sentence begins with a verbal clause, the very next word should be the word it modifies. That word should answer the questions who or what is doing the action.

The following show some dandy danglers:

> *When painting in oils, the canvas should be placed on an easel.* (Can a canvas paint at all?)
> *While using many colors, the palette should be cleaned regularly.* (A palette generally doesn't use colors.)

> *Having finished for the day, the painting should be covered.* (A painting's work is never finished.)
> *Leaving the building, the radio continued to play soft music.* (A radio most certainly would not leave the building.)

Here's how to make those sentences work and show which nouns are doing what:

> *When painting in oils, the artist places the canvas on the easel.*
> *While using many colors, the artist needs to clean the palette regularly.*
> *Having finished for the day, an artist may want to cover the painting.*
> *Leaving the building, someone forgot to turn off the radio.*

One of the ways a writer can benefit from reading a sentence aloud is to discover sentence construction that may not come out the way it was intended. The following sentences seemed logical when they were written, but read them aloud and notice the confusion.

> *The witness responded to the prosecutor looking as if she were about to faint.* (Who is about to faint?)
> *The child ran quickly to her mother crying wildly.* (Poor Mom! Or is the child crying?)
> *While instructing the program, I am sure Dennis had the interest of students at heart.* (I didn't actually instruct the program; Dennis did! But the sentence doesn't make that clear.)
> *Rubbing my hands to keep them warm, the bus finally arrived.* (Now really!)
> *Having broken his arm, the doctor operated for three hours.* (Ouch! Tough doctor?)
> *Having let the students out early, the school stood quietly.* (Can a school let out the students and then stand quietly?)

TO SUMMARIZE BLING (MODIFIERS)

Good writers select adjectives carefully, just as hot dressers select bling carefully. Modifiers can be overdone, or rather over-used. (See how it works? *Overdone* would best be used in the context of a barbecue.)

Use specific adjectives to define specific nouns and spice up your writing as you bring it to life. Specific modifiers often pin down responsibility. When you want to avoid pinpointing a culprit, skip the bling. Take this basic sentence…

People were accused of skipping out on debts.

…and bring the culprits to terms, by specifying exactly how many, what kind, which ones. Expose the details by means of modifiers:

Twenty-two **people** *between the ages of 16 and 28* **were accused** *directly by mall store owners of irresponsibly* **skipping out on debts** *that amounted to thousands of dollars during the period immediately following holiday spending.*

LITTLE WORDS (Glue)

(Conjunctions, Prepositions, Articles, Interjections)

Size doesn't matter when you discover the little connectors that form the stickum that holds sentences together. Just as in anarchy, where little people overturn the heavy-handed "rulers", the little words in U.S. language are the workers: Conjunctions, Prepositions, Articles, and Interjections. (Okay, the labels are long, but they represent the little words!)

Because these glue words are little, don't think they're pushovers. Most of the time, they're cooperative, but oh those moments when *pushover* comes to *shove*, they, like successful anarchists, can be nuisances.

Conjunctions are the glue that connect similar parts of language: nouns with nouns, verbs with more verbs, modifiers with additional modifiers, and sentences with other sentences.

Prepositions are the little words that glue phrases onto nouns and verbs.

Articles are both small and few, serving as identifying adjectives for nouns.

Interjections stick in comments that hold thoughts together and express opinion at the same time. Big jobs for little words!

Conjunctions should be easy, yes? How many are there anyway? *And, or, but, nor*? Sure, but don't forget: *for, yet*, and *so*, just for a start. Then we have conjunctions that introduce clauses: *if, when, where, although, while, since,* and *as*. Add the conjunctions that introduce ideas: *therefore, nevertheless, however, otherwise, thus, yet,* and *sure*. How many? (More than half of the last 40 words).

Prepositions certainly are easy. They're the little words that introduce phrases that answer the questions of *where, when*, and *in which direction* and probably were the first parts of speech you learned. These often-used words give direction (*up, down, in, out, over, under, between,* and *above*), for starters. But watch out; they can be tricky if you let them.

Articles were discussed briefly in the Adjective Section, since they modify nouns, the same way other adjectives do. *The, a, an, one* are the usual articles, easily recognized. *The* is called a "definite article" while *a / an* are indefinite articles. But don't forget *this* and *that*, sometimes operating as definite articles.

Interjections aren't exactly sticky words, nor even necessary at times, but they add color to writing as they communicate feelings. *Oh yeah*! Or *Ouch*! Sometimes referred to as Expletives or Wow Words, these are the words that add emotion to writing — or make it look ridiculous, depending on how the interjection is used.

CONJUNCTIONS

Conjunctions are the joining words. As chief connectors, they can join two words, two phrases, two clauses, or two sentences. In other words, they connect ideas. The things being connected can be subjects or objects (Nouns), Adjectives or Adverbs (Bling), or Verbs (Do-Be's). This grammar chemistry produces compounds: compound nouns, compound verbs, compound modifiers.

The "easy" conjunctions are *and, or, but, neither, nor*.

The owl *and* the pussycat are friends. (connects subjects)
They hoot *and* purr. (connects verbs)
An owl has soft *but* drab feathers. (connects adjectives)
The pussycat has *neither* feathers *nor* fins. (connects objects) *But* it often preens its fur *and* paws as if they were feathers *or* fins. ("But" connects sentences; "and" connects nouns *fur / paws* and "or" connects nouns *feathers / fins*".)
The owl flies in *and* out of its nest regularly. (connecting prepositions)
You could say it was *either* in the air *or* out of the tree. (connecting phrases)
The pussycat agreed to leave the owl alone, *for* it had other birds to watch. (connecting sentences)

You'll find more talk about compound sentences in the Sentence Section. For now, note that simple sentences can be joined in at least two ways to form compound sentences: with a comma and conjunction, or a semi-colon.

The colorful fish swam in circles; the yellow-finned wiggler escaped.
The colorful fish swam in circles, and the yellow-finned wiggler escaped.

Sometimes compounds refer to a singular subject. *The painter and sculptor is married to the mayor.* The mayor's spouse is both a painter and a sculptor. If the sentence used the verb "are", there would rise hue and cry about the mayor's bigamy.

When adverbs are used as connectors, they connect the ideas of two sentences and usually appear at the front of the second sentence. Punctuation is arguable; you can decide for yourself when you get to the Comma Section. The predominant guideline is to skip the comma for one-word connectors as long as it makes sense. The adverbs under discussion include: *however, consequently, therefore, nevertheless, while, since,* and *moreover*. Use them carefully to convey the precise meaning you want.

> *Jazz music is creative; however, many consider it disjointed.*
> *Jazz music is creative; nevertheless many don't get it.*
> *Jazz music is creative; therefore jazz must be used with care.*
> *Jazz music is creative; moreover, it stirs the independent soul.*

Beware! (an interjection.) Different meanings are attained by using different connectors. *Nevertheless* means "in spite of, however"; *therefore* means "in addition to" or "as a result, consequently". *Furthermore, besides, moreover* mean "in addition to". *Otherwise* means "in other ways". *While* means "during that time". And *since* means "at a time in the past" or "from the time in the past". Each connecting adverb carries its own shade of meaning.

CONNECTORS THAT COME IN PAIRS

You've already noticed that some connectors come in pairs. Two connectors go together to make it work: *either / or, neither / nor, both / and, whether / or, not only / but also*. Like many couples, the pairs need to accompany each other.

> Independent voters lean *neither* to the left *nor* to the right.
> *Not only* the Federalists *but also* the Tories tried to influence them.
> *Both* the Independent *and* the Royalist failed to make their points.
> We'll know in a century or two *whether* we understand them *or not*.
> or: We'll know in a century or two *whether or not* we understand them.
> They'll *either* talk each other to death *or* join forces to do something.

When using connectors, try to keep them equal.

> *You will either join us or fight us.*

If the first connector is followed by a verb (join), use a verb following the second word (fight).

> *You may become either an anarchist or a wimp.*

If the first connector is followed by a noun (anarchist), use a noun after the second word (wimp). Aha! You are saying, "Now I know why that sounds better!" Parallelism is a big topic in the Sentence Section.

ADVERB CLAUSES THAT CONNECT

Independent Clause is the fancy way to say "sentence"; it contains both a subject and a verb (Thing / Noun and Do-Be / Verb); it can stand by itself. A *Dependent Clause* cannot stand by itself because it's dependent — lacking either a subject or a verb. An Independent Clause may contain one or more of those Dependent Clauses. Translation: a sentence may contain one or more clauses.

Some of the indicators of the words that connect dependents to independents: *if, when, where, whether, although, while, since, after, before, provided, because, unless, until*, and *as*. When a dependent clause is connected to a regular sentence, what results is a complex sentence. (More about this too in the Sentence Section.)

The adverb clause modifies the verb of the primary or main sentence. Like other adverbs, an adverb clause answers questions of *why, where, when, to what degree, for what purpose, with what result*.

> *If the gardener weeds well, she'll remove everything but the flowers.* (The introductory clause modifies the verb *remove* and answers the questions "to what degree?")
>
> *When only the flowers remain, you know the job has been done right.* (The introductory clause modifies the verb *know*, explaining "with what result?")

Now let's turn around these sentences and you'll see how that clause works. Note that the comma is missing when the clause is placed at the end of the sentence.

> *She'll remove everything but the flowers if the gardener weeds well.*
> *You know the job has been done right when only the flowers remain.*

The sentences above include both a simple sentence ("She'll remove everything but the flowers" and "You know the job has been done right") and dependent clauses ("if the gardener weeds well" and "when only the flowers remain").

When a clause appears at the beginning of the sentence, it is called the Introductory Clause and is followed by a comma. The comma gets lost when the clause *follows* the independent sentence. Some grammar sticklers will tell you to re-name that kind of clause *nonrestrictive*, meaning "it can be eliminated and you'd still have a complete sentence" (although perhaps not your complete thought).

Now here's another choice for you. When the introductory clause is a single word or two, many writers opt to dump the comma. An anarchist can decide whether the sentence makes sense without the comma and choose to delete it — or not. Your choice will be easier after you learn more about commas in the Punctuation Section.

Would you delete the commas in the following sentences? You can if you choose to.

The ring seemed inconsequential. Nevertheless, he asked for it back the next day. Until then, she didn't want to remove it from her finger.

ADJECTIVE CLAUSES THAT CONNECT

Connectors are also used to introduce adjective clauses. And what does an adjective do, class? "Adjectives modify nouns and pronouns... period." So do adjective clauses. Some of these adjective conjunctions are: *who, which,* and *that*; they head up clauses that come in two flavors: Necessary and Unnecessary.

A necessary clause contains information needed to identify the noun it modifies. In short, leaving out the clause would leave the rest of the sentence inunderstandable (how's that for a new word?).

The auditor *who was honored for his work* turned out to be a bigamist.
The wife *who filed charges* said she lost her dignity.

Both of the clauses above are *necessary* in order to identify the subject noun (which auditor and which wife?). Note: no commas. That auditor is the one being honored; that wife is the one who filed charges. You'll discover the difference in the Comma Section.

An unnecessary clause contains information that is *not* needed in order to properly identify the modified noun. This clause may be set off with commas, but leaving them out would not render the sentence misunderstandable. (Don't you just love new words?)

> The auditor, *who was honored for his work*, turned out to be a bigamist.
> The wife, *who filed charges*, said she lost her dignity.

You may leave out those clauses between the commas and the sentences still make sense. See the difference? The auditor turned out to be a bigamist (not necessary to know that he was an honored auditor). And the poor wife said she lost her dignity (not necessary to know that she had filed charges). While these clauses may add meaty information to a sentence, they are grammatically unnecessary.

Now watch how those commas can make a difference, however subtle they may appear.

> My beef was with the department supervisor *who had red hair*.
> My beef was with the department supervisor, *who had red hair*.

In the first sentence the supervisor is identified as the one with red hair, not the bald guy or the blond. In the second sentence the hair color doesn't really matter. The beef was with the department supervisor — and it isn't important to know about the red hair.

Sometimes a clue turns up in the use of certain words. Using *that* and *who* as adjectives offer clues as to whether the reference is to a person or a thing. *Who* is used to refer to a person; *that* refers to a thing.

> *My favorite is the one that has long droopy ears.*
> *My favorite is the one who has long droopy ears.*

Now you know that the first one is probably a dog or a donkey; the second refers to a person (poor fellah or gal).

Here's another clue to the subtle difference between *that* and *which*. When used as pronouns, they can be interchangeable, and usually are:

> *The bike that has brass handlebars is a valuable show piece.*
> *The bike which has brass handlebars is a valuable show piece.*

But: *The bike, which has brass handlebars, is a valuable show piece.*

In the first two sentences, the appropriate bike is identified. In the third sentence, the commas make a major change to the sentences (converting the necessary clause to an unnecessary one that simply adds information about the bike).

The raucous Dirtbikers, who ride Harleys, are careful drivers.
The raucous Dirtbikers that ride Harleys are careful drivers.

The first sentence contains additional information (unnecessary clause, *who ride Harleys*). In the second sentence, the clause is necessary to identify the careful drivers — the ones who all ride Harleys. Note how the word *that* can be used with groups. When you want to identify someone or something in a group, substitute *that* for *which* or *who* and omit the commas. Thus, the clause becomes an identifying necessary clause and not a clause offering supplemental information.

The motorbike that was in the accident was a total wreck.
The motorbike, which (or that) was in the accident, was a total wreck.

In the first sentence, the bike is the one in the accident and no other. The second sentence indicates that the bike was a total wreck; that it was in the accident is extra info.

NOUN CLAUSES

Conjunctions can lead off noun clauses too. Such a clause is always dependent, since it may function as a subject or an object. This kind of clause also can function as a description of a subject called "a subject complement". Conjunctions used in this way include *that, why, what, whatever, which, who,* and *whoever*.

Think of a noun clause as a multi-word subject. To decode it, look for the verb (*which makes it a clause*) and then find who or what is doing it.

What she believed turned into exactly what he expected. (Verb: *turned into*; subject: *what she believed*)
He didn't expect her to believe *whatever she liked*. (Verb: *expect*; object: *to believe whatever she liked*)

The actor is *whoever the director wants him to be*. (Verb: *is*; object: *whoever the director wants him to be*) Do you recognize the subject and object are equal, reversible? *Whoever the director wants him to be* is the actor.) *Whatever the actor did* was *what the director told him to do*. (Here's a double whammy clause — both subject and subject complement are noun clauses, equal and reversible.)

SO / SO THAT (CONSEQUENTLY)

The word *so* can function as both a connector (adjective or adverb). When used as a connector to join things, the meaning is "with the result that". (*Bring on the barbecue so we can eat.* Or, *bring on the barbecue so that we can eat.*) Many grammarians propose limiting the use of *so* when it is meant to replace *so that*. Try it both ways, Anarchist! Decide which you like better.

Many writers become aware they overuse the word *that* and work to drop it, irritating those who bemoan the use of *so* by itself. This is one debate that remains open to choice. Decide for yourself and note it in Your Style Manual.

Here are examples of *so* and *so that* when introducing a clause that give reasons for some choices.

The teenager's bag was so full nothing more could be stuffed in.
The teenager's bag was so full that nothing more could be stuffed in.
Her mother asked her to clean out the bag so she could launder it.
Her mother asked her to clean out the bag so that she could launder it.

YET

Oooh, this one is sticky. Another decision for Your Style Manual: to comma or to semi-colon, that is the question. (Who but a grammar anarchist would dare use *comma* and *semicolon* as verbs?) The impact of a semi-colon seems greater than the simple comma. While this probably holds true for most connectors that join simple sentences, it is particularly true for *yet*. What do you think?

The directors all hated naptime, yet they participated eagerly.
The directors all hated naptime; yet they participated eagerly.

Whether you use the comma or the semi-colon, the impact is worth considering as you decide.

AND OR *BUT*?

Serious writers understand the psychology behind the use of most words. *And* and *but* are two of those words. *And* signals a direct connection: *you and I, the tall and the short, the prosperous and the deprived. And* joins things; *but* judges. In first drafts, *but* appears more often, used subconsciously by the writer. Now change the *but* to *and*, then read what happens to a statement. Read these sentences and feel the *but*.

> *Your tie appears handsome, but it is red.*
> *Your resumé sounds intriguing, but it is short.*

The clues about judgment suggest that whatever follows *but* is a lie or a put-down. "This appears okay, but..." "The food is fine, but..."

An exercise in increasing harmony is to replace the *but* with *and* to change the impact.

> *Your tie appears handsome, and it is red.*
>
> *Your resumé sounds intriguing, and it is short.*

Your anarchist psychologist has spoken.

PROVIDED / PROVIDING

Not usually considered among the connectors are the words *provided* and *providing* when they are used to mean "if" or "as a condition". Grammar teachers prefer *provided*, but this is another anarchist choice.

> *The sun felt warm, provided (or providing) you wore a sweater.*
> *Providing (or provided) you were tall, you could see over the wall.*
> *The flowers grew tall, provided (or providing) they were watered regularly.*
> *Children learn quickly, providing (or provided) they are given the opportunity.*

UNLESS

An old mistake is confusing the preposition *except* with the connector *unless*.

> The door will not open *except* you use the right combination. (old!)
> The door will not open *unless* you use the right combination.

BUT WHAT

Another ancient mistake that is going the way of the corset is using *but what* as a connector instead of *except that*. *But what* is stiff and inappropriate in today's world (just like the corset).

> I would go for a walk *but what* it is snowing. (old!)
> I would go for a walk *except that* it is snowing.
> Even better: I would go for a walk, *but* it is snowing.

WHERE OR *THAT*

Use the word *where* to refer to a location, a place. Do not substitute *where* for *that*.

> The children saw *where* the alphabet had 26 letters.
> The children saw *that* the alphabet had 26 letters. (better)

More appropriately:

> The children saw *where* the teacher had gone. (location)

PREPOSITIONS

Prepositions are very important little words that introduce Prepositional Phrases. You probably know most of them already: *up, down, in, out, over, under, between, among*. Their primary purpose is to give direction.

The most troublesome of the prepositions are *among* and *between, in* and *into, up* and *upon, like* and *per* (ugh!). Other troublemakers show up as prepositions that follow verbs or adjectives to convey a specific meaning; these include *even, only, just, ever*, and *so*.

What makes prepositions important are their functions. You may gain a new respect for these little words and the way in which they shift meanings very subtly. The word *up*, for instance, may have some meanings that will surprise you. As will that little word *down*, which you already have seen assumes the function of just about every other part of language.

> ### Find Subject / Verb
> *Remove the prepositional phrases — all those direction-minded words; 2) identify the subject (what we're talking about); and 3) the verb (what is happening). The basic sentence is what remains.*

Prepositions indicate a relation to things and ideas. In addition, they introduce the phrases that modify nouns and verbs, assuming the roles of adjective or adverb phrases.

When we get to taking apart sentences, you'll recall the sage advice to remove prepositional phrases when searching for the nouns and verbs. This is a great help when you're trying to match subjects with verbs. You may then deduce that prepositional phrases provide additional information to a sentence.

> *The candy store down the road, under the drawbridge, and across from the specialty shops (appear/appears) shabby in this neighborhood.*

1) Remove the prepositional phrases (*down the road, under the drawbridge, across from the specialty shops*); 2) identify the subject (what we're talking about, *the candy store*) and 3) the verb (*appear/appears*, choose one). You end up with a basic simple sentence: *The candy store ... appears shabby....*

In the anarchist's echoing words, "Simple, huh!"

You'll use prepositional phrases easier if you recall they are descriptions: they require a noun / pronoun object (from Column B in the Quick Pronoun Menu), and they are expendable as part of the basic sentence. They modify nouns/pronouns and verbs by telling direction and relationship.

But beware! Good writing rests on the ability to use these little word phrases to enhance your writing rather than detract. And when you overuse them, the enhancement gets lost. A rule of thumb is to avoid using more than two or three prepositional phrases in a row.

Mother watched for the school bus (1) down the road (2) in the afternoon (3) after three o'clock (4) with her baby (5).

Five prepositional phrases are too many. A re-write may take two sentences to incorporate all those phrasal ideas — or some of the phrases could be eliminated without great loss.

Mother watched for the school bus after three o'clock. She held her baby as she watched.

Note that the phrases "in the afternoon" and "down the road" were eliminated. It would seem reasonable that three o'clock was in the afternoon, and school buses use the roads.

Place Modifiers Carefully

Modifiers need to be near the words they modify.

Location! Location! Location! Of primary importance in positioning prepositional phrases is to locate them near the words they modify.

Mother watched for the school bus with her baby down the road. (Oops! The babe got away!)

DOUBLE PREPOSITIONS

There are times when two or more prepositions are used for specific meanings: *according to current statistics; apart from ordinary numbers; instead of using charts; because of constant rain.*

There also are times when the temptation arises to use double prepositions when they aren't necessary. Just because they're small, we think we can pop them in just any old place, which leads to over-using them.

The toddler fell off of the chair.
Where have all the cushions gone to?
Don't tell me where they're at! (Mercy, mercy!)

Save the Prepositions! Try instead:

The toddler fell off the chair.
Where have all the cushions gone?
Don't tell me where they are!

ENDING WITH A PREPOSITION

For ages, you've been warned against ending a sentence with a preposition. The purists even evoke the words of Winston Churchill, the former prime minister of Great Britain. He said sarcastically, tongue firmly planted in cheek, "This is something up with which I will not put." The sentence would make much more sense with the preposition at the end ("This is something I will not put up with"), but anarchists hadn't yet entered the grammar world.)

Having had our giggle with this "rule" (not ending a sentence with a preposition), take another look. It doesn't always work because of the contortions necessary to follow that silly "rule".

Here's a Policy Statement (guideline):

Whereas many prepositions are used with verbs as part of the verb;
And whereas these verbs sometimes appear at the end of a sentence;
Therefore, let it be here recorded that it is okay to end a sentence with a preposition. To do otherwise could become awkward. The Grammar Anarchist has spoken.
They had dreams they wanted to hold onto.
They had dreams onto which they wanted to hold. (Whew, stiff!)

or

The dreamers nevertheless were people you could depend on.

The dreamers nevertheless were people on whom you could depend. (Veddy, veddy formal!)

Take another look at those prepositions that demand being placed next to the verb: *put up, hold onto, depend on*. What you see is a complete verb, NOT a verb and preposition. Now do you see what makes for strange wording when you try to separate them? (For more fun, look further in this section to the uses of "up" and "down".)

Troublesome Prepositions

Many of the common prepositions are used so casually they can get you into trouble. What follows are some of these that need your attention. They are the words we hear every day that cause grammar purists to heave sardonic sighs as they wave their feathered fans and reach for the ammonia bottle. What may be worse are the employers and social leaders who view missteps in grammar on the same level as wiping your mouth with your sleeve.

So pay attention to the following suggestions.

ALL, ANY, **OR** *BOTH*

A common usage that may be difficult to purge is the extra preposition used after the adjectives *all* and *both*. Usually, if a noun follows, the preposition can be eliminated. If a pronoun follows, use the preposition.

> *Gather all (of) the flowers from the garden.*
> *Gather all of them from the garden.*
> *When both (of) the large blossoms are together, they overwhelm.*
> *When both of them are together, they overwhelm.*

AMONG / BETWEEN

Between requires a minimum and maximum of two people. That is, only two people can have anything going on *between* them.

> *Between us, Gary is the more outspoken.* (There are only two of us, Gary and me. Note also the use of "more", also indicating comparison of two things.)

Among requires a minimum of three, with no maximum. It takes a group to use "among".

> *The noise is greater among the youngsters.* (You can't be sure how many youngsters there are, but we know it's three or more and they are noisy.)

Here's another problem with the prepositions *among* and *between*. Objects of prepositions take pronouns from Column B (Quick Pronoun Guide), which should settle the problem of which pronouns to use. *Between* and *among* always — always — take pronouns from Column B (the object).

> *The race was between you and me* (or *you and him* — or *you and her*).
> *The responsibility is divided between them and me* (or *her and him* — or *them and him*.)

Courtesy requires a writer or speaker to put the first person pronoun at the end, as in: *The debate is between him and me.* (Certainly not: *me and him* or *me and them*.)

IN / INTO

Confusion develops between these two seemingly alike prepositions, *in* and *into*. *Into* implies movement, as moving into a situation or place. *In* indicates a position already inside.

> *We walked into the room; we then were in a strange place.*
> *While we were in this state of consciousness, we cannot go into a trance.*

LIKE / AS

An easy way to remember which word to use is to visualize. Use your mind to imagine what something is *like*. If you get a picture, use *like*. If you get a feeling, use *as*.

Here's another hint: as a preposition, *like* is followed by a noun or pronoun (not by a clause). *As* is followed by a clause.

> *He behaved perfectly, like a model child.* (noun follows *like*)
> *He behaved perfectly, as we knew he would.* (clause follows *as*)
> *They dance like other people.*

> *They dance as other people walk.*
> *He had a deep voice like Darth Vader, and as Darth Vader, he depicted a scary being.*
> *The pendant was shaped like a heart.*
> *The pendant was expensive, as we had expected.*

Like is a dangerous word that needs careful handling. It will get more attention when we talk about it the Word Section. This little four-letter word can take the role of seven of the eight parts of speech, some acceptable and some... well... faddish. No wonder it gives us trouble. Try to avoid wincing when "like" is overused, *like maybe like a preposition like something that like works its way like into a like sentence.*

PER (UGH!)

"Per" is a perfectly good preposition that means *through* or *by means of*. However, it has lost its original Latin usage in ordinary conversation. Consider using *per* mostly in connection with numbers:

> *The carpenter used three board feet per unit.*
> *The cost is $500 per hour.*
> *Racing cars move up to 400 miles per hour.*

The fact is that *per* sounds quite pompous: "as per my instructions", or "as per my household rules", or "as per the minutes of the board meeting". Perhaps that is why some business people throw in a *per* every time they want to sound official.

Don't! Please don't give in to the temptation to sound imperious. Use instead more congenial wording: *according to* or *as found in*.

> *According to my instructions....*
> *According to my household rules....*
> *As found in the minutes of the board meeting....*

Save the Latin usage when using legal verbiage. *The quota was set at $4 million per annum.*

The same careful usage applies to other Latin phrases: *per diem, per capita, per mill, per rata, per se.* Each has its own meaning in the technical, legal language of business.

UP

English grammar teachers around the world enjoy the word *up*. Some believe that it gives newcomers to U.S. language more trouble than some of the big words. "Up" means *to go the opposite of down, to rise, to incline, to move in a vertical way towards the sky.*

How then can you explain its use in the following:

Please write up your reports at once.
Don't give up on the secretary.
She'll be tied up until long after closing.

Look at the differences — and similarities — between the following pairs of words: *shut up* and *shut down*, *burn up* and *burn down*, *get up* and *get down*, *turn up* and *turn down*, *up the street* and *down the street*, *slow up* and *slow down*. These, fellow anarchists, fall under the clever all-consuming label: *idioms*.

Many verbs acquire an *up* tagged onto their backsides: *ante up, clean up, close up, do up, drink up, hurry up, join up, keep up, line up, live up, lock up, make up, mix up, offer up, pay up, play up, ring up, set up, stop up, sum up, tie up, tidy up, tilt up, turn up, wake up, wash up, work up, wrap up, up to now, up to us,* and even *listen up*.

> ### JOHNNY'S IN TROUBLE!
> When John **makes up** a story to explain the **makeup** on his collar, he'll **make up** with his wife while she **makes up** their bed and **makes up** her face after crying.

Some words have been used together for so long that they have been pushed together, becoming compound nouns with their own separate meanings: *cleanup, closeup, lineup, lockup, makeup, mixup, tieup, wakeup, workup, wrapup*.

Then there are the reversed words. Some of the combos retain their meanings; many don't. Consider: *up ante, upbeat, upbring, upbuild, upgrade, upgrowth, upheave, uphold, uplift, upkeep, upmarket, up play, upraise, uprise, uproot, upscale, upshift, upspring, upstage, upstart, upthrow, upthrust, uptilt, upturn*.

Computer language is setting a trend that places the preposition in front of the verb to make an entirely new verb. Now we can *download, upload, offload, input, output, outdate, update, upscale, downscale,* and *offclear.* To a grammar-conscious listener, some of the language sounds weird. To a computer techie, it's perfectly understandable.

Simple reversal of the words doesn't always retain similarities with original definitions. There is no connection between the meanings of *sweep up* and *upsweep* (one requires a broom, the other a comb or an upward motion.) *Set up* means "to build"; *upset* means the opposite. *Hang up* is a direction from your mom; *hangup* is the life result of too many such directions. Oh dear!

DOWN

Then we come to *down!* This word enjoys the same overuse and confusion as *up,* with the additional ability to pose as a number of other parts of language: noun, verb, adjective, adverb, and preposition. Count how many of the various parts of speech that "down" assumes.

Come on down to the downside of the house and follow us downstairs as we watch the downturn of our favorite team that can't make a first down to save their downy little hides.

Down

Down participates in jazzing up other words. One can download, downplay, downgrade, downshift, downsize, downswing, and downturn (verbs). Nouns include a downer, downbeat, downdraft, downfall, downgrade, downside, downstairs, downtime, downtown, downtrend, and a downturn. Down, as in down under pin-points Australia and New Zealand and has become a proper place noun, identified with capital letters: Down Under.

One of the funny things about U.S. English is the multiple roles of many words. You'll find many glue words that operate as other parts of speech. One such word that carries the burden of almost every part of speech is the word "down". Usually thought of as "just another preposition", "down" sometimes wears the garb of *noun, adjective, adverb, verb, preposition, conjunction* and *interjection*! Like most interjections, the word *down* can make up an entire sentence if spoken loudly: "Down!"

> The *down* on the duck's belly feels soft. (noun)
> The *down* belly of the duck feels soft. (adjective)
> The duck feels *down* unless someone strokes its belly. (adverb)
> A duck may *down* worms when it's hungry. (verb)
> A duck waddles *down* the path to the pond. (preposition)

The Grammar Anarchist, fed up with mangled language, faced the crowd and yelled, "Down! Down with 'rules'!" (interjections)

As a preposition, *down* is often used with other prepositions: *along, around, through, toward, in, into,* or *on:*

> *down along the river*   *down around the bend*
> *down through the age*   *down toward the bottom*
> *down in the pond*   *down into the depths of the pond*
> *down on your knees*   *down among the sheltering palms*

IDIOMATIC EXPRESSIONS

Idioms are like candy to The Grammar Anarchist. Idioms defy more "rules" than have ever been written. Every language has them; U.S. language has more than most. In fact, a good guess might be that U.S.-ers use more idioms per capita than anybody else.

Take a look at how idioms mess up what some call grammar "rules". (Hee-hee! Here's one you cannot blame on The Grammar Anarchist.) When prepositions attach themselves to other words with no particular reason, they become idioms — the peculiarities of language.

If you have ever studied another language, you already know there is only one way to learn idiomatic expressions — memorize them. When you come across some words that don't fit the guidelines you have learned, consider them idioms. Do an Internet search and believe half of what you read.

ARTICLES

If you're wondering, yes, Articles — *the, a, an* — are considered adjectives. However, the Grammar Anarchist considers them among the important Little Words that form the glue of sentences. Take a look!

The points to a specific item, as compared to just any old thing. *The* store means the one we're talking about, as opposed to *a* store — just any old store. *The* topic, as opposed to *a* topic — just any old topic.

The difference between the uses of *a* and *an* depend on the noun that follows. The single *a* is used before a noun beginning with a consonant (*a tree, a stone, a waterfall*). The *an* is used before a noun beginning with a vowel (*an elm, an emerald, an apparition*).

EXCEPTIONS WITH ARTICLES — ME-OH-MY!

Of course there are exceptions! This is U.S. grammar after all.

The letters "h" and "u" have multiple sounds that mess up the tidy "rules" of proper English. Many like to treat words beginning with "h" as a vowel-starter. That works fine with h-words where the "h" is silent (*an honor, an hour, an hors d'oeuvre*), but it does not include the h-words where the "h" is pronounced (*a house, a horror show, a high forehead, a heavy foot, a head, a hey-nonny nonny*). Don't fall for the haughty pronunciation that silences the "h" in *history, humble*, and *homage*. The "h" is pronounced in each (unless you go totally balmy and pronounce *homage* as ohm-ahj).

The "u" also has double-pronunciation problems. When the "u" sounds like "ewe", treat the word as a consonant, as if it started with "y" (*a utility, a use, a union, a uranium mine, a uniform, a unicorn, a unit, a universe*). When the "u" sounds like "uh", treat it as a vowel-starter (*an uncle, an ultimatum, an ultra-conservative, an umber umbrella, an underworld bum, an uptight personality*).

MULTIPLE DUTY

What happens when you have two nouns in a row (compound nouns), one that begins with a consonant and one with a vowel? Choose the article(s) to match the nouns.

> *They want to hire a lawyer and an accountant.*
> *Settle only for an agreement and a plan of action.*

However, if you want one person to handle both roles, then use one article:

> *They want to choose an accountant and lawyer.* One person handles both jobs. This is one of those dramatic, grammatic moments when you can impress someone (who had "rules" drummed into them back in grade school). Most people wouldn't notice. But now you will know and *they* will gasp in awe. Anarchists love to make 'em gasp!

INTERJECTIONS

"In-ter-jec-tions" is the song from "Sesame Street" that sticks in your head like glue once you get to singing it. Sometimes called *expletives* (but not often on "Sesame Street"), interjections add color to writing. That's why you seldom find them in formal reports and "serious" pieces.

Interjections spice up dialog in ways no other words can. *Ouch! Oh yeah! Right on! Whoopee!* They're the words that add emotion to writing — or make it look ridiculous. How interjections are used (when they matter) and how many are used (sparingly, please) determine the message.

An interjection can be one word or several. Sometimes there is a string of words that expresses an emotion. When that emotion becomes more powerful, it is in danger of becoming an expletive (you know, the #%$*&##$s of language). With a shady reputation, "expletive deleted" has become as easy to recognize as the popular "bleep" of radio and television. An expletive may contain a profane or extreme interjection.

The ordinary, garden variety interjection (actually named an *ejaculation* in British grammar) expresses surprise, annoyance, fright, wonder, confusion, and pain. It represents a sudden and strong feeling, sometimes expressed as an author comment (neato!).

Sometimes an *imperative verb* passes as an interjection, as in the case of: *Don't! It may be too hot.* (The single verb, "don't", implies the subject "you" and is called an imperative — as if there isn't time to use the more courteous "you".) When yelled out in haste — and loudly — interjections rock!

> *Whoopee*! We won the game.
> We came from behind. *Gee whiz*!
> You almost cost us the game, *dunderhead*!
> *Ouch*! You needn't be so rough.
> *Darn it all*, that ball dropped, *thump*, right in the middle of the play.

Because of the manner that an interjection is glued into writing, it is often accompanied by an *exclamation* point (an appropriate name). But not always. A word of caution (attributed to the author, Elmore Leonard): do not use more than one exclamation point for every ten thousand words. A bit extreme, perhaps, but good advice nonetheless.

Other words, acceptable words, pass as interjections to augment an idea or to strengthen a sentence. They include: *really, for example, that is, yes, no, in fact, well.*

> *Really*, you could have told me earlier.
> I knew... *gee*, I thought I knew... what time to start.
> *Yes*, of course you did.
> *No*, I truly did know. *In fact*, I emailed my information.
> *Well*, I didn't receive it.

IT / THERE

Two words — *it* and *there* — have turned into interjections by way of popular usage, meaningless usage. You have become familiar with "it" as a neutral pronoun and "there" as an adverb telling where. But over-usage has brought these words into a bad writing habit that causes them to lose their identity.

Try to identify what is meant when these words are used in the following sentences. Then replace them with more appropriate words to trim down your writing and empower it.

> *There is a chance of rain today.*
> *It is still a nice day.*
> *There isn't a cloud in the sky.*
> *Could there be a mistake in the forecast?*
> *It's possible.*

By using more specific words, not only do meanings become clearer, but the rhythm of the words improves and gains depth. Listen!

> *Rain has been forecast for today, although the skies remain clear and cloudless. Could the forecaster have been mistaken? Yes, that is possible.*

Specific words are usually better that the mamby pamby use for *it, there, nice*, and the ever-popular verb *is*. Specific words are always better when replacing the interjections *it* and *there*.

Similarly, find more expressive words to replace *it is*, another of those wimpy habits. *It is raining* (what is raining?); *it is a beautiful day* (what is beautiful?)

LIKE

When wrestling with *like* as a preposition, did you realize it could also serve as an interjection? *Like really!* (Is that a modifier to an interjection?) or: *Like!* (Not an interjection, but a space filler.) In recent years, the word has become a major part of the interjection repertoire.

> *Like, I'd never have thought of it like that way, like I'm sure! Like, you didn't think I'd like forget!*

Interjection of Anarchist: Ugh! (But you decide.)

Part 2

Punctuation
(Grammar's Road Signs)

Commas, Commas, Commas
(The Reflective Pause)

Colons, Semicolons, Periods
(Headlights, Dots With Tails, Full Stops)

Question Marks (?)
Exclamation Points (!)
(The Voices of Writing)

Parentheses, Brackets
Quotation Marks
(Enclosures of the Word Kind)

Apostrophes, Ellipses,
Hyphens, Dashes, Diagonals
(Dots and Dashes)

Punctuation

(Grammar's Road Signs)

The Grammar Anarchist sits in hog heaven when discussing the mess that's been made of U.S. punctuation. Those little curly-cues, dots, and lines cause more consternation for writers than an anarchist at a tea party. Where do you put the commas? When do you use a double quote mark and when a single? Why does an apostrophe go there? And what difference does it make whether a dash is short or long?

Reasons abound. And every linguist has their own set of them. In this section, the various choices and the reasoning behind them will remove some of the angst.

Think how you would manage moving about a place without signs or with signs that show only an illustration. If you've driven in another country, you're aware of the pitfalls. True, there is that international signing system. But what the heck does *that* European sign mean — the one with the man who appears to be running. Does it warn of pedestrians? Does it direct you to a stairway? A running path? An upcoming marathon? Or an exercise gym?

Of course it helps if you know the language! The same applies to learning punctuation — the *sign language* of writing. Without those little dots and dashes, readers become confused. And make no mistake, U.S. language has its own style.

When speaking face to face, you can shrug your shoulders, whisper, sneer, smile, scowl, hesitate, scream, chatter, drawl or clip, adding emphasis or de-emphasis to what you're saying. In writing, all these nuances must be — and can be — done with punctuation and strategy. The more you read the work of good writers, the more you learn about the techniques. The more you practice the techniques, the more adept you become at expressing yourself through written communication.

Some people are orators, speechmakers, swayers of vast audiences with their voices. They know and practice good punctuation, verbally. Only the great writers know how to practice good punctuation on paper to get a similar effect.

This section looks at the punctuation signing system, using familiar terms and examples. The key to using punctuation effectively is to use punctuation consistently. Just because you have choices doesn't require you to vary the options. Choose the guideline that best fits your work and follow it consistently: C-O-N-S-I-S-T-E-N-T-L-Y!

The catastrophe of a misplaced pauser — the comma — is sometimes a surprise to the writer who has been dropping the little markers into their writing with abandon all these years. Commas are the punctuation road hogs, taking up the greater share of punctuation guidelines.

Periods indicate the complete stop at intersections; colons are the headlights that point out what lies ahead; semicolons are the California stop that is longer than a comma, but shorter than a period. (Replace "California" with your neighboring state.)

The *voices* of writing are the question and exclamations marks that supply sound. They provide inflection to the written words that make the trip interesting.

Enclosures are discussed — quotation marks, parentheses, and brackets. You'll discover a variety of functions that each contributes to written communication.

In addition, notice that some dots and dashes offer their own special meanings to written language — apostrophes, ellipses, hyphens, dashes and diagonals.

Typesetting symbols and road signs are slightly different from typewritten or handwritten symbols. Some of these differences are pointed out for computer users to enlighten the typesetting ways that have been standard since the days of Benjamin Franklin.

Don't underestimate the power of the tiny punctuation marks. More litigation than one would anticipate is brought into courts to contest their uses. Effective writers know not only how to read the road signs, but they know how to use them to the best advantage.

I hear you anarchists who refuse to use certain — or any — punctuation marks. "I've read books that use no quotation marks." However, notice the earlier books of these writers. You'll find the writer who eschews quotation marks, for instance, knows the basics and is very handy with words to keep the reader apprised of who is speaking to whom.

The moral of this section: learn the various punctuation marks available and how they are used by most U.S. writers. Then, when you're brave and skillful with words, use them to your advantage or omit them altogether. Remember, be consistent — and you too can become a grammar guru.

COMMAS, COMMAS, COMMAS

(The Reflective Pause)

The bane of writers is the comma. And that's too bad, because the tiny little comma doesn't mean to be a bane. If you look closely, you'll discover that the comma offers the most fun, probably because it is the most important punctuation mark of the bunch. It paces words, communicates details, refines meaning, and fine-tunes reasoning.

HOW MANY ARE TOO MANY?

Some writers use too many, dropping them in like raisins in a scone, at random, whenever the mood strikes, and they don't care where, or if, they land.

Other writers like James Joyce never use commas or any other punctuation for that matter preferring to let the reader guess where the pauses should be which can be equally confusing.

Re-read the last two sentences, removing all the commas from the first and placing them randomly in the second. Like this:

1. *Some writers use too many dropping them in like raisins in a scone at random whenever the mood strikes and they don't care where or if they land.*
2. *Other writers, like James Joyce, never use commas, or any other punctuation, for that matter, preferring to let the reader guess, where the pauses should be, which can be equally confusing.*

Notice that some sentences are quite readable without the commas. Others make the reader work to understand them.

When a writer loses control of the comma, all manner of havoc can break out, including schisms in relationships, misunderstandings, and even lawsuits. National conventions have been held up while the Rules Committee works out details of comma placement. Legislators hire people to decide the punctuation of proposed laws. The comma has become so important that whole books are being written about them and debates are held to clarify them.

Can you deduce the difference between the following sentences?

1) All children who can read will be promoted to the next grade.
2) All children, who can read, will be promoted to the next grade.

How many children will be promoted? And will yours be among them? In the first sentence, only the children with reading skills will be promoted. In the second sentence, all children will be promoted because they all can read. Do you see the difference now?

Consider:

If you'll teach Jasper, the class average will go up. (Jasper is the slow one holding back the average.)
If you'll teach, Jasper, the class average will go up. (Jasper could help the class average rise by teaching them himself.)

Oh nuts, I don't have any sugar. (Darn! I'm out of sugar.)
Oh nuts, I don't have any, sugar. (Darn! I'm out of nuts.)

Life would be so much easier without having to guess where to put the slippery commas. While "rules" might help, there are many exceptions that are determined by what the writer has in mind. It makes complete sense, then, to provide some guidelines to lead writers to the conclusions that will transmit their intended meaning.

As you discover these guidelines, you'll become equipped with the tools you need to add emphasis, deflect attention, describe details, assign responsibility, and identify speakers. What follows provides the framework of guidelines with which you can provide your own cosmetics, remembering that, like makeup, less is better.

COMMAS IN A SERIES

Don't bother with commas when using a connector for two things (*apples and oranges, boxers or briefs*).

Do bother with commas when listing a series of three or more items, clauses, or phrases. Separate the final item with a comma before the *and* — or not. This is where you can choose; there will be times when the comma is critical and other times when it just gets in the way.

> **Commas In a Series**
>
> *If you get in the habit of using the comma before the **and** in a series of three or more, your readers won't need to decide whether or not it belongs.*

Here are some instances where the comma makes a major difference in the interpretation of meaning.

> *All the babies — Kaitlin, Katy, Kelly, Kevin, and Kenny — were entered in the Pretty Baby Contest.* (Clearly five children were entered in the contest.)
> *Pretty Baby contestants, Kaitlin, Katy, Kelly, Kevin and Kenny — walked off with the trophies.* (If you know there were five trophies, you know they all received one. If you suspect there may be only four trophies, you'll believe that Kevin and Kenny shared one of them. Maybe they were twins!)
> *Pretty Baby contestants, Kaitlin, Katy, Kelly, Kevin, and Kenny — walked off with the trophies.* (Now we're sure there were five trophies, enough for all the contestants. Happy babies; happy parents.)

Here is a legal f'rinstance:

The company co-workers — Mark, Melody and Morgan — agreed to share the lottery winnings of $3 million.

Mark could claim that he gets half ($1.5 million) while Melody and Morgan share the other $1.5 million. Melody and Morgan can each demand a third of the prize, a full million each, as equal winners, but a comma would have negated the need for legal wrangling. What a difference a comma makes! Attorneys regularly earn their fees by arguing such claims, thus adding another party to lay claim to the prize.

While the following example might not get into the courts, it could make a difference to your stomach.

The $20 holiday special includes nachos, veggies, meatballs, beer and coffee.

The question might revolve around whether or not the consumer receives both beer and coffee or whether a beverage choice is included in the special price. A simple comma after *beer* would assure the guest a beer before dinner and a cup of coffee afterwards.

COMMAS IN A COMPLEX SERIES

When parts of a series contain commas of their own, use a semicolon to separate the primary parts of the sentence.

Please contact one of the officers: Cleveland Adams, president; Charlotte Jefferson, vice president; or Trenton Livingston, secretary.
Send the memo to the branch offices in Cleveland, Ohio; Charlotte, North Carolina; and Trenton, New Jersey.

AFTERTHOUGHT COMMAS

Writers like to add information to clarify or identify. These afterthoughts are set apart from the rest of the sentence by commas. If you remove the afterthought, the main sentence will still remain intact, subject and verb.

1) *Call the artists, Wendy and Will, an hour before the opening.*
2) *The gallery, Art For You, opens with a gala next Sunday.*
3) *The curator, Mandy Garfield, will host the event.*
4) *She might find the task, greeting visitors, overwhelming.*

Notice that you can easily remove the words between the commas and still have a complete sentence. If you need a grammatical name, call them *unnecessary* or *restrictive commas*. What they do is more important than what they're called.

Commas: Necessary Or Not

Have you met my husband Elliot? If I have only one husband, I don't need commas. However, if I have more than one husband, I may need to point him out by using the commas: "my husband, Elliot, and not my (other) husbands, Michael or Timothy".

The following sentences contain necessary, or restrictive, phrases and can be grammatically referred to as *appositives*. These are phrases that must be included in order to complete the thought. No commas here.

Call the artists Wendy and Will an hour before the opening. (The artists' names are Wendy and Will; there are no other artists to be called. In Sentence 1 above, the instructions are to call only Wendy and Will, and no others. This is pointed out clearly by the commas.)

The gallery Art For You opens with a gala next Sunday. (It appears there is only one gallery around, and it is called Art For You.) In Sentence 2 above, this particular gallery has been selected from among others.

The curator Mandy Garfield will host the event. (In Sentence 3 above, the commas indicate there are other curators. The only one hosting the event is Mandy.)

She might find the task greeting visitors overwhelming. (In Sentence 4 above, Mandy's tasks include greeting visitors, among others. Without the commas, the task of greeting visitors overwhelms her.)

Aren't commas fun? The little dot-with-a-tail may surprise you with its power to change meaning.

Notice the following sentence pairs:

> *1a) The trouble that you caused cannot be overlooked.* (Necessary clause)
> *1b) The trouble, that you caused, cannot be overlooked.* (Unnecessary clause)
> *2a) The diamond necklace is for the pretty woman who loves beautiful jewelry and me.*
> *2b) The diamond necklace is for the pretty woman, who loves beautiful jewelry, and me.*
> *3a) The fourth graders who ate peanut butter sandwiches came down with tummy aches.*
> *3b) The fourth graders, who ate peanut butter sandwiches, came down with tummy aches.* (The entire class!)

In Sentence 1a, the subject is "the trouble that you caused". In Sentence 1b, the subject is "the trouble". The possibility that you caused it is irrelevant.

In Sentence 2a, the object is "the pretty woman who loves beautiful jewelry and me". In Sentence 2b, the necklace is for "the pretty woman" ... and me. Oh yeah, she happens to love beautiful jewelry.

Sentence 3a tells about tummy aches suffered only by the fourth graders who ate peanut butter sandwiches. Sentence 3b indicates that all of the fourth graders got tummy aches because they all ate the sandwiches.

PARENTHETICAL IDEAS

Ideas that come along in the middle of a sentence, like this, are set off with commas. It only makes sense, we believe, to assume as much. If you object, however, you may want to eliminate the little nuisances. But you may, for sure, expect trouble.

Re-write the above sentences without commas and you get:

Ideas that come along in the middle of a sentence like this are set off with commas. It only makes sense we believe to assume as much. If you object however you may want to eliminate the little nuisances. But you may for sure expect trouble.

If it reads well without the comma, leave it out. Yeah, commas don't cost anything; you can use them or not — sometimes. *Who'll notice if there's a comma or not? After all, it's just a little mark!* Oh my, how much difference one little comma can make and how much trouble one can cause when it is inappropriately inserted or omitted.

COMMAS TO JOIN SENTENCES

Remember that a *simple sentence* contains a subject and verb (sometimes called an *independent clause* because it has been liberated) and needs nothing else to make it stand. There are a two ways to join two or more of these sentences together: 1) connect with a comma followed by a conjunction, or 2) use a semicolon without the conjunction. The two sentences being joined should be so closely related that you want them kept closer together than if they were separated by a period.

Combining Sentences

Combine sentences with similar ideas; use a semicolon between the two rather than a period (and capital letter). Or: use a comma, followed by a conjunction.

In terms of driving a car, the comma compares to a slow-down for the reader; the semicolon offers something between a slow-down and a stop (hence the use of both a period *and* a comma).

1. The two cars collided at a busy intersection; no one was injured.
2. Two cars collided at a busy intersection, but no one was injured.
3. Two cars collided at a busy intersection; headlights were broken and fenders were dented on both cars; no injuries were reported.

In Sentence 1, the two independent clauses are connected with the semicolon. In Sentence 2, a comma and conjunction (*but*) connect the two bits of information. Sentence 3 shows the ease of combining three separate sentences with the semicolons.

COMMA AFTER INTRODUCTORY ADVERB CLAUSE

Notice the word "introductory". This guideline applies only to adverb clauses or single adverbs at the beginnings of sentences.

Since the weather is changing, let's eat indoors.
While we're eating, keep an eye out for intruders.
After we're finished, we'll go out to a movie.

When you place an adverb clause at the end of a sentence, omit the comma.

Let's eat indoors since the weather is changing.
Keep an eye out for intruders while we're eating.
We'll go out to a movie after we're finished.

COMMA AFTER INTRODUCTORY VERBAL CLAUSE

The verbal clause is followed by a comma and the subject that is being modified. That second part (subject being modified) often gets lost or misplaced and provides some ludicrous misplaced modifiers.

Determined to be popular, she sang her heart out.
Electing to go first, he grabbed the microphone.
Disgusted, she sat down and sulked. (Even a one-word clause can deserve a comma.)

The verbal clause at the end of the sentence does require the comma.

She sang her heart out, determined to be popular.
He grabbed the microphone, electing to go first.
She sat down and sulked, disgusted.

That embarrassing misplaced modifier usually happens when it is added as an afterthought rather than connected to the word it modifies. You probably know them as "dangling modifiers".

She sang until he grabbed the microphone determining to be popular. (Just how popular can a microphone expect to be?)

Try this:

She sang, determining to be popular, until he grabbed the microphone.

COMMA AFTER ONE INTRODUCTORY WORD

One-word modifiers may merit a comma at the beginning of a sentence, but not at the end. This is one of those places a writer can choose. Remember that the function of a modifier is to modify something.

Reluctantly, she gave up the microphone to her opponent.
Slowly, she walked off the stage.
Sadly, he never even noticed her demeanor.

Place the single modifiers next to the modified word and you can forget the comma.

She gave up the microphone reluctantly to her opponent.
She slowly walked off the stage.
He never even noticed her demeanor. (The "sadly" is a comment made by the writer and may not belong in the sentence.)

Just as editorial comments (like the "sadly" above) can be added at the beginning of a sentence, so can interjections and expletives. They too require that comma.

Yes, she did have a jealous bone in her body.
Indeed, he wasn't aware she was watching him.
Honestly, do you think he cared?
Darn, she should have seen it coming.

COMMAS IN MULTI-MODIFIERS

When a string of adjectives or adverbs are used to modify a single word, the writer may indicate those that are similar and separate them from one another. All of the following modifiers describe the attitude of the job applicant, yet each is slightly different. Separate them with commas.

> *The job applicant was friendly, witty, energetic, and skilled.* Each modifies "the applicant".

Now consider her appearance.

> *She had curly brown hair and large blue eyes.*
> *Her curly, kinky hair defied straightening.*

In the first sentence, "curly" and "brown" both modify "hair", but in different ways. Thus, no commas. In the same way her eyes are both *large* and *blue*. The commas used in the second sentence show that her hair was *curly* and also described as *kinky*.

OTHER USES FOR COMMAS

While you probably haven't even noticed, there are many kinds of uses for commas. They're as useful in many ways that don't take much thought. Commas are used in addresses, dates, titles, measurements, and all manner of odds and ends.

> ### Her birthday is on the 15th.
> With complete dates, do not use *th, st, rd,* or *nd* unless you omit the month. You'll pronounce it May fifteenth, but write May 15. Use the *th* only if you omit the month and use only the date.

Use a comma in addresses between the street, city, and state. His address is: *3030 Private Lane, Hollywood, California.* If you use the two-letter postal state abbreviation, you can skip the comma: *Hollywood CA.* And you add the zip code as well without commas: *Hollywood CA 90011.* (The post office asks for the use of all capital letters and no punctuation in addresses on business envelopes.)

Separate the date from the year with a comma, only if both the month and day are used: *May 15, 1952*. Do add a comma if only the month and year are used: *May 1952*.

Use a comma to separate a name from a title: George Washington, President; Harry Truman, Vice President; Patty Murray, senator. Do not use commas if the title precedes the name: President George Washington, Vice President Harry Truman, Senator Patty Murray.

Use commas in measurements to separate various components: 6-feet, 3 inches; 13 pounds, 7 ounces; 47 years, 6 months, and 14 days; 51 yeas, 49 nays.

COMMAS CLARIFY AND PREVENT MISINTERPRETATION

Whenever a sentence can be misread without a specified pause (indicated with a comma), you'll need to place one. This happens when writers use words that can be both noun and verb (*record, draft, cover, top, bottom, joke*). The choice of commas lies with the writer. The best way to catch such situations is to read the sentence aloud (or read it several hours after writing it).

Some of the following confusion could have been avoided by using these suggestions. You place the commas:

> *I'm sorry it's not loaded Sonya.*
> *Mark said he wanted to be a hit man.*
> *Expecting visitors she didn't want to be caught without her makeup.*
> *Delighted he brought chocolates for the hostess who didn't expect him.*
> *I'm not sure she even knew about that Jane.*
> *While I froze my friend raised her umbrella and hit the assailant.*
> *They recognize the dilemma as a misunderstanding and plan to keep their lives open from here on thanks to caring neighbors.*

COLONS SEMICOLONS PERIODS

(Headlights, Dots With Tails, Full Stops)

The little dots with tails are often described as essential to the road signs of writing. The one you know best through its use in smiley faces appears on your computer on its side, the side that is defined as a Colon :). In some computers, the smiley face actually appears automatically when you key in the colon and the close-parenthesis.

As described in the previous section, the dot with the tail (at ground level) is called a comma. Now put that comma together with the colon and you get… ta-da!… a Semicolon (;), and no smileys appear when you key in those two things.

COLONS (:)

SOMETHING LIES AHEAD:

Notice that the colon resembles headlights, turned on the side, but headlights that proclaim "something lies ahead". When you want to list several things in a series, begin with words such as: *such as, as follows, the following, these things*, and follow with the colon.

> *Punctuation is used as follows: to direct the reader, to separate similar words, to inform the reader when the end is reached, to get the reader excited, and to raise a question, among other things.*
>
> *You have three choices: agree, disagree, or remain neutral.*
>
> *The joyful story ends as follows: "And they lived happily ever after."*

However, if your list follows directly after an indicating verb (calling for action), do not use the colon.

> *What I enjoy most about stories* include *the lilting rhythm of the writer, the wild action words, and the music of the sentence.*
>
> *A musical sentence* contains *modifiers that enhance the mood, sad adverbs, happy adjectives, or vibrant descriptions.*

Whether or not a capital letter is used after the colon or indicative verb depends on two factors and the writer's choice:

1) if what follows is a quotation *("That's what it's for.")* or
2) if you think what follows is important enough to merit a capital letter (*The only direction for a writer is this: Know what you mean to say.*)

There are occasions when what follows an indicator is only a word or two. You may then consider using the long dash (m-dash) instead. Some punctuation gurus consider the dash to be more informal than a colon — use your own judgment and see the Dashes Section.

> *Only three people responded to the questionnaire — all boys.*
>
> *Heaven knows why teenagers love glitz — especially girls.*

QUOTATIONS — LONG AND SHORT

When a quotation is short, just a sentence or two, precede it with a comma.

The professor was precise with directions, "Don't copy!"
Every student muttered words of agreement, such as "Yeah, Of course, Sure".

When a quotation is longer, you may want to use the colon. Whole passages or long dialogs may follow the colon, as long as the indicator words (*such as, the following*) are used as well.

Directions were given by the quizmaster as follows:

Keep your eyes on your own paper and remember to fill in all the blanks. Any questions left unanswered will be excluded from the grade. Be sure to watch the clock. Each section is carefully timed; you will be given a one-minute warning when the section time is ending.

Often, a long quotation is set off with a change of margins or with a change of font (*italics*, for instance). And note that the quotation marks may be omitted when the quotation is indented.

MORE USES FOR THE COLON

Oh yes, there are other uses for the colon.
Use the colon to separate hours from minutes, when referring to time.

Meet me at 11:30 a.m. We'll discuss this until 2:30 p.m.
Your best running time is clocked at 1:28:30.

Use the colon to indicate ratios.

The polls showed a 3:1 lead.
Interest in the project was expressed by a 5:4 vote against.

Use the colon to depict chapter and verse or subsection.

The reading came from Proverbs 21:3.
Look up RCW158:17 for the law that applies here.

Use the colon in subtitles for books or magazine articles.

The Angry Angel: A Story of Retribution
"Fragile Marble: The Picture of Our Environment"

Use the colon in (some) salutations, when you want to be formal.

Dear Fellow Anarchist:
Henrietta Jones:

Now try it with commas and notice the difference. Somehow it seems inconsistent to use the stern colon with such a term of endearment as "Dear".

Dear Fellow Anarchist,
Dear Henrietta Jones,

See? Either is acceptable. You choose and record it in Your Style Manual.

SEMICOLONS
(THE CHOOSE-YOUR-STATE STOP)

In the West, we call it the California Stop. In Wisconsin, it is called the Illinois Stop. In New York, it's the New Jersey Stop. Seems like every state considers drivers from the nearest state as irresponsible, corner-cutting anarchists.

The semicolon, however, reflects what they mean — a kinda, sorta, nearly stop, but not a full stop, and not a very long one. The semicolon is best used to keep two similar thoughts together when each has its own sentence (independent clause, if you want to get technical).

Semicolons sometimes get mixed up with colons (because of their names), but each has its own special use. The semicolon takes on the troublesome compound sentence with its two distinct parts. Some refinements here might surprise even a seasoned writer.

THE CONNECTOR SEMICOLON

When the semicolon connects two complete sentences, it acts as the connector between them. This keeps two similar thoughts kinda, sorta together.

As in:

Oak trees bear acorns; squirrels love acorns.
The managers met for three hours; they reported their findings immediately.
France is a beautiful country; tourists flock to it every year.

The previous sentences could be written separately:

Oak trees bear acorns. Squirrels love acorns.
The managers met for three hours. They reported their findings immediately.
France is a beautiful country. Tourists flock to it every year.

They also could be written with a connector preceded by a comma:

Oak trees bear acorns, and squirrels love acorns.

The managers met for three hours, and they reported their findings immediately.
France is a beautiful country, and tourists flock to it every year.

> **Sentences With Semicolons**
>
> When two simple sentences are related, use a semicolon to connect them. Options: 1) stop the first sentence with a period and begin the second sentence with a capital letter; 2) use a comma followed by a connector.

The thing to look for is the completeness of each clause. Is there a subject and verb in each part? The semicolon indicates the relationship between the two sentences and the need to keep them connected in some way.

TRANSITION WORDS

The semicolon is considered the peacemaker among ideas, holding them together, clarifying meanings, and indicating shifts. The easy transition word is "and", but many others can accomplish the same task, such as: *however, yet, therefore, moreover, still, as a result, in addition, in summary, on the contrary, besides, consequently, for example, for instance, accordingly, thus, also*, and many more.

The dinner was delightful; however, the restaurant was overcrowded and uncomfortable.
The salad was large; as a result, many couldn't finish theirs before the entrée was served.
The dessert was scrumptious; moreover, the wine accompaniment fit perfectly.

While the comma usually follows a transition word, it often can be eliminated after one-syllable transition words. For example:

The moon shone brightly; yet visibility was limited.
The friends watched the moon rise over the lake; still they didn't want to jump in.
A midnight swim can be refreshing; or it can bring an evening to a quick conclusion.

Before rushing to use the semicolon, make sure that both sentences are able to stand by themselves. Also make sure the transition word(s) is not just a parenthetical expression — set off by commas or included within parentheses. The following are *not* pairs of simple sentences; they include parenthetical expressions.

Red is a color of high emotions, an example of both love and hate.
Yellow, a bright sunny color, invites good cheer, as well as happy thoughts.
Blue sets moody people to the depths of sadness, especially those inclined toward depression.

LISTS THAT CONTAIN COMMAS

The semicolon is used to separate items in a list when the items include commas of their own:

The trip included stops in Chicago, Illinois; Hannibal, Missouri; Austin, Texas; and Los Angeles, California.
Making the trip will be Joan Hendrix, president; Maureen O'Hara, treasurer; John Appleseed, secretary; and the office assistant, Claudia Smith. Stops will be made overnight on Tuesday, March 2; Thursday, March 4; Saturday, March 6; and Sunday, March 7.

When used in this manner, the semicolon clarifies a less-than-clear series of items, often found in very long sentences, like the following:

The purpose of the trip is to review transportation systems; interview possible interns, who would be helpers in the new project; collect ideas, to be used in the new project; and submit a report, within three weeks, supporting the request for transportation funding.

Note that in this long, involved sentence, the subject is repeated toward the end to remind the reader what the heck is being talked about. Sometimes, in an eagerness to get everything in, we forget that the reader easily becomes lost in lengthy complicated sentences.

PERIODS (.)
(THE COMPLETE STOP)

Everything comes to a stop when you use the dot by itself, the period. Or, as it is sometimes known: a *pip, tittle, jot, speck, blip, pixel, decimal point, multiplication sign, spot, dot matrix, musical notation, zit*, and a *dowry*! (Okay, look it up! Look up "dot" and you'll find it was considered a lady's dowry in terms of Middle English, among other things.) Each of these weirdly named dots has its own use. And now, computers have brought us a new use — as in *dot.com*.

When the word *period* was adopted into Latin from the Greek, it took on the meaning of "a punctuation mark used at the end of a rhetorical period (of time)". In terms of time, the period became the *full stop* (British term) that ends a sentence.

Back in second grade (or was it first?), you learned to end a simple sentence with a simple dot — a period. As a grownup, you can now call that "a rhetorical statement".

> **Question**: So how much trouble *can* a little dot cause?
> **Answer**: As much as an unexpected stop in traffic (oops! rear-ended!).

Like driving in traffic, you won't get into trouble with the period-that-stops as long as you use it when necessary. What's interesting about the close look at the period is the discovery that there are many instances, similar to traffic, when it should *not* be used.

> What you learned in second grade was the use of the period after a simple sentence, a statement, request, or a command.
> *Mary had a little lamb.*
> *Its fleece was white as snow.*
> *It would be nice if the lamb followed Mary.*
> *Lamb, keep up with Mary.*

Now comes The Anarchist's opportunity to choose. The bold utilize periods after sentence fragments, something your second grade teacher warned you against. "Do not write incomplete sentences," she cautioned. Well, there are many times a fragment resembles a complete sentence:

> *Certainly, like this.*
> *Definitely understandable.*

ABBREVIATIONS

The period indicates an abbreviation: *Ms., Mr., Jr., Sr., etc., e.g., i.e., Inc., Ltd., Corp., Jan., Feb., Mar., Sun., Mon., Tues.* Computerization usage removes the periods from most abbreviations. Do NOT use periods in easily recognized acronyms: USA, NATO, YWCA, UFO, FDIC, IRS, FBI, AAA, FAA, CPA, nor in easily recognized small-letter abbreviations: rpm, mph, rbi, mpg.

Postal state abbreviations do not require periods (WI, CO, KS, MN, OH, MD, FL, WA). In fact, the post office seeks addresses without periods (123 ELM ST, WOODVILLE NY USA). Wait for it... here's the exception. If you use the standard state abbreviations, use the period: Wis., Colo., Kans., Minn., Md., Fla., Wash.

> **Caution**
>
> *Some abbreviations carry several interpretations. MS, for example, can mean multiple sclerosis, manuscript, master of science, millisecond, military science, motor ship, Mississippi, or a courtesy title for a woman. Best to explain.*

As technology changes, new abbreviations arrive, some without written usage guidelines. In the case of "facsimile transmission", is it FAX or fax, F.A.X. or f.a.x. — capitalized or not? Does the abbreviation take a period... or not? The guideline offered here is this: as long as the word is not a registered trademark, spell it with small letters — fax, without periods.

When using abbreviations of something that all readers may not easily understand, spell out the word(s) with the abbreviation in parentheses. Thereafter, use just the abbreviation. Whether the parenthetical abbreviation comes before or after the spell-out is unimportant. Just keep your readers clued in.

Once a year, every worker fills out an IRS (Internal Revenue Service) form.
Once a year, every worker fills out an Internal Revenue Service (IRS) form.

THE DECIMAL POINT

The decimal point is actually a period with a pseudonym (alias) that interacts with the world of math and science. Use it in dollars and cents, percentages, anything that uses a base-10 numbering system. However, use the European comma when referring to euros.

Expenses for the project amounted to $125.89.
That paid for 30.8 percent of the project.
In euros, that amounts to $14,95.

Use the period when numbering an outline — if you wish.
1. *Grammar*
    A. *Words*
    B. *Punctuation*
        1. *Comma*
        2. *Period*
        3. *Parenthesis*

Another method suggests the use of parentheses for the numbers or letters. In those cases, you can omit the period... or not.
1. *Dots*
    a) *Period*
    b) *Colon*
2. *Dashes*
    a) *Hyphen*
    b) *Long dash*

BUT! Place a period after the heading only when you list complete sentences.
    a) *The night was long.*
    b) *The sky was blue.*
    c) *That's why I told you I loved you.*

INSIDE / OUTSIDE? WHERE DO YOU PLACE THE PERIOD?

Easy answer: place the period at the end of a sentence. If that sentence is a quote of dialog, place it inside the quote marks.

1. Little Red said, "What big eyes you have, Grandmother."
2. Grandmother replied, "You think I have 'big eyes', you should see my teeth."

In the first sentence, Little Red is speaking.

In the second, Grandmother is quoting some of Red's words (in single quote marks).

In the following sentence, neither Grandma nor Little Red is speaking.

3. Grandmother's tone caused Red to look closer at her "big eyes".

If a complete sentence lies within the quotation marks, place the period (and any other punctuation) inside the quote marks. If quote marks are used with the final words of a sentence but are NOT quotations, place the period *outside* the quote marks.

When using the period with the parenthesis, follow similar guidelines. Place the period inside the parens if the sentence is complete. (*Parens* is short for "parenthesis".) If the addition is part of the sentence, place the period outside the closing *parens*.

Look closely at the previous paragraph before dashing off to the Parenthesis Section.

MISCELLANEOUS DOTS

How often do you get to the end of a sentence and wonder if it is *legal* to use two periods? Perhaps it was this morning, about 10 a.m. You see, it is unnecessary to add a period if the sentence already ends in one (as with the abbreviation *a.m.*). Please note that the preceding sentence includes the "abbreviation" dot *inside* the parenthesis and the "sentence-ending" dot *outside*.

QUESTION MARKS (?) EXCLAMATION POINTS (!)
(The Voices of Writing)

What's a good anarchist without the tools of questions and exclamations! Weren't you delighted to learn that you have a bunch of marks to end a sentence? You probably yelled out loud, "Wahoo!" After learning that the basic ending of a sentence is a period or possibly a semi-colon, you have (at least) two more options: a question mark and an exclamation point.

Question marks mark questions. What else! The problem is the placement of the mark. Is it inside or outside a quote mark? Inside or outside a parenthesis? In the middle of a sentence? All these questions will be answered in this section.

In the same way that question marks signal questions, exclamation points mark exclamations. Of course! Again, placement is the problem. Inside or outside the quote marks or parenthesis? But, Writer, ask yourself: *when is enough too much?*

If you keep in mind that question marks and exclamation points represent the sounds of your voice, you will get the hang of this more easily. When speaking, our voice rises at the end of a question, doesn't it? (voice slides up) When speaking, you can slam your fist or shout to drive home your exclamations!

QUESTION MARKS (?)

When you don't know something, when you wonder about an idea, when you can't believe a statement, you ask a question. And, you close that sentence, independent clause, with a question mark. Shouldn't that be simple enough?

There's more. Sometimes you may make a statement, then add the question at the end. In a case like that, end your statement with a comma or semi-colon, then ask your question, isn't that reasonable?

You told me a long story, but is it believable?
I thought it was funny, didn't you?
You weren't home last night; did you stay with your friend?

You might even pose a question without the standard questioning words (who, what, why, when, where). If you mean the sentence to be a question, make it one by using the question mark.

You're a single mother?
You have three children?
Now you tell me you have a job too?

Other times you may make a *statement* that contains an indirect question. Omit the question mark in this case.

The employer asked if she understood the requirements.
The employee asked where the coffee machine was.
The manager wanted to know if she could use overtime.

THE RHETORICAL QUESTION

When is a question not a question? When you don't expect an answer. Here are a couple of examples, usually spoken by parents or people in authority. Use the question mark, but please don't expect an answer.

Are you going to give us answers?
Why in the world would you say that?

Is it any wonder you can't keep your employees?
When can we expect to see the records?

MORE THAN ONE QUESTION

Sometimes questions just tumble out, one after another. Does each deserve (or need) a separate sentence? and therefore its own question mark? or can you ask several questions in one sentence? do you notice you're reading such a sentence now? with multiple questions?

Oh yes, it's possible, although you may have to convince your computer not to capitalize the words following the question marks. Usually, these strings of questions occur when you have just one subject. Do you hesitate to use individual sentences with question marks? or use one long sentence with several question marks within it? You are the writer; you have a choice.

Why didn't you call me? or come to visit? or write me a letter? (understandable)
Why didn't you call me, or come to visit, or write me a letter? (also understandable)
Why didn't you call me? Why didn't you come to visit? Why didn't you write me a letter? (yup! This is understandable too)

WHERE DO YOU PLACE THE QUESTION MARK?

This conundrum occurs when you use a question in tandem with quotation marks or parentheses. Inside or outside, that is the question. Part of the answer lies in the writer's intent. What do you mean when you write it?

If the question is what is being quoted, for instance, the question mark belongs nestled inside the quotation marks.

The officer asked, "Are you planning to park here?"
The driver responded, "Is there a law against it?"
The bystander commented, "Are you harassing the officer?"

If the entire statement is a question, place the mark outside the quotation marks.

> *Did you just tell me to "mind my own business"?*
> *Will you tell me again, "There's no law against it"?*
> *Who wrote this ticket saying, "I broke the law"?*

Now, what if you have a question within a question that is inside a quotation? (Stay calm; it happens!)

> *Who asked, "What am I supposed to do?"*
> *Why did everyone want to know, "Where do I go now?"*
> *How did the story end without answering the question, "Who dunnit?"*

A question inside a quotation that's inside another question takes only one question mark, *inside* the quotation marks. But know there are those who believe the second question mark is necessary.

> *Who asked, "What am I supposed to do?"?*

The Grammar Anarchist doesn't think so.

The same guidelines apply to question marks inside parentheses. There are occasions when the question is inside the parentheses only.

> *The routine trip was brief (just how many days?), but enjoyable.*
> *You took three weeks (or was it four?) for your vacation.*
> *Your tan from your vacation (or was it a tanning salon?) is lovely.*

A LESSON IN TACT

When you want to schmooze someone to ask for a favor, leave out the question mark and begin your request with "will you" or "would you" (and *please* wouldn't hurt either). It sounds like a question, but it also includes an assumption that the answer is "yes".

> *Would you mind closing the door when you leave.*
> *Will you please pass the sugar.*
> *Would you like to take me dancing some time.*

UNCERTAINTY?

In essays or reports, it happens that a fact may be questionable. Use the question mark to express that to your reader.

> *The number of felons loose on the street (aged 28-40?) is the reason for the new law.*
> *Martha Washington was born in the early 18th century (1732?).*
> *At least 600 (?) attended the demonstration.*

But use just one! Resist: *At least 600 (????) attended the demonstration.*

ANOTHER LANGUAGE

Question marks vary according to the country you're in. The Spanish use an upside-down question mark (¿) at the beginning of a sentence and the right-side up question mark at the end. Just to be sure?

> *¿Como esta, Juan?*
> *¿Bueno, y Usted?*

EXCLAMATION POINTS (!)

How much emotion can you take? The exclamation point has something to do with that. For instance: you're driving along peacefully listening to your favorite jazz when another car pulls around you and cuts in front of you — without signals, without easing over, without any concern for your well being. What do you yell out? "You stupid *#$%&^!" or words to that effect, ending with an exclamation point!

REMEMBER THE BOY WHO CRIED "WOLF!!!!"

Be careful that you don't overdo the surprise mark in your writing. You can be surprised only so much. Like the boy crying "Wolf!", the exclamation point is overused in much of today's writing. Watch a television commercial! Notice the wham! bang! whoopee! — the noises that accompany the exclamation points on screen! After too many, the impact diminishes!

> ### One / Ten Thousand
> *One big-time writer warns against using the exclamation point more than once in every 10,000 words.*

Used with care, this mark expresses strong feelings, deep emotions. This is just the right place to suggest "less is more". The less the exclamation point is used, the stronger the impact on the reader when it appears.
Consider the following passages.

> *Your last memo concerned me! I'm disgusted! Yes! disgusted with the anger! I saw it as impatient!! Obviously you don't understand a dire situation clearly!!! In short, you need help!!!!*
> *Your last memo concerned me. I'm disgusted, yes disgusted with the anger. I saw it as impatient. Obviously you don't understand the dire situation clearly. In short, you need help!*

Strong words — *disgusted, anger, impatient, dire.* Let them work for you by themselves, without relying on marks. In a way, using the exclamation point with restraint has the impact of a silent person who withholds comment until the right moment, then says something important — *you need help!*

Confession: A writer once confessed that the urge to use exclamation points led him to take drastic steps to cure himself. Now he piles them up and tosses them into emails and tweets. A good way to dispose of them!

PLACING THE EXCLAMATION POINT

The exclamation point is placed in a way similar to other sentence-ending punctuation. Whether it appears inside or outside quotation marks or parentheses depends on what the writer means: if the surprise is spoken, the point is inside quotation marks; if the surprise is a comment written as an aside, place it inside parentheses.

> *"I won't go just because you say so!" he yelled at his mother.*
> *"I'm trying to be patient, but you're tempting me!" Mother yelled back.*
> *"Help!" the child responded.*
> *The mother stood glaring at the boy (he was scared!), then walked away.*
> *What a way to treat each other!*
> *So much anguish rose from the cry for "help"!*
> *Now that was a scary movie (Thirteen Days With a Monster)!*

PARENTHESES BRACKETS QUOTATION MARKS
(Enclosures of the Word Kind)

Often discounted as unimportant, the parenthesis and brackets add or detract from a piece of writing.

1. **Parentheses** enclose disconnected elements that you want to de-emphasize.
2. Use them to insert an *aside* (please avoid *ha-ha*).
3. Use them to clarify legal figures that follow the spelled out number.
4. Use them to enclose a series of numbers or letters that introduce narrative lists.

Some punctuationists are adamant about including both fore and aft parens with numbers. Some prefer just the aft. Your choice.

    Brackets are used in academic and technical writing. They will enclose words added by an author in the midst of quoting another author, something like an *editorial note*. They're sometimes used to set off a parenthesis within a parenthesis.

While it may seem obvious to use **quotation marks** to set off words that are quoted, there are questions about where to place the marks, when to use them, and how often to use them. Do the quote marks go before or after the period, question mark, exclamation mark? This offers a good place to review other associated quandaries.

PARENTHESIS ( )

The Parenthesis is an enclosed expression that you feel holds enough importance to be included, but is not important enough to deserve its own sentence. Sometimes this information explains or defines. Sometimes it comments. Parenthesis (singular) refers to one or both of the marks that enclose such an expression. Multiple *pairs* of these marks are spelled: *parentheses*.

Within another sentence, the parenthetical expression does not call for a capital letter (to begin) nor a period to end.

The storm hit at mid-day (right in the middle of lunch hour) and caused considerable damage.

When the parenthetical words come within a sentence that requires a comma or other punctuation, place punctuation after the closing parenthesis.

The rain descended in torrents (a devastating experience), flooding the streets.

When making references, do not capitalize the referral word *see,* or not.

Damage was extensive (see: The Tribune newspaper) throughout the city.

Damage was extensive (See: The Tribune newspaper) throughout the city.

In the following example, the question mark points to the question within the parentheses; the period marks the end of the sentence.

I visited Rainville during the last storm in May (or was it April?).

If the parenthetical information is composed as a sentence, it is punctuated within the parentheses. (This is fairly simple to understand.)

The storm continued for hours. (My own house remained undamaged.) The entire city lost electrical power.

NUMBERS AND LETTERS

The parenthesis sets aside numbers and letters when used to list a series of ideas or things, or when outlining. This can be done in a number of ways. Simplification in today's business world accepts a single parenthesis instead of both (usually the closer). Just be consistent in which choice you make.

> *The plan called for (1) a committee to be named and (2) a visit to the site, and (3) affirmation by the entire council.*

The following example uses the single parens:

> *The plan called for 1) a committee to be named and 2) a visit to the site, and 3) affirmation by the entire council.*

Or   *The plan:*

> *1) Name a committee*
> *2) Visit the site*
> *3) Take it to the council*

FORMAL / LEGAL PARENTHESIS

In formal writing, usually in connection with legal documents, the parenthesis is used to clarify information:

> *The Party of the First Part (Adam J. Stone) and the Party of the Second Part (Eve G. Garden) enter into this agreement.*
> *The amount paid in compensation amounted to Thirty Thousand Dollars ($30,000.00), to be paid in one lump sum.* (Note that legal folk love to add the zeros in the cents column. They usually aren't necessary.)

PARENTHESIS TO DE-EMPHASIZE

In many of the above examples, the parenthetical information could have been set aside with commas or dashes. By placing the information in parenthesis, the writer is playing down its importance. In the section concerning dashes, you'll see how dashes set off information, play it up, emphasize it. Choose your strategy and use the appropriate marks. Notice the difference:

1. *You may receive this offer for a small amount — only $9.95 — for a limited time only.*
2. *You may receive this offer for a small amount (only $9.95) for a limited time only.*

You'd want to use the first if this clearly is a for-real bargain. Let's say it is an article you usually would pay twice the amount to own.

However, if this is a gadget worth a much smaller amount, you'd want to play it down, place it in parenthesis, as in the second sentence. If you feel so-so about it, you may choose to set off the price with commas. This tidbit of information on the psychological effects of punctuation is particularly useful in preparing *sales* messages.

BRACKETS [ ]

Brackets are not just square parentheses. They have some uses all their very own. The best part is that you, the writer, can choose how you want to use them.

INSIDE REMARKS

Use brackets when you have a parenthetical remark within another parenthetical remark.

> *Trees such as these are found in warm climates (in North and South Carolina, Georgia and Alabama [especially the Gulf Coast region] and in Florida). Timber from these trees is particularly long-lasting. (Some suggest even longer-lasting than mahogany [see page 35] when used in furniture.)*

Brackets are useful in setting apart the comments of one writer when quoting another and in adding information to quoted material.

> *Employees at the saw mill stated in their request, "We want everyone to know that Arnie [Line Supervisor Arnold R. Matson] has agreed with our need for a new saw."*
> *The article stated, "This group wants to request $15,000 [that figure has since been reduced to $12,000] for new equipment."*

BRACKETS FOR [SIC]

When quoting a piece of writing or a spoken statement, it is necessary to repeat it exactly as written or spoken. Occasionally, you'll find words that are misspelled or misstated that you may want to note as such. The way to do that is to write the Latin word *sic* and place it in brackets behind the misquote. That tells the world you are only copying as delivered.

> *The class sang, "Row, row, row your coat [sic], gently down the stream."*
> *"Tell me, Josiph [sic], do you care about me?" she wrote on her lilac stationery.*

Without the bracketed *sic*, you run the risk of having words corrected by an editor, or having your knowledge questioned by the reader.

Spelling clarification is the greatest use for *sic*. Occasions arise where the writer needs to show a spelling discrimination or an on-purpose misspelling.

> *People who live in Tacoma WA, and attend Tahoma [sic] High School know what this means.*
>
> *My daughter wrote: "I luv [sic] you, Mommy."*

"QUOTATION MARKS"

Quotation marks come in pairs: an open quote and a close quote. They also come in sets of singles and doubles. They resemble uplifted commas, except that they can also appear upside-down. Open quotes look like upside down commas ("). Close quotes look like right-side-up commas on helium ("). On the typewriter, there is no such distinction because the inch mark (") is used for quotations. In the computerized typeset copy used by word processors, there is a distinct difference.

QUOTED WORDS

Quotation marks are used to set off quoted material. No surprise there. They usually are reserved for the exact words.

> *Mandy told her client, "I can't work any faster."*
> *The client retorted, "I have an appointment in exactly 30 minutes."*
> *"My work demands plenty of time," Mandy came back, "and requires you to sit still."*

A quotation does not have to be the entire sentence. There will be times you'll want to use only a few words. Use quotation marks around the quoted section only.

> *Mandy repeatedly was told she needed to "take her time".*
> *She was attempting to learn "patience".*

In normal written dialog, each speaker receives a new paragraph. Notice in novels how you can follow the conversation without the speaker being mentioned each time it changes.

> *"Mary, you know I love you."*
> *"You say you do, but how can I be sure?"*
> *"Trust me."*
> *"Oh Joe, you know I do."*

In business correspondence (minutes, legal proceedings, report writing) the guideline to denote a speaker becomes more important.

Supervisor Teton spoke first. "I am the boss in this factory," he said.
"And I am a respected employee," Jamey spoke back.
"When I give an order, I expect it to be carried out."
"I did that," responded Jamey, "and I carried it out right down the line. I don't see what this fuss is all about anyway." Jamey turned his back at this point and appeared to walk away.

As long as one speaker is continuing, or as long as you are writing about that speaker, keep it in the same paragraph. The paragraph immediately above belongs to Jamey.

Do not use quote marks if you are not quoting.

She asked if everyone was all right.
He answered with a simple no.

SINGLE QUOTE MARKS

Sometimes you'll find a quote within a quote.

Penny offered, "I'll tell you right now that she said, 'I want to go along.' Those were her exact words: 'I want to go along'."

Use the single quote within another quote. And don't forget to close them both at the proper place. Always close the single quote first.

Yes, if there is a quote within a quote within a quote, you return to the double quote marks. But please try to avoid this kind of confusion. Writing, by its very form of words on paper, is difficult enough to translate without adding further confusion about who is saying what.

ALTERNATIVE QUOTATION USES

Long quotations can be handled in several ways. One is to maintain the same type style and continue quoting. In this case, begin each new paragraph with open-quote marks. Do not use close quotes until the end of the final paragraph. The open quote marks tell the reader that the quotation continues. Don't disappoint them before the end.

> **Ration the Quotes**
> *Save the quote marks when using long quotations.*

Long quotations can be set in a different type style. The material may be indented, single-spaced, written in italics or bold-faced. In this case, you won't need any quotation marks at all. The type change tells the reader this is a quote.

This kind of change is particularly effective when quoting newspaper articles or information from a letter or a report. Credit for the quote can be given either at the outset or in a line by itself at the close.

> *MADISON, WI September 1, 1979—Citizens of the city were shocked this morning to learn a large section of Madison was doomed to be torn down.*
>
> *Righteously up in arms, the townspeople are preparing today to march on the State Capitol, challenging the right of the City to destroy history.*
>
> *Legislative Representative Leona Morgan told the crowd, "I know nothing of this transgression, but I will look into it."*
>
> *The angry crowd is expected to stage a major protest march on Saturday night, moving to the rotunda to confront the Legislature.*
>
> —**State Newspaper, September 1, 1979**

SPECIAL WORDS

Sometimes a writer wishes to express special meaning to words. Slang, coined words, and euphemisms are so treated.

> *The pilot was careful to note the location of his "little black box".*
> *When the plane took off for the first time, the navigator, "a greenhorn", shouted with glee.*

We have to note in the records that these "changing times" are killing our budget process.

It's impossible to hire any more "account executives" when what we need are "salespeople"!

Along with word processors came the ability to italicize words easily. In typewritten messages, words are underlined for emphasis. With word processing, the words are *italicized*.

Some quoted words may read better as italics. Technical words, for instance.

The Board of Directors was asked to provide *attitudinal neutralization equipment* throughout the office (meaning the office staff "needs more coffee machines").

By using both techniques in one sentence, the quote mark tone suggests that somebody is playing with somebody's head when they could have spoken more clearly in the beginning. Use the same technique to define words or terms.

Attitudinal means "to harbor an attitude".

TITLES OF NEWSPAPERS, BOOKS, MAGAZINES, ETC.

Here's one that you learned about and promptly dismissed from your mind. You've probably been wondering ever since how to write the title of a book as opposed to the title of a magazine article. Do we underline? italicize? quote?

Whole works (books, magazines, newspapers, long musical works, plays) are italicized in print. When italics are unavailable, underline or write all capital letters. You may have to choose one of these alternatives when keying directly online.

Type: My favorite novel is Gone With the Wind.
Or: My favorite novel is GONE WITH THE WIND.
Print (Word Processing): My favorite novel is *Gone With the Wind*.

Short works, portions of longer works, are written with quotation marks: *chapters, articles, news items, short stories, songs, one-act plays,* and *poems.*

> I enjoyed your article, "How To Write With Your Left Hand", as printed in *Livelihood Magazine.*
> The news item, headed "Left-hand writing is tough", caught my eye in today's *Sun Times.*
> You ought to title your song, "Write Left-handed and Cry".

APOSTROPHES (')
ELLIPSES (...)
HYPHENS (-)
DASHES (—)
DIAGONALS (/)

(The Dots and Dashes)

The little raised dot-with-a-tail, called the **Apostrophe**, combined with the word *its,* raises more havoc in written communication than any other mark. When do you insert it and when do you not? Here is a review of possessives and contractions; those are the primary places that apostrophes are used — and misused. An apostrophe is used to indicate omission of letters or numbers, some of which result in *contractions.* An apostrophe may be used to form the plural of a number, letter, symbol, or certain abbreviations. This is the writer's choice, another place to exercise your anarchist genes.

The **Ellipsis** is a lesser known mark with a single use. The three little dots indicate a pause or something missing... such as part of a quote.

Dashes come in three sizes, with a separate purpose for each. The **Hyphen**, shortest of the three is used to divide words, in one way or another. Sometimes they're used in compound adjectives, and sometimes they divide words between syllables at the end of a line (a disappearing art in itself).

The **M-dash** and **N-dash** are identified by their size, the N-dash the width of an "n" and the M-dash the width of an "m" (or did you guess that).

A kind of tipsy dash is called a **Diagonal**, among other things. Still, it has uses all its own.

Each of the dashes has a life of its own, although they share a few elements. M-dashes are more powerful and used to set off expressions you want to emphasize. Use the dash before a summary set of words, to indicate an afterthought, to set off an interruption clause, and before a word or phrase that is repeated for emphasis. The N-dash combines units that may contain both numerals and letters. And the diagonal is used to give the reader a choice, usually of either / or.

These dots and dashes are invaluable to a writer who knows how to use them. They provide clues to meaning, directions for the reader, and intent for the story teller. Take a look.

THE APOSTROPHE (')

The Apostrophe has a few varied uses that don't produce much of a pattern. The high-strung, raised comma is used as a single quote mark (a quote within a quote), to form possessives, to form contractions (they fill a spot where a letter or letters have been removed), and on certain occasions, to form a plural (with numbers, letters, and other symbols).

Please refer to the Noun Section where the apostrophe is used to show possession, and to the Pronoun Section where it is *not* used to show possession.

The most helpful thing to remember about the apostrophe is that, like X, it marks the spot. Usually it is a spot where something is missing. The clue to knowing the power of the apostrophe is to notice its placement. So pay attention! Much can be learned from your choices.

NOUN POSSESSIVES

Add an apostrophe-*s* ('s) or single apostrophe (') to nouns to indicate possession.

The civic leaders' dinner was an event of its own.
The city manager's division was in a turmoil.

PRONOUN POSSESSIVES

Do not use an apostrophe in personal possessive pronouns (*hers, theirs, its, ours, yours*), the ones found in Column C.

Its main consideration was the cities' electrical power.
The distraught council confused ownership—theirs, yours, and ours.
However, the problem was theirs, not the committee's.

Use the apostrophe with the other pronouns — the pronouns that don't look like pronouns — *one, another, somebody, someone, anyone, anybody.*

She selected one scarf's color and another's size to use in her new creation.
It was anybody's guess as to what to call its new form.

PLURAL POSSESSIVES

Some people think that pluralized possessive nouns (with the s-ending) should have yet another apostrophe *s* at the end. You decide.

The Morrises' names kept getting mixed up.
The Morrises's names kept getting mixed up.

CONTRACTIONS

Writing a sentence without contractions appears formal and is not the way someone usually speaks the words. Contractions appear less formal, make reading, and often understanding, easier. To form a contraction, use the apostrophe to hold open the space where the letter or letters are removed.

Don't = *do not*
Can't = *cannot* or *can not*
Won't = *will not*
Shouldn't = *should not*
She's = *she is*
There's = *there is*

A designer *cannot* understand why *it is* important to conduct analysis sessions that *will not* continue too long.

A designer *can't* understand why *it's* important to conduct analysis sessions that *won't* continue too long.

The same guideline applies to any number or letter that may be removed.

In the '50s (instead of 1950s), *banks seldom opened before 10 o'clock* (of the clock).

NUMBERS AND LETTERS

The apostrophe is used to help readers identify plurals of numbers and letters. Such use is completely optional. Use it or not, for clarity.

1. *Mind your p's and q's.*
2. *This was a 1970's saying. This was a saying of the 1970s.*
3. *Be careful about using too many even's in your written copy.*
4. *These are powerful do's and don'ts in good writing.*

In the first sentence, confusion would rain down if the apostrophe were not there (*ps* and *qs*). With numbers, the apostrophe offers another meaning. In the second sentence, the apostrophe (1970's) implies a possessive; without it, *the 1970s* indicates the plural.

Sometimes the apostrophe is overused. Omit the mark except where it is *absolutely necessary* in order to clarify meaning.

The above examples could have been written: *'70's* or *don't's*. Two apostrophes in one word is over-use; no apostrophes may be confusing. To write *dos* and *donts* would give the reader pause to grasp the meaning. Moderation! Moderation in all things, including the use of apostrophes.

APOSTROPHE IN MEASUREMENTS

In technical writing, the apostrophe may be used to represent measurement in feet: The room was 9' x 12'. (The room was 9-feet by 12-feet.) Note that these apostrophes do not have the bump on the ones in previous paragraphs. The "measuring" apostrophe is different and generally found in the Symbols Section of your computer program.

FOOTNOTES ON APOSTROPHES

Clever ads get our attention. And advertisers know the value of proper punctuation.

A clever company named Saturday's Wearables once used the apostrophe to promote its products. A giant billboard read:
Saturday's Are For What?
An advertiser named Gai's wanted customers to recognize its name. In a popular television commercial, a little girl spelled out the company name in her childish sing-song voice, mispronouncing the word *apostrophe* to keep up the cadence of the jingle. She spelled: *G-A-I-APOS-TER-OPHEE-S.* It worked. No one is likely to misspell that company name.

THE ELLIPSIS (. . .)

Three little dots in a row are considered an Ellipsis, which comes from a Greek word meaning "to fall short or leave out". The ellipsis (singular word) indicates that something is omitted, whether it is in the beginning, middle, or end of a sentence. An alternative symbol of the ellipsis is a triple asterisk (***).

> *The nominating chair spoke at length "…to present a slate of new officers that will be… acceptable to the entire assembly."*
> *Her words began, "It is my honor to…."*

If the ellipsis ends the sentence, add a fourth dot (a period).

Some style manuals insist that no spaces shall exist in an ellipsis. Others suggest a space either before or after; the purpose is to avoid unwieldy spaces when all the words attached to the ellipsis are carried forward to the next line. You decide.

Another option is to use spaces between each of the three dots: . . . rather than…. Again, you decide.

A word about technology. As word processors replace typewriters, new skills in using them affect both keying and the way the product prints out. Most word processing programs contain a separate key for the ellipsis. Check yours to see how to make all three dots show up simultaneously.

HYPHENS (-)

Let's talk semantics (words). A Hyphen may look like an itty-bitty dash, but it is not. Its width is the smallest of the horizontal lines and has a key to itself, although shared with the two dashes. (The "dash" key is the one at the top right of your keyboard that also forms an underline, sometimes called the "minus" key.) A hyphen separates words or parts of words to avoid confusion and is formed by using the dash / minus / hyphen key. Dashes get attention later.

THE HYPHEN IN COMPOUND WORDS

The evolution of compound words (a single new word made up of two or more individual words) once took years to complete. Now, new compound words seem to appear overnight. You can guess a person's age by asking them to spell *brownbag*, as in lunch. If they spell it as two words, they're probably collecting Social Security. If they use a hyphen, they are baby boomers in their 50s. If they spell it as one word, they learned it in the last 20 or 30 years.

That's what happens to compound words. They begin as two words and are used together often enough to slide into one word.

Yes, there's a guideline for knowing when to hyphen and when not to hyphen. If the first part of the compound word has a single syllable, write both parts as one word (as long as it is easily understood).

The following words began as separate words, then were hyphenated for a time before becoming single words.

Bookkeeper	Taxpayer
Footnote	Bookstore
Boombox	Textbook
Bedroom	Teenager
Homemaker	Househusband

If the first part has more than one syllable, use a hyphen, or separate the words without a hyphen. Sometimes this guideline works; other times you have to use your imagination and write it your own way.

Baby boomers   *Baby-sit*
Kitty litter   *Doggy bag*
Trouble maker   *Light house*

This is a guideline. The only way to be sure about some compound words is to consult a current dictionary. Compound words pose several problems. The word *pastime* is often misspelled as past-time, with a different meaning. The title of *vice president* does not include a hyphen (unless the title represents the *president of vice*). Better not hyphenate vice regent, vice chancellor and vice consul, or vice president.

THE HYPHEN WITH ADJECTIVES

Several adjectives can be used to modify a noun. If all of them apply directly to the noun, commas are used to separate them.

The hyphen is used mostly to indicate compound adjectives. When other modifiers are used to form compound adjectives, the hyphen is the only little mark that stands between understanding and confusion (sometimes catastrophic, sometimes just silly). The clue is the way the *other modifiers* relate directly to the noun or to the other adjective(s).

Where could hyphens be placed in the following sentences to make sense?

> *The second hand painted bowl sold for $358.*
> *That $11,000 figure represented the small car sale price.*
> *The team won the pennant with an extra base hit.*
> *Four architects submitted small scale designs.*
> *The judge's bigger is better decision was instantly apparent.*

Hyphens tell the reader that certain words go together, and certain ones do not.

> *The second-hand painted bowl sold for $358.* (A used bowl.)
> Or *The second hand-painted bowl sold for $358.* (There were two bowls.)
> *That $11,000 figure represented the small-car sale price.* (The car was a mini.)
> Or *That $11,000 figure represented the small car-sale price.* (The price was a steal.)

The team won the pennant with an extra base-hit. (They needed only a base-hit.)
Or *The team won the pennant with an extra-base hit.* (The hit was a three-bagger.)
Four architects submitted small-scale designs. (Itty-bitty designs.)
Or *Four architects submitted small scale-designs.* (The designs were drawn to scale.)
The judge's bigger-is-better decision was instantly apparent. (Bigger-is-better is treated as a single modifier to "decision".)

If the hyphenated adjective combinations are placed *after* the word they modify, the hyphen is omitted.

The bowl was hand painted.
The architects submitted designs that were on a small scale.
The judge believed bigger is better.

THE HYPHEN WITH PARTICIPLES

Remember the verbal *participle* and how it can function as an adjective? This is the place. When one element of a compound modifier is a participle (a verbal ending with *ing* or *ed*), a hyphen works best.

However expensive, that is a good-looking car.
The driver is grabbing a much-needed rest.
Let him remain a not-awake dozer, since he may not be a law-abiding citizen.
We've rehearsed this fine-tuned drill a thousand times.

If you re-read these sentences without the hyphen, they may make no sense at all the first time. The hyphen says the words *have to* be used together.

Here's the helpful guideline: if the participle is modified by an adverb ending in *ly*, you won't need the hyphen. It will be a *perfectly clear* statement.

Hers was a finely tuned classic car.
The driver grabbed a sorely needed rest.

Let him remain a barely awake dozer, since he may not be a law-abiding citizen.
We've rehearsed this finely tuned drill a thousand times.

Guidelines to use or not to use a hyphen in a two-or-more-word modifier.

1. Check to see if one of the words is a participle (*ing* or *ed* verb form) If it is, use the hyphen.
2. Check to see if the word modifying the participle is an *ly* adverb. If it is, leave out the hyphen. If it isn't, add the hyphen.

If you read the sentence and it is perfectly clear without the hyphen, leave it out. If you had to pause to be sure how to read it, put the hyphen in.

THE HYPHEN WITH VERBS AND PREPOSITIONS

When verbs and prepositions are combined to make a single-meaning, they can either be one word or hyphenated. Here again, you need to decide if the words written as one make an understandable new word, or a jumble.

	takeover
	tipoff
	dropout
	putdown
But:	*put-on*
	come-on
	get-up
	tie-off

If the last four were spelled together, they would read: puton, comeon, getup, tieup—making the reader work hard.

Warning: When using these same words as a verb *and* preposition, do not use a hyphen. Write them this way:

take over	*put on*
tip off	*come on*
drop out	*get up*
put down	*tie up*

Beware the compound words that have multiple meanings.

If the members take over the gym, it is not necessarily referred to as a *takeover.*

If new players come on the floor, it is not necessarily a *come-on.*

THE HYPHEN WITH PREFIXES

A good dictionary is a must for making sure about these words. Most dictionaries carry inset words using common prefixes (word beginnings): *co, in, over, pre, re, un.*

Here are a few guidelines:

Co before a noun usually is hyphenated: *co-counsel, co-author, co-chair, co-star* (noun). But put *co* in front of a verb and they may run together in a readable way: *cooperate, coordinate, costar* (verb).

Self generally takes a hyphen when it is used as a prefix: *self-evident, self-centered, self-esteem, self-explanatory.* Some exceptions are *selfsame, selfish, selfhood, selfless* (each is a single word).

Anti gets along without a hyphen except when it is followed by a root word beginning with *i (anti-inflation, anti-inflammatory)* or when it is followed by a proper noun *(anti-Communism, anti-Capitalism, anti-West).*

When using *re* as a prefix, use a hyphen if it means to do something again: *re-finish, re-start, re-type, re-state.* Do not use a hyphen in words such as *renew, renovate, remake.* This may help to understand the difference between *remark* (comment) and *re-mark* (to mark again). Again, use the dictionary, make your decision, and record it in Your Style Manual.

Because *ex* has its own meaning (as in *I want you to meet my ex*), use a hyphen to indicate something from the past: *ex-partner, ex-soldier, ex-star.* Some believe that *ex* isn't dignified enough for some positions. Use *former* when discussing has-beens in rarified fields: *former president, former chief of staff, former secretary of state..*

When more than one word is connected to a prefix, the hyphen is used at the end of each prefix: *three- and five-year leases; pro- and anti-choice; semi- and full-circle events.*

THE HYPHEN AS WORD CONNECTOR

The hyphen is used to connect two words that are joined to form a new idea, usually proper names. In a time when women and men both retain their family names, the hyphenated name is taking on great popularity (*John and Mary Smith-Jones*).

Hyphens are used in some trade names (*Alka-Selzer, Alpha-Bits*) and the spelling out of words: s-p-e-l-l-i-n-g.

The hyphen joins:

number words, i.e.: *twenty-two, fifty-seven;*
fractions, i.e.: *three-fourths, one-half;*
numerals to other units of measurement, i.e.: *6-foot ladder, 2,000-year-old man;*
and written numbers to dollar amounts, i.e.: *eight-thousand seven-hundred twenty-five dollars.*

THE HYPHEN AS WORD DIVIDER

The hyphen separates words at the end of a line that must be divided in order to fit the typesetting. (This is becoming a lost art since computers have assumed this function.)

You may have called it *syllabification* as you proudly claimed this long word. It means to divide words according to syllables, so if a word doesn't quite fit at the end of a line, some of it can be placed on the following line. Your computer already knows all of them by heart.

The prime guideline is to follow common sense. Use the division as far into the word as you can: (*investiga tion, impracti cal*); don't divide abbreviations or combinations of numerals; don't divide one-syllable words; divide between syllables (repeat the word out loud if you have to); avoid leaving one or two letters on a line (*un necessary, agend a*); avoid ending more than two consecutive lines with hyphens; avoid dividing proper names; and never leave a hyphen at the end of a page.

Divide words between double consonants (*unneces sary*).
Divide words between the root word and the ending (*aveng ing*).

Do not divide before a vowel that makes up its own syllable (*infatua tion, initi ate*). If the one-letter syllable is part of a recognized suffix, keep the suffix together (*poss ible, incap able*).

Divide hyphenated words only after the hyphen (*first- rate*).

When in doubt, look at a good dictionary. Words are presented in obvious syllables.

If you rely on a computer, re-check a printout of the copy for too many hyphenated words. These can easily be changed by placing a return in front of the hyphenated word. The wrap effect of the computer automatically carries the word to the next line.

Some programs allow you to turn off the automatic hyphen, thus avoiding all word breakups and relying on yourself. When formatting, choose the "left-margin" rather than "justification" to avoid embarrassing spacing of words.

DASHES (M– AND N-)

Now we come to the two dashes: the N–dash (sometimes spelled "endash" or "en dash), and the M—dash (sometimes spelled "emdash" or "em dash). The n-dash is as wide as the letter "n"; the m-dash is as wide as the letter "m". These terms are derived from the old days of hand-printing.

THE M—DASH

The bona fide long dash is called an *m-dash*. That is, it is twice as long as the hyphen. The typist, therefore, uses two hyphens to equal a dash. The word processor has a special key to produce this useful punctuation mark. Debates abound on the subject of whether or not to place spaces before and after the dash. Most professional printers do not use spaces. Some do. You decide and add it to Your Style Manual.

Mac computers use the OPTION/SHIFT/HYPHEN keys in Word. The PC uses CONTROL/ALT/HYPHEN.

Occasionally, an expression that you might consider placing in parenthesis will do a better job following a dash — just for emphasis. The parenthesis diminishes an idea; the dash augments it, plays it up.

The bowling team — the new champions — plays on Thursday nights. Come and watch Sidearm Johnson (last year's runner-up) do his stuff.

A definitive phrase following a noun is sometimes — not always — set off with dashes. Dashes are especially useful when the definition contains commas of its own:

Four members of the team — Davenport, Downing, Davidson, and Denver — showed up for practice.

The dash is helpful too in summing up a preceding series.

Gutter balls, line errors, dropped balls — all of these have turned into problems.

The dash may indicate an afterthought — if that is relevant.

Emphasize a word by repeating it after a dash.

The outcome was successful — successful in that the other team didn't show up.

The dash sometimes replaces the colon in introducing an expression. The words following the dash are such words as *for instance,* or *namely.*

We'll try to raise another team — for instance, in about ten years.

The dash is often used as a credit for a long quote. The dash precedes the name of the author or the publication being quoted.

"*Good words are worth much and cost little.*" —George Herbert

Like the exclamation point, dashes can be overdone. Generally, a good comma will do the same thing as a dash. Use the m-dash with care — when to do so would be most effective.

THE N–DASH

An embarrassing moment came when a grammar teacher was asked, "What is an n-dash?" He didn't know, had to look it up, and had a devil of a time finding it. His dictionary entered it under "e", as in "endash". (His grammar book didn't even mention the difference between the en- and em-dashes.)

Check your computer guide to make an n-dash. Mac computers use the OPTION/HYPHEN keys in Word. The PC uses CONTROL/HYPHEN keys.

The usage guideline for the n-dash is to connect numbers, times, dates, places, possibly even those family names.

The Writing Group will meet Tuesdays, June–August, from 2:30–4:00p at the Sunny–Smiley Café. (Signed) Margot James–Taylor.

Thus endeth the dashing tale of the horizontal lines.

DIAGONALS, OR VIRGULES (/)

Next, we take up the story of the slightly vertical, slightly horizontal line called the *slant, diagonal, forward slash, stroke, separatrix,* or *virgule*. No matter the name, it's the mark found in the lower right corner of your computer keyboard.

Its opposite, the *back slash, reverse slant, reverse solidus,* or *backwhack* (that's a favorite) is primarily used by as a typographical mark, mainly in computing. Strangely, this mark also as its own key (although one seldom used by writers).

DIAGONAL = AND / OR

The comma, remember, is often used to replace the word *and*. In the same way, the slanted diagonal mark indicates the use of either *and* or *or*. Sometimes called a *virgule* (there's a word to toss off at the next cocktail party!), it is placed between words that show alternatives, sometimes opposites.

> *Your lunch consists of sandwich, coffee, soup and / or salad.*
> *Notice this is not an either / or choice, but an and / or.*
> *They want to appeal to your physical / emotional senses.*
> *The religious / scientific implications are best left to the experts.*
> *The slant / diagonal / virgule is a popular piece of punctuation.*

The diagonal / virgule also indicates relativity, replacing the word *per*.

> *The space ship traveled at 2,500 miles / hour.*
> *Using the guage, the tapestry contains 846 stitches / inch.*

Notice that the examples used here do not reflect a choice of *his / her*. This attempt to avoid sexism is pathetic in the least and not half as effective as the alternatives (*See*: Unbiased Language).

THE BACKWARD DIAGONAL (BACK SLASH)

The backward diagonal has become a part of coded computer language. The symbol with a key of its own, has long been questioned by keyboard users. What other use is there for a backward slash?

The Secret of Punctuation

As mentioned at the beginning of this section, the key to handling punctuation is to make your choices and then use them consistently. Because The Grammar Anarchist recognizes the need for some kind of order (without those darned "rules"), consistency covers it.

Be daring, be original, be brave, courteous, and true, but Be Consistent with your choices. After all, you know best how to frame your words. Believe me, few — if anyone — will notice. Choose the best words, then use punctuation to make them work for you. That is The Secret to good writing.

> **Warning:** If you are editing or writing for (and being paid by) someone else, clarify which of the many style manuals they wish you to use. Then do it.
> Your Style Manual is for use when writing what you want, for yourself, your way.

Part 3

Putting It All Together
(Assembling the Parts)

Words

Sentence Structure

Paragraph Building

Spelling

Numbers

Unbiased Language

A Writing Style of Your Own

Your Style Manual

Grammar Glitches

Putting It All Together

(Assembling the Parts)

No respectable *anarchist* would begin a project without planning. Likewise, no respectable *writer* would begin a project without planning. This section highlights the craziness, the problems, the wonderfulness of words, and the ways they are put together. Oh, you thought writing was delivered to your head from someplace "out there" all ready to be printed and read? Not a chance. While writing may be considered work, it still offers variety and fun when you're aware of the intricacies — rather like solving a crossword or sudoku.

The Anarchist's Guidelines in this section look at words that become sentences that become paragraphs that become entire works, whether a company memo, an article for a major magazine, or a book.

Here's the qualifier: Because The Anarchist considers emailing to pals, blogging, writing letters, Tweeting, IMing, and all those other personal messages to be off-limits to linguistic guidance, these are not discussed. Tweet away with your shorthand! IM with secret codes! Use up all the extra exclamation marks in your emails!!!!

What will be discussed here are guidelines for improving writing done in the course of business, writing done for publication, writing to show off your talents, writing for hire. Since different writing requires different approaches, The Anarchist covers many angles.

What good are all these hints and tips and guidelines if writers attempt to copy the style of other writers? Why they would do that remains a conundrum, but some do. Come on, Writer, trust yourself to create your own writing style by eschewing the "rules" and accepting your freedom to soar.

The purpose of this book is to offer guidelines — solutions to the conundrum of which "rules" to follow. The best solution for writers is to create Your Own Style Manual. When you have digested this section, return to the beginning and set up Your Style Manual.

This section shows how to incorporate the individual parts of writing that finish your work, give it polish, make it shine.

WORDS

Word usage reflects the writer. Every writer has favorite words, ways of putting them together in sentences, and combining those sentences into cohesive paragraphs. Each of these steps is included in the following pages.

SENTENCE STRUCTURE

Some writers pour sentences onto paper as easily as they pop raisins into their mouths. Others struggle, sweat, and fret over each sentence as if it were their last. However you write your sentences, some guidelines will help.

PARAGRAPH CONSTRUCTION

Those same sweating writers construct their paragraphs with similar precision, carefully placing topic sentences and forming connections. Are there really "natural" writers or are they just lucky?

SPELLING

The bane of U.S. writers is spelling, especially those words translated from other languages. The question remains: which of "alternative choice" spelling to use. Spelling is the main reason for rebelling against "rules". How can there be "rules" when many words have multiple spellings?

NUMBERS

Another area of indecision in written U.S. language is that of numbers. Separate guidelines apply to fiction and nonfiction writing, for use with narrative, and for use with measurements and dates. Is it any wonder that this confusion has led to anarchism of the word kind?

UNBIASED LANGUAGE

A responsible anarchist understand that English and all its versions was developed and recorded by men — in the days when women weren't considered bright enough to handle words. The don't-bother-your-pretty-little-head syndrome caused men to hold women back from education, caused men to compile the early dictionaries, to make the decision to assume the world (and everything in it) is masculine until proven otherwise. The grammar anarchist will clear up some of these sexist language issues.

A WRITING STYLE OF YOUR OWN

Here are guidelines that attend to the differences between business writing and fiction writing (although some contend it often appears the same). Business writing and most nonfiction writing follow formal guidelines. Fiction offers more freewheeling opportunities. Still, the results need to be readable, even if not always understandable.

YOUR STYLE MANUAL

The most creative action you can take to improve your writing is to compose Your Style Manual — your very own. Here you will record your choices of the iffy bits of U.S. language (the things the pros cannot agree on). Take your time; build your manual to suit your use. Directions included below.

GRAMMAR GLITCHES

Finally, this section concludes with a series of Grammar Glitches, those pesky words that foul up writing, keep editors working, and prevent many writers from success in business or publication.

Fasten your safety belts. We're off to tie up all the pieces of U.S. language into presentable, readable, prolific, exciting, writing that uses words to communicate with clarity, ease, and originality.

WORDS

(Wimpy and Wonderful)

The crazy way that U.S.ers use words reflects an anarchistic state of mind that boggles grammarians. It's not as if we are proposing to change that. Take a look at how bold writers develop a freedom to use words without fear. You'll find words can be troublesome, wonderful, specific, vague — anything a writer wants them to be. There is further talk of dictionaries and style manuals in this section, as well as ways to play with words and make up new ones.

The primary components of writing are words, obviously. So obvious, in fact, that writers forget to realize the importance of the ways word usage changes within the culture. Why not make up a word with a specific meaning just for you and your *communicatees*? (There, I just made up a word!) Words are wonderful, aren't they! You'll never look at them again as just components.

If words are the material of communication, then writers must be free to use them. Words are meant to shape and fine-tune information, not only in standard usage, but in creative ways. Become a grammar anarchist, lose your fear of words, and gain control over them. Become familiar with dictionary meanings of words, their wide ranges, and their possibilities.

OH THE DICTIONARY!

Do not consider the dictionary as the last word in words, but only a first word, a guideline. If word usage were restricted to dictionary definitions, we'd end up speaking like newcomers to the American language — using single words to express needs and little else (*me eat, you wait*). The dictionary is a guide offering basic meanings, pronunciation, root derivations, grammar functions and, sometimes, examples of usage. The rest is up to you.

Most United States dictionaries use English as a language base. They trace words to origins, dating them and locating where they came from. Dictionary prefaces are full of information about words and language. Read the explanations at the front of your dictionary and be impressed with how much is known about words.

You'll be impressed, only if it is to discover your dictionary is outdated. Yes, dictionaries get old. Old U.S. dictionaries don't contain the thousands of words that are added to vocabularies each year. They don't contain words constantly being added to the language as people from other countries join the U.S. party.

When dictionary people are informed about a "new" word (oh, you didn't realize dictionaries are compiled by *people?*), they investigate — just like detectives. They find out who uses the suggested word, where they use it, how they use it, and why they use it. Some words take months, even years, to track down the source and precise meaning. Then, and only then, will it appear in the next edition of the dictionary — that dictionary. Possibly other dictionary people are doing the same detective work, but won't accept the same word until later.

Dictionaries judge words too. Not exactly the dictionary itself, but the people who put the words together. Words are labeled according to their acceptance in polite society (and academia). You'll find dictionaries attach such labels as *dialect, slang, idiom, postulate, substandard, obsolete* and *archaic*. Look up the same word in another dictionary and you'll find that various editors differ on which words belong with which labels. How long does it take for a word to go from *idiom* or *slang* to *archaic* or *obsolete?*

THE THESAURUS CONNOTES

The thesaurus is another tool for word users. Such a book offers shades of meanings to words. Where the dictionary provides *denotative* meanings, "the basics", the thesaurus offers *connotative* meanings, "the side issues". Ask a half dozen people for their definitions of a word like *peace*, and you'll receive half a dozen variations of meanings. Finding those connotative variations is the work of the thesaurus.

> **Note**
>
> *Dictionaries offer alternative spellings for the words **denotive** and **denotative** when used as adjectives: **connotive** and **connotative**. You choose; I did.*

The computer revolution has affected the way we use words. Many young people don't even remember the typewriter. No, that's not exactly accurate. When the typewriting machine was invented, the word *typewriter* was given to the (usually male) person operating the machine, later called the *typist* (usually female). Almost a century later, the verb *to type* has given way to another new verb, *to keyboard*. This new verb — keyboarding — probably developed because men were averse to *typing*. As the computer became the communication mainstay, it became necessary for both women and men to type.

> **Irony**
>
> *Once men were the only typewriters, then women became typists, now computer users (men and women) spend their days keyboarding.*

Most computers also bring with them spelling and grammar checking programs. They are great for catching the obvious errors, but please don't depend on them. After all, you're smarter than that computer program! It fails at times and offers such messages as "can't find" or "no such word". You don't have to accept that message as final. Read on.

PLAYING WITH WORDS

Different people use words in different ways. Word artists (poets, fiction writers, advertising copywriters) play with words, expand them, squeeze them, misspell them, pile multiple meanings on top of one another, change word functions, even create new ones.

Many of the new verbs beginning to appear in dictionaries are the result of an ad copywriter's whim. Where else could we have found the verb *prioritize* that came from the noun *priority*? Creative spelling and word usage once came only from poets. (Who else would try to rhyme *rain* with *again* simply because they are similarly spelled?)

The new spelling for the word *light* already is included in most dictionaries with its "alternative" or "slang" spelling *lite*. How many other words will follow, reducing the onus of *crazy* spelling? *Adjusting* spelling makes sense. New words often appear in all the places that people look for spelling hints — on television and on their computers.

Night has made it to *nite*; why not turn *tight* into *tite*? Or *right, sight, might* to *rite, site* and *mite*? Oh-oh! Another problem pops up; the last three words (*rite, site, mite*) have different meanings all their own.

MAKE UP YOUR OWN

If you can't find the word in the dictionary, make it up. You probably never heard a grammar teacher give this advice. (More likely, you were told that if it isn't in the dictionary, it isn't a word.) The Grammar Anarchist knows, however, that unlike the chicken and egg scam that's been enticing for years, the dictionary did not come before the word. It came after, and it still does. "In the beginning there was the word..." remember?

How do you make up a word? Actually, there are two ways. One is the way most words are devised: by finding a root word and altering it (*medicine/Medicare*). Another is to find two or more words that belong together and combine them (*back + head = backhead*. Definition: the place you'll never see without a mirror).

Here's another example. Imagine: you need a noun to show what happens when someone tells a funny story about politics. *Funny story* or *joke* doesn't quite fit the bill. You want a word that defines the kind of story as well as the way it is told. You try *political humor, politico-comedy, politico-joke, joke-politico*! Not quite. You want the essence of *story* in there. Look up *politics* in the dictionary. Learn that the root comes from "the people, the government". Look up adjoining combinations of words — *politicalize, politicize* (politi-sighs), *politick* (from the noun *politicking*). Now there's a word to play with. *Politick, politrick, politruck*. Check the thesaurus and find alternatives for story (*tale, plot*). Put them together and come up with *politale*, "a funny story about politics". Not bad for a first try.

A friend with a new home has made a quasi-pet out of the squirrel that plays in her yard. She calls it her *yardsquirrel*. While the word isn't in her dictionary, it adequately describes the animal.

More likely, new words come from what feels natural. It's one of those there-oughta-be-a-word experiences. One author writing about a society where women and men share equal standing came up with the word *equalitarian*. It plays off the word *egalitarian* from a French word which means the same thing. But this author uses a spelling that comes closer to the exact meaning she wishes to imply.

Hey, communicator. You can do that too. There's no law that declares if you find a better word, or a better combination of words, you can't share it with other communicators. If they like it, they'll use it. And possibly, one day a dictionary will print it. If no one else likes it, the word will come to a natural and deserved demise.

Here are some familiar words you may recognize: *doozie* (it's in a dictionary), *intersomnambulists* "people who dream the same dreams" (not in the dictionary, yet). Two new words in some dictionaries: *wanna be*, "a hopeful copy-cat"; and *bungee jumping*, "a suicidal recreation" (author's judgment).

Be assured that when you use words in a new way, someone will caution you about following the dictionary: "You can't use *ain't* because it isn't in the dictionary!" When that happens, just ask them if they understood what you wrote. If they did, congratulations! You have coined a new word. Besides, *ain't* now *is* in the dictionary.

Words are fascinating when you take a close look at them. There are many words that sound alike but have several spellings and meanings (*wise / whys; whose / who's; reel / real; pair / pare / pear; bare / bear; roll / role*). There are words that are spelled alike, but have different meanings (*put, take, up, shade, flower, monitor, jack-ass*). There are words that have a variety of meanings according to the way they are pronounced (*record, produce, progress, project, polish*).

TECHNICAL LANGUAGE (LANGUAGE OF THE FIELD)

Legal people use words in almost a backward way. They go to the dictionary as the authority for word meanings, build sentences with words that are made to fit together according to some "rules", and squeeze more long words into long sentences than any document should be made to bear. That is the art of *practicing* law. (Interesting use of the word *practice*.)

Don't blame the lawyers. Vague, multi-meaning, misleading, duplicitous words are the language of the law. In other words, that's what attorneys do.

Every field of endeavor has its own technical language. Put a sports writer with a military strategist and they might understand one another because their technical languages borrow from each other (*officer, bomb, target, fight, win*). But put a sports writer with a chef and the two might not be able to exchange a single idea (a *bomb* is a chef's success, not a sports writer's loss).

Architects, health care providers, insurance underwriters, plumbers, street pavers, street people, automotive servicers, kitchen workers, painters, musicians, movie makers, police officers (10-4). All of these people have languages that are unique to their work.

How do imposters get away with their scams? They learn to talk the language of the field they wish to impose on. Remember how you had to learning to talk a new language when you took on a new job in a new field? The Ph.D. who takes a temporary job pumping gas or driving a taxi has to learn an entire new language. The taxi driver or gas pumper who takes a job parking cars at an elegant hotel has to learn an entire new language. The short-order cook who finds work as a chef, or vice versa won't survive without new words.

Words tell who we are, or pretend to be. They give us away as surely as clothes do. Written words tell even more, for they reflect what is going on inside as well as outside the body. Words give away geographic origins, educational background, and emotional outlook on life. Just think of a nattily attired young man, well-groomed, handsome, standing tall, and appearing regal. Then he opens his mouth and out comes, "Me and him ain't gonna wait no longer."

There used to be a man in show business who frequented talk shows with his act — guessing where people came from just from hearing them talk for a few minutes. He listened for word clues and judged word pronunciation, then identified the accent so well that he could often tell where a person was born, where they grew up, and where they currently were living, just from the words.

Psychologists depend on words to uncover hidden meanings and repressed trauma in patients. The words flow from the feelings and provide clues to what's going on inside a person.

Believe it or not, you can tell a person's approximate age by listening to their word choices: *groovy, right on, hubba-hubba, I'm hip, I'm hep! twenty-three skidoo!*

SELECT WORDS CAREFULLY

Pay attention to word meanings. Become intimately connected to your dictionary, thesaurus, and other written word information sources.

Read profusely. Notice how other writers use words. Try to get inside an author's mind and unlock the feelings and intentions of the writer while the writing was being created. It is very easy to read a paragraph, skim the words, and pull out a superficial meaning. But how much more rewarding it is when you can re-trace the thought process of the writer and determine what were the feelings at the moment the words were placed on paper (or into the computer). This illuminates especially well when reading the classics.

Know who you're writing to. Different messages require different words. The selection of words must fit the reader. What words would you choose to send a scathing memo to your boss, a make-nice memo to your staff, a request note to your spouse, an apologetic note to the principal, and a report to the board of directors. How would your words differ?

EXTRANEOUS WORDS

Watch for unnecessary words. Read over what you have written and determine which words can be eliminated to keep your message succinct, yet flavorful. Look at the following phrases as examples of over-wordiness.

Too Much	Better
As per your request	As requested
Until such time as	Until
We respectfully solicit	We ask
We are this day in receipt of	Today we received
In the event that	When / If
In regard to	Regarding
An invoice in the amount of $58	An invoice for $58
The foregoing	These
In reference to	Referring to
Under separate cover	Separately
Would you be so kind as to	Would you
For the duration of the year	For the year
At the present time	Presently
At your earliest convenience	Soon / Promptly / Immediately
Enclosed herewith is	Here is
At a later date	Later
It is to our mutual interest	It is mutually
To spell out	To clarify
Due to the fact that	Because of
Mutually agreed upon time	At a convenient time
The above	This / these
Thanks and please advise	Please let us know

Yet, these extra words pop up in much of today's correspondence. Remove them and increase your I.Q. in the eyes of your readers. Here are more useless combinations.

Let's cooperate *together*.
I know you write stories, poems, articles, *and* etc.
The sculptor cut a piece off *of* the marble.
Please meet a friend *of mine*.

The table was reserved *exclusively* for the big wigs.
The program continued *on* with unabated boredom.
They said *that* the work was produced on a *more* sounder basis.
In my opinion, I think she was wrong.
Each and every report was carefully recorded.
The speech was meant to get people off *of* their duffs.
It was the *general* consensus of opinion that it worked.
The audience rose *up* to speak shaking their fists.
The speaker responded *very* briefly.
The opponents had nothing in common *with each other*.
The whole encounter *actually* took only about five minutes.
We must *first* report this before we leave.
It happened *at* about 7:30 *p.m.* last night.
We'll let you know *later* how it turned out.

THROWAWAY WORDS

What is worse than too many words is the use of the wrong words or the use of non-words. Every day, we hear some of the following, which have no reason for being.

Not so hot!	**Better**
Anyways / Anywheres	Toss the "s". *Anyway / Anywhere*
Being that / Being as how	*Since*
Coulda / Woulda	Save for tweeting.
Could of / Would of	*Could have* and *would have*.
Exsetera	*Et cetera* is pronounced like it's spelled. It means "and so forth".
Enlargen	*Enlarge*
Enthused	The adjective is *enthusiastic*.
Gonna	Sqwushing of "going to" (use prudently)
Had / Hadn't ought	*One ought to* or *ought not to*.
In regards to	If you are referencing, use *in regard to*.

Irregardless	No such word! (The prefix and suffix mean the same thing.)
Unmerciless	Ditto above.
Momento	This is Spanish, meaning "in a moment". Do you mean *memento*, "a souvenir"?
Portentious	*Portentous*
Presumptious	*Presumptuous* is what you mean.
Prophesize	The verb is *prophesy* (sigh); the noun is *prophecy* (see).
Secondhanded	Toss away the *ed*.
Somewheres	*Somewhere*
Undoubtably	*Undoubtedly* misspelled!
Unequivocably	*Unequivocally* misspelled!

FUN TO TRY

Make a list of technical words you had to learn to get along in your field of work.

Keep a notebook where you can list words you never heard before. Are they in the dictionary? or did someone make them up? (Thank you, Auntie Mame.)

Start a collection of your own words (ones you make up to solve a deficiency).

Establish a checklist to cover areas you need to monitor in your own writing. The list could include such things as: spelling, overuse, double verbs, extraneous words, verb / noun agreement, proper pronouns, overuse of commas, too many hyphens, too many dashes or ellipses.

EXERCISE YOUR WORDS

1. Strictly for fun and profit (you'll gain a wealth of information about how words work), convert the words below into as many kinds functions as you can. For instance: *Profit* is a noun. Change it into an adjective, verb, adverb, or anything else you can: *profitable* (adj.) *profit* (v.) *profitize* (v., why not?), *profitably* (adv.)

Not all the words are nouns. But they might be converted if you try.

discovery	generous
compare	beautifully
desire	lonely
describe	apparently
accident	similar
analyze	defiantly
grammar	humid
resent	ecstatically
miracle	efficient
confide	jokingly
apology	frivolous
exclude	apathetically

2. How many meanings can you devise for the following words (without consulting the dictionary

light	down
up	round
run	break
object	blood
roll	well
commercial	mother

SENTENCES

(How To Structure Them)

Most likely you've learned some nefarious "rule" that a sentence "must have" a subject and a predicate, and the predicate "must" contain a verb, and…

Yes, there are some basics to putting a sentence together, but you can leave out that word "must"! The distinction between the function of words and the names of the parts of speech is confusing. A *noun* can be a "subject" or the "object of a preposition" or the "direct object of a verb". And what the heck does "predicate" mean? When you complete this section, draw a picture of the different kinds of sentences. Rather than recalling the old-fashioned *diagram*, try using a computer flow chart.

The foundation of good writing is sentence structure. A responsible grammar anarchist will wail about words, such as "structure", "must have", "correct" and other such bothers. How easy it is to pick up clues to writing the three kinds of sentences: *simple, compound* and *complex*. And what difference does it make anyway? In this section, you'll learn to write grownup sentences. You'll review clauses, phrases, parallel construction, misplaced modifiers and sentence overload. You'll also look into the pitfalls of double-verbing, a nasty habit that is perpetuated in much of today's business correspondence.

All of this without pushing "rules" on you. If there were one perfect, serves-all sentence, don't you think it would have been flashed around the world by now?

WHAT IS A SENTENCE?

A sentence is a collection of words that focuses on a separate idea or on closely related ideas. It can take the form of a statement, a question, a command, a wish or an exclamation. A sentence can be very simple or very complex.

Take a simple subject, add a simple verb to tell what the subject is doing; add an object to tell who or what is being done to; then throw in a some phrases and a clause or two to describe the nouns and verbs. Presto! You have a sentence.

But what if you need a phrase or clause to form the subject? Or a phrase or clause to define the verb? Now you're talking grammar! Don't faint just yet; we're clarifying, remember?

This is a sentence:

Something is happening. (Subject / Verb)

This also is a sentence:

Something or other which I can't put my finger on is happening or about to happen or did happen to me and others in my family who so far have forgotten to tell me about the event which I probably will find out about in due time or at the time when it is my turn to know about such things.

Would anyone in the class like to parse this one? Parse, dissect, diagram, explain, describe the component parts? Come back after you finish this section and try it again.

The following paragraphs are samples of several different ways to write sentences, from the simple to the verbosely complex. They depict various styles of writing and degrees of complexity. Look them over carefully to determine how each has its place and each has its own style.

SIMPLE WRITING:

A house is for sale. The house belongs to the Morgans. The Morgans are a family of four. The house has three bedrooms. It has two bathrooms. The house also contains a living room, dining room and kitchen. A basement is finished for use. The lawn needs work. A garage will hold two cars. It is attached to the house.

GROWNUP WRITING (NOTICE HOW DATA IS COMBINED INTO LONGER SENTENCES):

The house belonging to the Morgans, a family of four, is for sale. The house, which contains three large bedrooms and two bathrooms, also has a spacious living room, a dining room that will hold large family dinners, and a well-equipped yellow and white kitchen. In addition, the basement, finished with extra rooms, and the lawn, which needs some work, are added assets to this fine house. Still more; a two-car garage is attached to the house.

SHORT WRITING (LEAVE OUT THE DETAILS):

The Morgan house, containing three bedrooms and two baths, living and dining rooms, kitchen and finished basement, is for sale. A two-car garage is attached to the house. The lawn needs work.

EVEN SHORTER:

For Sale by family of four: 3 br/2 bath, lr, dr, kitchen, finished basement, 2-car garage.

PRETENTIOUS, VERBOSE, FLOWERY WRITING:

The Morgan family, a respected family of four — mother, father and two lovely children — is selling their beautiful well-designed Tudor home. Three large, friendly bedrooms and two full baths have provided a wonderful living space for the family; they are heartsick about having to sell it.

The wide-open living room is lighted naturally by two elegant picture windows that invite the afternoon sun. The ambience of the large family dining room awaits the holiday banquet as easily as it encourages simple family meals. Adjacent, the early sun floods the yellow and white kitchen with delightful effect on morning coffee.

Below, a fully-finished basement begs for attention — a den, office space, private hobby room, recreation room. As if this weren't enough, a garage, big enough to hold two family autos, is attached at the side of the house, keeping occupants dry in rainy weather. No dash to the door for the lucky family that purchases this house.

All of this magic — grownup writing, parallel writing, understandable, idea-producing, explanatory writing — is accomplished by using all three kinds of sentences, simple, compound and complex (or a combination of any of them). Just what are they? How can you put one together?

SIMPLE SENTENCES

The idea of a simple sentence is to include one *subject* and one *predicate*. Oh-oh! What's a predicate? Does anyone know? Okay, then; if the *subject* is what you're writing about, call the rest of the sentence the *predicate*.

A simple sentence contains "the subject and the rest of the sentence". The rest of the sentence contains a verb, which makes this sentence a clause, often called *an independent clause*. (It stands on its own.) The sentence could have several phrases, but in the end it comprises only one independent clause. All of the following are simple sentences; the verb is "held".

> The company *held* a picnic.
> The ABC Company <u>with all its six branches</u> *held* a picnic <u>in the park</u>. (The underlined portions are prepositional phrases.)
> The ABC Company, its employees and officers, *held* a picnic and family outing in the park. (Compound subject and multiple objects, but only one verb.)

Take one subject, add a second verb:

> The company *held* a family outing and *presented* the annual report during a picnic in the park on Saturday. Compound verbs (*held* and *presented*) and objects (*family outing* and *annual report*), additional prepositional phrases: *during a picnic, in the park, on Saturday*, but only one subject (*company*), maintaining its status as a simple sentence.

The prime requisite of a simple sentence is that it has only one independent clause and no dependent set of words (clause) containing a verb of its own. It may contain modifying words and phrases.

A simple sentence may use an action verb or a stop-action verb. The action verb requires a direct object (and perhaps an indirect object).

The stop-action verb may be followed by an adjective (that describes the subject), a compliment (that completes or repeats the subject), or an adverb that describes the verb. A stop-action verb does not have an object.

The company held its picnic for 300 employees. (Action verb is *held*; direct object is *picnic*; indirect object is *300 employees*.)
The day felt warm. (Stop-action verb *felt*, and adjective *warm* describes *day*.)
The day was Saturday. (Stop-action verb *was*, and its complement, *Saturday*, which repeats *day*.)
All those people were served easily. (Stop-action verb *were served*; adverb *easily* describes *how*.)

COMPOUND SENTENCES

A compound sentence is simply a connection of two simple sentences, (two independent clauses). They can be joined in four ways: 1) a comma followed by a conjunction, 2) a semicolon, or 3) a semicolon followed by a conjunction. 4) A very short compound sentence may be connected with only the conjunction.

Two simple sentences: *The food was the best part of the picnic. Every department contributed some of it.* Here are four ways to turn them into compound sentences.

1) *The food was the best part of the picnic, and every department contributed some of it.*
2) *The food was the best part of the picnic; every department contributed some of it.*
3) *The food was the best part of the picnic; and every department contributed some of it.*
4) *The food was the best part of the picnic and every department contributed some of it.*

COMPLEX SENTENCES

To form a complex sentence, simply add a clause — the phrase that includes a verb. Phrases were reviewed in the Modifiers (Adjectives and Adverbs) Section, and in the Conjunction Section. A complex sentence contains one independent clause (the main simple sentence) and one or more dependent clauses (they need the sentence to exist).

A clause adds information about a subject, object or verb and is joined to the simple sentence by a conjunction. That's all. Not as complex as it sounds, is it?

The following are complex sentences to learn more about that picnic (above) and about adding clauses.

1) The hotdogs and beans were furnished by the Accounting Department, *who did all the cooking themselves*. (Adjective clause modifying *Accounting Department*.)
2) The salads, *which were made by members of Shipping*, tasted fresh and appetizing. (Adjective clause modifying *salads*.)
3) *Although we didn't expect it*, the beverages were supplied by Management. (Adverb clause modifying *were supplied*.)
4) Pies were the dessert *furnished by Sales*. (Noun clause complementing the subject, *pies*.)
5) The contribution *made by the receptionist* was the cake. (Noun clause identifying the subject, *contribution*.)

The last two examples, noun clauses, are on the borderline of the complex sentence. They are included here to show how close they come to the edge. Technically, a clause includes a verb. When the subject clause fits that requirement, it becomes a contributor to a complex sentence.

If we omitted the verb in the clause, the sentences would be simple sentences:

4) Pies were the dessert from Sales.
5) The contribution by the receptionist was the cake.

A cause and effect sentence shows that something happens as a result of something else. Try using a complex sentence (with a clause) instead of a compound sentence with an inappropriate connector. Rewrite the compound sentence replaced by the awkward *so* or *but* with a reversed sentence that begins with a clause.

Avoid:

*The speaker noted the hour was early, so he continued taking questions.
Everyone in the audience was tired, so they applauded and got up to leave.
The orchestra hadn't rehearsed but they played well.*

Cause and effect:

*Noting the hour was early, the speaker continued taking questions.
Because everyone in the audience was tired, they applauded and got up to leave.
Although they hadn't rehearsed, the orchestra played well.*

Reversed:

*The speaker continued taking questions, noting the hour was early.
The audience applauded and got up to leave, because everyone was tired.
The orchestra played well, although they hadn't rehearsed.*

COMPOUND-COMPLEX SENTENCES

Ready? Here's the big one, combining the elements of both compound and complex sentences.

Re-check the requirements for both the compound and complex sentences. Compound sentences require two independent clauses (two simple sentences); complex sentences require a dependent clause or two. Put them together, just like in science or math, for the finished product.

*If you want to take over the company, you need at least $5 million; clearly, a small down payment and a promise might get the paper work started.
The Board of Directors heard about the takeover, but failing to act immediately, they lost the advantage.
Mergers and takeovers cause problems over and above what occurs daily; yet, the emerging company always comes out stronger.*

CLAUSES, PHRASES

Clauses and phrases make simple writing more grownup by adding variety. If you wrote in simple sentences all the time, life would get boring. This is what clauses and phrases are for: to spice up the writing, make it interesting, understandable, and clear.

Vital writing contains both long and short sentences. Vary them as you would vary herbs in stews, riffs of jazz, or sites of anarchistic uprisings. After writing a few longs ones, throw in a short sentence. It works. (See?)

PARALLEL WRITING

Take an idea, identify what you are talking about (subject), choose the verb that best tells what is going on, and the object that receives the action. Carefully select the phrases and clauses that modify and connect these ideas. When you connect several elements, make sure you choose the same kinds of words in the parts being connected.

Making sure that the parts are parallel is as important as fitting the right pieces of pipe together in plumbing. If the parts come from different manufacturers or are made of different materials, there may be an interruption of flow.

Rather than:

The idea *supported* the plan and *identifies* the project.

Use either two past-tense verbs:

The idea *supported* the plan and *identified* the project.

Or two present-tense verbs:

The idea *supports* the plan and *identifies* the project.

Keep the tense of verbs equal, in the same time zone. Be sure that both *belong* in the same time zone! If you discover that one part belongs in another time zone, sometimes it is best to give it a separate sentence.

I visited San Francisco and found it was a beautiful city.

Actually, San Francisco still is a beautiful city. That *was* should be *is*.

I visited San Francisco and found it is a beautiful city.

This appears to defy the parallelism in order to maintain honesty, but it doesn't. Look at the active verbs. The *is* lies in the clause that is the object of *found*. The *visited* and *found* maintain the past tense in fine parallel form.

A huge problem in parallel writing arises when a series crops up. Sometimes the writer gets lost before coming to the end.

My decision was to ride the trolley, visit the museums, drive across the bridge, shop at the big department stores, and spending the rest of the day on the wharf.

Whoops! The verbs are: *ride, visit, drive, shop* and *spending*.

One of them doesn't belong. Can you tell which one? Of course you can.

My decision was to ride the trolley, visit the museums, drive across the bridge, shop at the big department stores, and spend *the rest of the day on the wharf.*

Yet, grownups put together series like this in much of their writing. It's the way we think. Knowing this, it shouldn't be too difficult to watch out for mismatched parts of a series in the future.

If you're hungry you can enjoy a snack of cheese and crackers, sipping on a milkshake, indulging in a yogurt sundae, or pick a few tomatos from the garden.

Verbs: *enjoy, sipping, indulging*, and *pick*. Choose verbs either with or without the *ing* and proceed.

Either: *If you're hungry you can be* enjoying *a snack of cheese and crackers,* sipping *on a milkshake,* indulging *in a yogurt sundae, or* picking *a few tomatos from the garden.*

Or: *If you're hungry you can* enjoy *a snack of cheese and crackers,* sip *on a milkshake,* indulge *in a yogurt sundae, or* pick *a few tomatos from the garden.*

The very ridiculous happens when we mismatch ideas. That is, combine two separate ideas in a sentence. Remember, a sentence needs to be focused on a single idea.

The picnic began with a rain shower that dampened the food and continued when the company president arrived to make a speech.

This item, if it appeared in a company newsletter, could cause trouble for the writer. Did the rain continue or did the picnic continue with a damp mood? Separate the two events to make clear that the president didn't have anything to do with the rain, or that the rain didn't have anything to do with the president.

The picnic began with a rain shower that dampened the food. The rain continued as the company president arrived to make a speech.
Or: *The picnic began with a rain shower that dampened the food. The picnic continued (even picked up) as the company president arrived to make a speech.*

Whew! That's better. Somebody's job is safe.

TROUBLESHOOTING IDEAS

Sentences must be checked just like computer disks to be sure some kind of strange virus hasn't invaded. Sometimes thoughts race during the writing process, resulting in sentences that contain diverse information.

The files are in a bad mess, and the receptionist is home sick with a cold. Three people from the front office are out sick and the telephones are ringing.

The above two sentences are somewhat related in the writer's mind, but not in the sentences. Relate them by supplying information in appropriate clauses:

*The files are in a bad mess because the receptionist who normally handles this duty is home sick with a cold.
Since three people from the front office are out sick, the telephones are ringing with no one to answer them.*

TOO MUCH! OVERLOAD!
The following paragraph contains one single sentence!

Occasionally, when we're in a hurry, we write too much in one sentence, cluttering it up with detail that should be relegated to additional sentences, which would place close ideas together and leave the other ideas for sentences by themselves, sentences that would read more easily because of the shorter format and the fewer details within a single sentence, causing readers to be able to extract the idea being communicated with less trouble than a sentence such as this causes a reader.

Pant, pant! Pity the reader who has to wade through such a sentence. Keep yours shorter. Leave out repetition, simplify sentences, modify what is necessary and leave out the rest.

Over-writing is simply unclear thinking (or academia). Get your act together and decide exactly what you want to say before starting to write. In academia, long cluttered sentences are par for the course — anything to require heavy brain waving.

On the other hand, you may want to attempt to write the longest sentence in the world. (Note: it can always be made even longer.) However, try writing a complete story with one sentence. Fun and eye-opening!

DOUBLE VERBS, MODIFIERS, NOUNS

Many communicators have such a shadowy idea of what they want to say that they grasp wildly for the right verb, often supplying a choice for the recipient of the message. This is understandable in spoken language, acceptable to a point.

However, in written communications, there is little excuse for double verbing, that is, grasping for the right verb.

A favorite example of double verbing:

I thought I would like to try to sit down to attempt to make up or produce a memo to you to start to explain the altercation yesterday.

Count the verbs: *thought, would like, try, sit down, attempt, make up, produce, start, explain!* Too many! Choose two, even three, but no more. Here's what that cluttered sentence is saying:

I'm attempting to produce a memo to explain the altercation yesterday.

Look over something you have written lately and pick out the double (or triple or more) verbs. Could the right one do the job? In much writing today, the message sender gives the message recipient choices.

I want to extend or direct *my apologies to you.*

Let's meet to plan and outline *the report.*
Over lunch we can interrogate and review *the new recruit.*

In each of the above sentences, the reader has to make the choice that should have been made by the writer. Here's your excuse: "I was writing so fast in my first draft that I didn't want to stop to decide which was the more accurate verb." Okay, now that you realize that, decide and reduce your verb-iage.

More direct sentences occur when the writer determines exactly what is being said — even if you have to go back to analyze each of your original words.

I want to direct *my apologies to you.*
Let's meet to outline *the report.*
Over lunch we can interview *the new recruit.*

Double adjectives and adverbs suffer the same malaise. In putting thoughts down quickly, a writer doesn't take time to sort and choose, ending up with sentences like the following:

She was *pleased and happy* to note the appointment.
When she sat down, she appeared *relaxed and contented.*
He admitted he felt *lonely and left out* when the group met.
After the *tall and rangy* man entered the room, it quieted down.

The emphasized words in each sentence are repetitious. They say nearly the same thing. By using more words than you need, you are asking the reader to choose the appropriate word, which slows down reading. Shame on you! Sentences appear much stronger when that choice is made by the writer. Here's where self-editing pays off.

She was pleased to note the appointment.
When she sat down, she appeared contented.
He admitted he felt lonely when the group met.
After the rangy man entered the room, it quieted down.

Sloppy writing occurs with unclear thinking and scant editing. Write down your message with all the choices on the first draft. When you're finished, go back and scope the *ands* to eliminate redundant words. You may find another alternative that is even better. The way you self-edit is an important part of your unique style.

MISPLACED MODIFIERS

Some of the world's best jokes come out of misplaced modifiers. When those pesky little things end up in the wrong place, we get sentences like:

We need a tool for fastening a mirror that is made with a small motor.
The clerk handed me the motor and turned to another customer carelessly.
The new instrument in my hand represented greater repair of our home with its red, shiny motor.
You only say it costs $14.98?

Modifiers must be placed close to the words they modify. Rewrite the above and move the modifiers where they belong:

We need a tool that is made with a small motor for fastening a mirror.
The clerk carelessly handed me the motor and turned to another customer.
The new instrument in my hand with its red, shiny motor, represented greater repair for our home.
You say it costs only $14.98?

Can't you just hear Teacher? "If I've said it once, I've said it a thousand times, always put the modifier next to the word it modifies."

PARAGRAPHS

(How To Build Them)

Putting paragraphs together is more like playing with blocks than you may realize. Each paragraph is a module of its own which must be made to fit smoothly into the format of the entire piece of writing.

DEFINITION OF A PARAGRAPH

A paragraph is a division of written material consisting of one or more sentences that typically deal with a single topic or quotations of one speaker's words. Paragraphs need a way to be separated from other paragraphs in a significant way: generally indented, although double spaces between paragraphs are used in some electronic printed material.

PARAGRAPH LENGTH

A paragraph can be complete with a very few words, a single sentence, or a series of sentences. Effective writing throws in a bit of each to produce a variety of paragraph lengths. Repetitious paragraph lengths works much like a sleeping potion, especially in business writing.

A professional writer tells how she discovered the deadly repetition of paragraph lengths when she switched to a word processor. For the first time, she saw her writing as a pattern on the screen and was surprised to find she habitually wrote four-line paragraphs. To avoid this pitfall, pick up a random piece of writing from your desk and turn it upside down. Do the paragraphs all look the same? If so, vary them; make some longer, some shorter.

A short paragraph grabs attention.

A longer paragraph draws that attention out, telling the reader there is much to be learned about this particular idea. That's one of the reasons for having a long paragraph. Another reason is to provide a canvas for a complete message, one that may be reduced or diluted if it were split up into several short paragraphs. The long paragraph definitely has its place in business writing.

Review the last two paragraphs. Notice the differences, the similarities.

Short paragraphs are used in newspapers and magazine text to make reading easier and faster. Fiction utilizes longer paragraphs to completely explore an action or a thought.

TOPIC SENTENCES

Surely, you recall learning about topic sentences in school. That may have been the day you first were exposed to the subject of paragraph construction. Perhaps you have since learned to construct paragraphs subconsciously; many writers get through long careers unaware of how they do it. If you are aware, subconsciously or not, that paragraphs have a form, your writing may utilize the notion without much thought.

With a solid sentence foundation, paragraph building becomes a cinch. A topic sentence sets the tone and subject of a paragraph. It may head up the paragraph, end it, or lie buried in the middle. Everything in that paragraph must define, expand upon, compare to or contradict that statement. A topic sentence can be stated more than once in more than one way.

Red

Red is a color close to my heart. Actually, it is the color of my heart, and blood vessels, and much of my body. Red is the color that means life and beauty, much like the pulsing of the vital organs, the throbbing of a heart. Because red is such a color of health and life, it is often referred to as a vibrant color—vibrant meaning "full of life". **Yes, red, a vibrant color, is close to my heart.**

The above paragraph carries the topic throughout — *red is a color close to my heart* — and the more definitive topic sentence is repeated at the beginning and at the end. A paragraph that follows on the subject of red might contain a topic sentence about the color red as found in nature, or in literature, or in music. Or it could describe the way a particular painter used the color red, or didn't use it. Can you see the flexibility, the space to move around with your topic sentence? The topic sentences in the following paragraphs are emphasized.

Red is a color found in nature. *Because it is bright, red is a favorite color of fruits and flowers, such as cherries, apples, raspberries, roses, hibiscus and rhododendrons. Tomatos and red peppers seem to be the only red vegetables, unless you count red cabbage and red celery. Animals too reflect the red color, as in red-tailed deer, red squirrel and red fox. The red coloring found in birds is also distinctive, usually found in males.*

Because emotions are strong, they elicit strong reactions. Anger, jealousy, rage are among the strongest. Sexual desire is considered a strong psychological reaction in humans. These strong emotions can be enhanced with the use of color. **Red is the color most often connected with strong emotions.**

When discussing red, the human body must be included. *Red is found in skin tones, hair coloring, and in a person's shy blush. Red is the color of blood and most internal organs. We even refer to some people as rednecks when they spout biased ideas.* **The human body contains many references to red, even artificially.** *Coloring is added to many human bodies in the form of nail polish, lipstick, and rouge. Even some eye makeup is colored red.* **Red is a significant color when attached to the human body.**

In the first of these three paragraphs, notice the topic sentence at the beginning, informing the reader what will follow. In the second paragraph, the topic sentence concludes the paragraph, summing it up.

In the third paragraph, you find a not-to-be-missed technique of ensuring understanding: topic sentences at the beginning, middle and end.

You can judge a writer's clarity by reading the first few words or first sentence of each paragraph. If you can understand what you're reading, the writer did it well. If you're confused, the writer has short-changed the reader.

TRANSITIONAL WORDS

In the construction of paragraphs, it is necessary to link them somehow. That is, it is necessary to provide transition words that tie the ideas of the sequential paragraphs together.

Here are a few techniques that may help:

Use words that automatically give direction to writing by setting the time or space of the topic, such words as: *yet, still, next, first, finally, however, moreover, thus.*

Use a pronoun in a paragraph's opening sentence that refers to a noun in the previous paragraph.

The catalog that comes with each machine tells everything about the fully automatic Multi-key Typewriter. A primary accessory is the error eraser.

Another of its *accessories is the adjustable set of keys.*

Pick up a word from the previous paragraph and use it early in the following paragraph.

You'll especially like the ease with which the automatic keyboard fits your fingertips.

This ease *will be reflected in the comfort you feel during the work day and the extra energy you'll enjoy after working long hours.*

Parallel construction is another technique for tying paragraphs together. Begin each paragraph with a similar sentence; then go on to fill out the paragraph to follow that topic.

Red is a wild color...
Red is a hot color...
Red is a sexy color...
Red is a warning color...
Red is a color with many intensities...

Read through pieces of business writing, newspaper items, and magazine articles, as you watch for the transition techniques. Become aware of how they are used by skilled writers. You won't have to make a conscious effort to build your paragraphs; by knowing how, the construction will fall into place easily.

COMPUTERIZED WRITING

Using the word processor to create pieces of writing is a snap when you utilize a simple system for outlining. Brainstorm. Write down a number of ideas that you wish to include in your piece and list them all on the word processor.

Brainstorming — Brainstorming is a problem-solving technique used in groups to produce ideas. One person is designated to write down everything said. The others come up with creative suggestions, which are written down without judgment. It's a spontaneous, no-holds-barred way of stimulating original thought.

Individuals can brainstorm in similar ways, writing down all the ideas you can drum up, without passing judgment on any thoughts. A quiet room and a yellow pad work for some. Others prefer a recording machine. Many writers use their word processors, darkening the screen or covering it up in order to free the brain to take off into flights of fancy and originality.

In a brainstorming session, the subject *red* turned up a page full of ideas. They fell into several areas of interest, listed below:

Chromatic Hue
Nature
Emotional Color
Political Connotations
The Human Body
Danger
Shades of Red
Red Words

Take this list, rearrange the ideas in whatever order that seems to work, and you have the outline for an essay on the color red. You can make that essay as short as a sentence:

The color red, the brightest of the colors, is found abundantly in nature, is an emotional color with political connotations, is a primary color of the human body, is used to signify danger, comes in many shades, and shows up in such word messages as redneck and red hot.

By completing each thought with a full sentence, you may construct a longer paragraph. Get carried away and write several paragraphs about each thought on the list to achieve a full essay. When you really get steamed up, you may try writing an entire chapter about each topic. That's how books are often planned and written. The best writers use this technique.

The computer, with its marvelous ways of expanding and its ability to move ideas around, provides fun in catching ideas. In addition you'll find them easier to edit.

Hint: After many years writing professionally, a friend suggested that the best place to find that important opening paragraph is at the end of your work. For some reason, the human mind likes to save the best part until last. Look at your final paragraph and decide whether or not to move it up front.

SPELLING

(Four Ways To Do It Better)

Why is U.S. spelling so darned hard? This section offers four guides to improve spelling: 1) Seek root words, 2) Understand prefixes and suffixes, 3) Know how to pronounce words, and 4) The look-it-up-and-memorize-it method.

Most attention in grammar seems to be aimed at spelling. If all the words are spelled *right*, we feel we've done a good job. Of course that isn't quite true, but the emphasis on spelling is extremely important. The first notion that must be erased from most bad spellers' minds is that they *are bad spellers*.

Recently a proud banner went up in a neighborhood shopping plaza announcing: Florist Comeing Soon! Two weeks passed before someone whited out the *e* to correct the spelling. Readerboards notoriously contain misspelled words. Of late, they're even showing up on crawl lines of television news shows!

Mention spelling (sometimes *grammar* will do it) and you hear, "Oh, poor me! I can't spell worth a darn. I've always been a bad speller."

With that attitude, you'll always be a bad speller.

The secret to becoming a good speller is simple — pay attention. Read and become familiar with words, lots of them, even if you don't always know what they mean. Become aware of how words are put together with suffixes and prefixes (endings and beginnings). Discover the world of root words, the places where words come from. Because U.S. language combines languages from cultures around the world, it's no wonder that spelling is a challenge. Some word people (lexicologists) estimate U.S. language contains contributions from more than 150 countries.

The spelling disease in the U.S. comes from the words themselves that arrive here in their original forms — the way they appear in native languages. A definite drawback to re-spelling in U.S. language is the transition from one alphabet to another. In Arabic, for instance, the "kuh" sound, as in "cat" and "keep" can be Anglicized with "c", "k", "qu" or just "q". So then, how do you spell the Islamic holy book? *Curan, Coran, Koran, Quran, Quoran, Qu'ran...?* Some dictionaries choose one, and others offer "alternatives".

Now add 150-plus languages with wide varieties of spelling similar words and you begin to understand the problem. Actually, it is not a problem at all, but a challenge. Here in this wondrous land is a unique language, one-of-a-kind, the only one like it in the whole entire world. It's no wonder there are difficulties, but the result is a language with unequaled opportunities: new words, new ways to put them together, new ways to use them, new ways to think about them.

Take up that challenge and wallow in the freedom to write your way. In the case of multiple spellings, variations, or alternatives, choose the one you prefer and write it in Your Style Manual.

FOUR GUIDELINES TO BETTER SPELLING

The four ways to improve spelling are:

- The Root Word Approach
- The Prefix / Suffix Approach
- The Sounding Approach (attention to correct pronunciation), and
- The Look-It-Up-and-Memorize-It Approach

Spelling is a visual skill. You need to pay attention with all of the senses and implant words into your visual memory forever, as securely as spelling your own name.

The four methods presented here are offered as helpers to anyone wanting to improve spelling techniques. No single method will work in all situations, but you may be surprised how often you will employ one or more of the methods. If one doesn't work, try another.

The Root Word Approach

You have noticed how often many words stem from approximately the same word. Medical: *medication, medicine, medicinal;* hypnosis: *hypnotize, hypnotic, hypnotical;* tense: *tension, tenseness, tensity, pretension, extension.*

The root word approach suggests that you find another related word that you do know how to spell and apply similar spelling to the word you're looking at.

If you wondered how to spell *medic_nal* (is it *medicanal, medicenal, medicinal, medicunal?*), you might look at *medicine* (which you are sure of) and apply the same spelling (choosing the *i*).

When you know that the *sci* in science is carried over into words like *conscious* and *conscience,* you won't have trouble with them anymore.

Do you spell *preten_ion* and *exten_ion* with s or t? Can you spell *tension?* Sure you can. Spell the others the same way, with the *s*.

The Prefix/Suffix Method

This system requires some sense of root words. It also employs a mathematical formula that's as simple as adding $1 + 1 = 2$.

If a prefix ends in the same letter that the root word begins, add them together and get two letters. (*un-necessary, ac-commodate, im-mediate, il-legitimate, in-novation*). If the prefix ends in a letter other than the beginning of the root word, there is no doubling: resistant, acoustics, recommend, disappear, renovation, ineligible).

The same mathematical formula works for suffixes (*common-ness, human-ness, certain-ness, grand-ness, civil-ness, logical-ly, final-ly, like-ly, grand-ly*).

The Sounding Method

Here's the one that Teacher taught for a few terms under the guise of "phonetics": "Sound it out". The catch is that many of us come from parts of the country that speak with different sounds. So it is logical for people to mis-spell words the way they mis-sound them.

Public schools seem to favor alternately, on an intermittent basis, the phonetic system and the spelling bee (memorize the way words are spelled). Many words can be sounded out and spelled accurately using any one of the smattering of spelling guides. However, recall that you probably learned the word *exception* in connection with spelling "rules". There always seemed to be more exceptions than there were "rules".

Now, how do you learn the different spellings of homonyms — words that sound alike but have different spellings, such as: *pair / pear / pare; bear / bare; fair / fare*? In some parts of the country, the following words may sound alike: *fear, fare, for, fair, far*, thus giving the willies to spelling teachers. Try *tear, tar,* and *tire* in the Deep South or Texas.

We had a President who probably could never spell *government* because he pronounced it with a "b" (gubment). Government contains three syllables: *gov-ern-ment*. Another U.S. President (and a lot of U.S. citizens) pronounce *nuclear* with an extra "u" (nu-cu-lar); another three-syllable word: *nu-cle-ar*. Wrong pronounciation increases the likelihood of misspelled words. Refer to dictionaries for sound help.

Realtors themselves seem to have trouble pronouncing their word correctly: *real-tors* and not *real-a-tors*. Athletes like to add an extra syllable in their label too: *ath-a-letes* rather than *ath-letes*. If you can't pronounce it right, you will have trouble spelling it right.

The big debate continues nationwide as to the pronunciation of *harassment*. (However, there need be no doubt, the word contains two *s*'s.) While not exactly scientific evidence, it seems men prefer the accent on the second syllable; women and British people prefer to accent the first.

Sound out the following words and watch out for the sneaky letters that seem not to belong there:

length, strength, height, perform, surprise, persevere, prescription, recognize, hindrance (only 2 syllables), *athletics* (only 3 syllables), *library, government, congratulations.* (How often have you seen a congratulatory sign on a high school readerboard spelled *"Congradulations"*? One can only hope it was placed there by a non-graduating student.)

The Look-It-Up-and-Memorize-It Method

The most useful way to become a good speller is to carry a dictionary with you and look up words you're unsure of. But promise yourself to look up a word only once. Then give yourself a system for remembering — the sillier the better.

> *Aberration* contains an *aber* and a *ration*.
> *Apparition* has an *ap* prefix with a *parition* root.
> *Accommodation* duplicates 2/5 of its consonants.
> *Pursue* is what you do when you see a purse you want.
> *Iridescent* descends (nearly) from the iris.
> *Privilege* stands on a leg and not on a ledge.
> *Contemptuous* is a relationship (con) that tempts u and ous.
> *Personal* means just for one (n); *personnel* concerns more (add the *nel* suffix).
> *Aqua* and all its watery derivatives are the only words that begin with "aq". The other similar-sounding words need the c-insert: *acquire, acquaint, acquit.*
> The only *ceed* words are *proceed, exceed* and *succeed.* All the others are *cede* words: *accede, intercede, precede,* etc. Don't forget *supersede,* which sounds like one of this family but isn't (two *s's* and no *c*)!

Certain words in your vocabulary probably have bothered you for years. Decide to look them up one last time. Make a rhyme or jingle to help you remember them (the naughtier the jingle, the easier you'll remember). Keep your dictionary close until you discover one day that you refer to it less and enjoy spelling more.

There is no "e" on the end of develop, but there is on the end of envelope (noun). The verb *envelop* (meaning to enclose) lacks the *e*. Here's one way to build memory — a rhyme:

Devel op is enough to see (see / op, get it?)
It doesn't have to end in "e".
Envelope may go express;
An antelope is hard to dress.

If no one else understands your jingles, don't mind. If they help you remember how words are spelled, only you have to understand them.

"I BEFORE E..."

The more people try to develop "rules" for spelling, the more mixed up they become. It seems that there are more exceptions to "rules" than there are standard uses for them. When challenged to state a "rule", some staunch adherents offer the "I-before-E" as an example. Not a rule if it adheres to the need for no exceptions. However, a few ideas may serve as guidelines to improve spelling.

I before E except after C
or when sounded like A
as in neighbor and weigh.

Just as quickly as you learned that rule-with-an-exception, you begin to unravel the numbers of *other* exceptions.

Either seize the weird counterfeit heights or use a sleight of hand.

Memorize this sentence and you'll know most of them.

ENDING IN O

A bunch of nouns end in "o". Grammar gurus have had a field day improvising "rules" for these nouns, separating the o-nouns into lists... and lists (no two alike). The lists, without rhyme nor reason, pluralize some nouns with "s" and some with "es". Anyone looking closely at those lists immediately realizes that not one single o-noun would suffer either mispronunciation or misunderstanding by using only the "s" ending.

Would you have a problem with: *potatos, tomatos, tuxedos, cargos, heros, torpedos, mottos, mementos, volcanos, vetos, banjos?*

ENDING IN Y

When a word ends in *y*, there are two ways to make it plural. If the *y* has a consonant before it, change the *y* to *i* before adding *es*: (company / companies; worry / worries).

If the *y* follows a vowel, the second way is simply to add the *s*: monkey / monkeys, journey / journeys.

SHORT VOWELS

When adding a suffix (*ed, ing, er*) to a word ending in a short vowel (the one that does not say its own name) and a single consonant, double the consonant to retain the short sound to the preceding vowel (*hop / hopping / hopped*).

LONG VOWELS

When doing the same with a word ending in *e* preceded by a single consonant, drop the *e* and add the suffix, thus retaining the long vowel sound (*hope / hoping / hoped; desire / desiring / desirable / desirous; spike / spiking / spiked; excuse / excusing / excusable*).

Words that sound a long vowel usually end with a silent *e*, which provides the clue as to when to remove the *e* and add a suffix. A word like *come* that nearly says its own name doesn't call for the doubling of letters (*coming, comer*).

A NOTE FOR NORTHERN U.S.ERS

The closer you get to the Canadian border, the more opportunities you have for lousing up your spelling. You see, Canadians are related to the

British who have their own way of spelling. They get the *s* and the *f* mixed up sometimes. They also use the *u* more often than we do. And they leave the *e* in places where the U.S. has removed it. (Remember the Revolution in the 1700s?)

Typical British (Canadian) spelling: *honour, colour, favour, theatre, centre, judgement, acknowledgement*. Typical U.S. spelling: *honor, color, favor, theater, center, judgment, acknowledgement*.

Many word endings that have been cluttered up with extra letters are now disappearing. Once spelled *cigarette*, the word has become *cigaret*. Others are the *gue* words, such as *dialogue, monologue, catalogue*. These now are spelled acceptably as *dialog, monolog, catalog*. The *ue* was retained after the *g* by the French to make sure we used the hard *g* sound (*guide, guess, guilt*). Little question remains that the extra letters have served their purpose.

But not in Spanish. Those wise people spell their words without double letters, except for the "l". Yes, even Spanish has its exceptions.

Don't dismay at this wonderful language of ours. Thomas Edison didn't. Take solace in his words: "It's a damn poor mind that can spell a word only one way."

NUMBERS

(How To Write Them)

Since many business people work with numbers, the subject deserves its own section. Confusion exists as to whether or not to use numbers as words, when to use them as figures, and how to write them. Here you'll review using numbers in dates, money, inventory, temperature, fractions and percentage, dimensions, weights and measures, and addresses. You'll also delve into the mystifying meanings and uses of cardinals and ordinals.

WHEN TO WRITE OUT NUMBERS

Numbers are used often in business writing, from an invoice to an annual report, and in personal writing, from baby's weight to the settlement of wills. Not much attention is paid to these numbers until they appear in courts of law or collection notices.

Generally, numbers from one through nine or ten are written out. Numbers 10 (or 11) and above are written in figures, numerals. (Yeah, the profs couldn't decide this one either. The Anarchist chooses to spell out "ten".)

The city has four hospitals and 490 physicians.
The 23 nurses at one hospital comprise less than five percent of the staff.

One guideline suggests that when you use a group of numbers in a particular context, either use all numerals or all words. The decision of which to use depends on the majority of the numbers. If most of your numbers are under ten, write out the one or two that are over. If most of the numbers are above 11, use numerals for the few that are under.

The package contained two scissors, four rolls of tape, six bandages and thirty aspirins. Bandages come in separate packages of 500, 250, 50, 30 and 6.

Incidentally, The Grammar Anarchist abhors the use of *over* when talking about numbers. *Over* refers to a physical location that is "above, on top of, hovering overhead". The preferred words with numbers are either *above* or *more than*. However, most number users sprinkle their work with phrases like *over 40, over $3 million, over two dollars*. The way of the user seems to set the standard on this one. You decide which you prefer and record it in Your Style Manual.

Business related injuries number over 3,000 a year and cost over $150,000.
Business related injuries number above 3,000 a year and cost more than $150,000.

Too often, the effect of a business report is lost to the cumbersome, monotonous recital of numbers, too long and too detailed to be understandable. This is the time to find an easier-to-read version and spell them out; choose indefinite words when summarizing the numbers:

Thousands of dollars were lost because of bad planning.
Letters numbered in the hundreds.
People in their twenties exude hope for recovery.
Give me a half minute to think.

You have learned a "rule" about not beginning a sentence with a numeral? You may want to avoid beginning a sentence with a number of any kind. When there is absolutely, positively, no... other... way... to... begin a sentence with a number, write it out, however cumbersome it may be. Most times, however, it is possible to re-cast the sentence to move the unwieldy number inside.

Rather than:

2,314 responses came from angry constituents.
Twenty-eight people attended the open hearing.

try:

Responses from 2,314 angry constituents were received.
The open hearing was attended by 28 people.

Solve the dilemma of writing two numbers back-to-back, when they could be misinterpreted, by using numerals for one. Select the shorter word for convenience and write it out.

Use: *66 six-passenger planes* instead of *66 6-passenger planes.*
Use: *two 22-foot red carpets* instead of *2 22-foot red carpets.*

When writing out short fractions, use: *one-third, three-fourths.* (You'll use figures, possibly from your Symbols File, when mixing fractions with whole numbers: 5-1/2% interest.)

Formal documents also invite spelled-out numbers — invitations, legal papers, announcements.

The wedding will take place at two o'clock at the church on Seventh Avenue. The dowry settlement amounts to Four thousand Fifty-two dollars ($4,052.00). (Lawyers prefer *everything* to be spelled out! They prefer numbers in both numeric and spelled-out forms.) Lawyers and salespeople, also like to add the zeros when no cent amount is shown.

NUMBERS IN DATES AND TIME

Dates are usually written with the month (spelled out), the day, and the year (in numerals): June 5, 2000. The longer months can be abbreviated in tight places: Dec. 25, 1950.

Be careful writing only numerals to indicate a date. Some errors might occur because of a misinterpretation. In some locations, dates are written European style, day/month/year: 5 June 2000 or 25 December 1950 (note the lack of punctuation). In the U.S., dates are written month/

day/year. When these dates are written in numerals, they become either *5/6/00 and 25/12/50* or *6/5/00 and 12/25/50*. The December date poses no problem since there isn't a 25th month. But the June date could be misinterpreted as May 6 (5/6) instead of June 5 (6/5). Make it easy on yourself. Write out the month, no matter which order you use.

In business correspondence (and probably personal as well), it's a good idea to include the year at least once per document. Because files and records are stored for years, these complete dates could prevent a problem in the future. A municipal records keeper notes the importance of keeping the year complete (1935 as opposed to '35). In older communities, property listed as built in '85 could easily be 1785 or 1885. Now in another century, the problem is raised again. Writing '09 could possibly refer to 1909 or 2009. My how time flies!

Do not use the ordinal (*th, st, rd, nd*) form of numbers when writing the complete date: *January 15 is the date for the examination.*

However, you may choose to use the ordinal suffixes if you write only the day: *The 15th is the date for the examination.*

Time is written in numerals (except in formal use) and is accompanied by a.m. / p.m. or am / pm or AM / PM or A.M. / P.M. Deciding on which form to use calls for a style manual.

Be consistent in using hour and minute figures. If you use *10:15 a.m.*, then use *2:00 p.m.* If you don't need the minutes, use *10 a.m.* and *2 p.m.*, or even *10 and 2* when there is no question about time of day. Remove redundancy by avoiding 3 a.m. in the morning. When else is 3 a.m.?

NUMBERS AND MONEY

Because much business writing pertains to money, invoices, payrolls and taxes, business people tend to use more numerals than short story writers. The same general guidelines apply: use figures for numbers above ten.

Most money figures are written in numerals, particularly dollars and cents. Omit the decimal and two zeros when writing round dollar figures.

The bill amounted to $80. When the tax was added, it came to $84.29.

Cents alone are depicted as *34 cents* or *34¢*, and not as *$.34* (unless in a column with other larger numbers). That symbol for cents (¢) is available on most computers.

Write big, big numbers in a combination of words and numerals: *$5 million, $1.2 million, $2.25 billion.* If the numbers are detailed into the thousands, go to all figures: *$4,275,000* rather than *$4.275 million.*

The psychological factor indicates a dollar figure looks greater with the zeros ($2700.00). Therefore, if you're trying to minimize the amount, scrap the zeros ($2,700).

Business writers, as a specific group, like to mix the very big numbers with letters. They're easier to read: *$2.5 million* (instead of *$2,500,000*) and *$45K* (meaning *$45,000*). Some business people use the letter *M* to represent thousands; some use *K*.

Receipts from the emergency room topped the $150 million mark. That averaged about $1.25 a month, or $40K for each patient.

MORE WAYS TO USE NUMERALS

Measurements, weights, temperature readings, stock market quotes, percentages and addresses are written in numerals.

Measurements require numerals used with other symbols.

The size of the lot was 120' x 80'. The worker was hit on the head by a 2 x 4. He was taken to the hospital in his own 4X4 pickup.

Weights also require numerals, sometimes used with symbols.

The worker weighed more than 200 pounds, considerably more than the 4-pound, 3-ounce board. That was because he regularly carried 2 gallons of water on his back.

Temperature is written with numerals, either with degrees in word or symbol (*62 degrees* or *62°*). Choose one and use it consistently throughout a document.

The poor fellow's fever ran up to 101.8°. He stayed cool since the outside temperature was a mere 40°.

Stock Market quotes appear without decimals,

The blue chip stock closed at 32 1/4, off 1/2.

Percentages are also written in numerals, with the word *percent* written out. Confine the use of the percent sign (%) to financial documents, tables, graphs, and charts.

The fund drive raised 38 percent of its goal, with only .03 percent received from new donors. The sales quota was 25 percent higher than last year. Recall that .25 = 25% (twenty-five percent) and .25 percent = twenty-five hundredths of a percent.

Numbered streets are usually written in numerals. Some exceptions suggest that numbered streets under ten be written out. House and apartment numbers always are written in figures.

The accident occurred on the corner of First Avenue and 45th Court. The victim lived at 105 45th Court, Apartment 6. The witness lived at 4516 Fifth Avenue.

Highway and route numbers also are numeralized.

The way to the hospital was on Route 1 by way of State Highway 536.

RELIGIOUS NUMBERS

There seems to be a religious connotation to numbers, having to do with rank and position. Numbers are referred to as *ordinals* or *cardinals*, and they come in *denominations*! Ordinals are the *st, nd, rd, th* words (*1st, 2nd, 3rd, 4th...*). *Ordinal* comes from the word meaning "to be ordained". *Cardinal* numbers are those used to count from one to whatever (*1, 2, 3, 4...*). *Cardinal* means "principal, of basic importance".

Write out ordinal numbers when they contain just one word: *third prize, tenth in line, sixtieth anniversary, fifteenth birthday.* Use numerals for the others: *the 52nd state, the 21st Amendment.* Street names above Ninth or Tenth (yes, capitalized) also call for ordinal numerals: *15th Street, 19th Place.*

When all this is digested and committed to memory, a third grade logic will probably be the best guide you have in using numbers. Along with "consistency". Consistency is the key. As long as you are consistent, other people will figure you know what you're doing.

The use of numbers in business writing is probably the best selling point for providing style manuals in offices. Check out the many good ones available through bookstores. Or, your office manager may decide to make up one for the entire office. However it is done, a style manual gives everyone within an organization the writing guidelines that result in consistency throughout the company. Style manuals save much unnecessary fretting.

UNBIASED LANGUAGE

(Include "Them")

Bias in language not only turns off many readers, but is illegal in many ways. Government agencies and businesses require written materials to be free of language that excludes. How is that possible? Certain words and phrases carry meanings that exclude, debase, or stereotype whole groups of people; this is called *sexism, racism, ageism, classism*... well, you get the point. This is how it works with sexism.

Sexist language takes three basic forms. It assumes the world is masculine until proven otherwise; it demeans and diminishes with word endings; and it stereotypes. Here are some very basic ways to eliminate sexism in writing — without reverting to the awkward *he / she* or the overuse of the word *person*.

The English language is a male-dominant language; terminology and words are weighted toward masculine usage. Today, this male-dominant language is called *sexist* if certain terms or words are assumed to apply equally to both sexes, and in fact do not.

Sexism in writing, particularly business writing, turns people off, personally, professionally, and legally. Great care must be taken to keep writing sexist-free, a topic not dreamed of not too long ago, and probably avoided for a long time because it means altering some precious "rules".

Fortunately, it is not difficult to keep writing unbiased and inclusive.

THE *MAN* WORDS

The assumption that the world is masculine until proven otherwise is reflected in *man words*, particularly the pronouns *he, him, his* to refer to people whose genders are unknown. Grammatically, this is easy to correct by replacing the third person singular masculine pronoun *he* (such a long introduction for such a little word). This is a fairly simple process.

1. Change writing to reflect first or second person singular (*we, our, you, your*).
2. Change writing to reflect the plural third person (*them, they*).
3. Restate the sentence and use the offending information in a clause or phrase.
4. Rewrite the sentence passively to change the subject into an object.
5. Eliminate the pronoun, replace it with the original noun, or replace it with the words *one* or *the*).

> **Man / Woman**
>
> *Isn't it strange that* **man** *is supposed to include "women" when the word* **woman** *does include "m-a-n"?*

U.S. language also utilizes many *man words* that once were expected to include women. Words such as: *mankind, salesman, businessman, penmanship,* and phrases such as: *man of the hour, man hours, brotherhood of man, man the torpedos*!

Words of this nature are easily replaced with words that more accurately describe the subject: *civilization* or *humankind, sales representative* or *sales agent*, executive or *manager, writing ability, script, distinctive person, work hours, kinship of humans, go to war*!

Do not confuse "man" words in the context of male-ism with the "man" words relating to "mano", the Latin word for hand (*manipulate, manifold, manage, manifest,* etc.) Don't eliminate a word because it begins or includes the letters m-a-n. Simply eliminate the m-a-n words that suggest that a w-o-m-a-n is not included.

DIMINISH AND DEMEAN

The second form of sexism is found in diminishing and demeaning words, the kind of words that separate women from the standard *man words*, portray women as objects, possessions, or as *little, less-than, second-class*. Words such as: *waitress, bachelorette, actress, little woman, cookie, girl, aviatrix, heiress.*

When women are treated as less-than through language, the consequences follow in other parts of life — economically, politically, academically. For centuries, women have not received the same educational opportunities that men have. Politically, women have been suppressed, overlooked and demeaned. Economically, the results of suppression have kept women in low-paying or non-paying work.

The word *girl* used in reference to a grown woman has probably done more to keep women in subservient positions than any other word. It implies "incompetency, little-girl qualities, cuteness, immaturity". When office people refer to "the girls in Accounting" or "the girls in the front office", they are suggesting that these workers are not serious about their work and therefore don't deserve a woman's paycheck. And why not? For many years, women were not considered as a serious part of the workforce.

Use adjectives that point to women's abilities and strengths, not their weaknesses (or perceived weaknesses) or their appearance. When describing women workers, talk about their skills rather than how blond, how shapely, or how tall they are.

Use women's names on a par with the way all names are used in the office. For instance, avoid calling the boss *Mr. Boss* if woman co-workers are called by their first names. Many women, who are called by their first names by male doctors, dentists, lawyers, and stockbrokers, still have difficulty calling these men by their first names.

Do not use word endings that point to women as also-rans or objects. Eliminate the endings that say: *the real word doesn't have this ending; this ending indicates "only a woman"*. Use instead the words that best reflect the intended meaning.

Instead of	**Use**
adulteress	adulterer
barmaid	bartender
camera girl	photographer
chairwoman	chair
girl Friday	flunky / assistant
goddess	god
housewife	homemaker (has nothing to do with being a wife)
laundress	launderer
meter maid	meter reader
mistress of ceremonies	host
murderess	murderer
post mistress	post office manager
sculptress	sculptor
seamstress	sewer
spokeswoman	speaker
sportswoman	athlete
stewardess	flight attendant

STEREOTYPES

The third form of sexism is found in stereotyping certain words or ideals for women and men. Picture the following people in your mind's eye: *bank president, lawyer, doctor, high school principal, teller, secretary, nurse, teacher*. Did you picture the first four as men? the last four as women? That is stereotyping!

Women are entering all fields of endeavor and succeeding in them, proving to the world that places in government, the military, medicine, law, business, sports, religion, and the arts are places for women and men, working side-by-side.

Avoid referring to secretaries, nurses, and teachers as *she* and to doctors, lawyers, and executives as *he*. Keep an open mind about gender until you find out whether the company president is a man or a woman, or the company secretary is a man or a woman.

Be careful to use appropriate titles when addressing letters. If a woman wishes to be addressed as *Mrs.* or *Miss*, she will say so. Otherwise, refer to her as *Ms*. Don't assume that the director of the traffic agency is a man or that the director of the health organization is a woman. If you have to use a title, find out which applies, or be neutral. If you don't have to use a gender title (Mr. or Ms.), don't.

Avoid referring to gender if it isn't necessary. Whether the lawyer is a woman or man probably isn't important. Know also that referring to her as a *lady attorney* or *lady doctor* is patronizing. First of all, it isn't important most of the time to make such a note. Secondly, the term *lady* is gratuitous. If she is a woman, say so. Don't hide behind alternative terms such as: *lady, gal, female*.

By eliminating sexist language from your writing, not only will you uphold the law, but you will make friends and respect people for who they are and what they do instead of whether they go to a hairdresser or a barber. (Many barbers count women as their clients; many hairdressers welcome men to their salons. As savvy business people, they are getting rid of gender and focusing on hair.)

Eliminating sexist language is not to suggest eliminating sex or gender from your life, just from your language.

A WRITING STYLE OF YOUR OWN

Isn't it time to develop a style that reflects you and you alone? You want to read the best writers and hope some of their style rubs off on you, but how much stronger your writing will be when you develop your own way of doing it. This section is where you may pick up the self-confidence to fly solo!

Here you consider such things as your purpose in writing; themes; openings / closings; the reader; formal / informal writing; and business writing. Serious freelance writers need to know how to seduce editors into printing their work. Here's where you develop your own style with your own rhythm and harmony, build your own style manual, and use the computer to its fullest.

Before you sit down to write, you need to have a message. How often a "writer" says, "I want to write a book. Wonder what I can write about"? You need to have a clear message or an urge before you even sit down. The best way to do that is to take the time to consider, "What's my message? What am I trying to convey? What are my writing objectives?"

When you rushed home from third grade to tell your folks about how you learned to write, you may have been confused about what "learning to write" entailed. You defined it either as "learning to write script, to handle a pen on paper" (remember the miles of scrolls and fence posts you practiced?) or as "controlling the rules of grammar long enough to string a few sentences together".

Writing is some of that, of course. But it is so much more than forming letters and memorizing "rules". Writing is communicating.

Writing is tapping into yourself and your ideas; writing is describing your emotions; writing is connecting yourself with the rest of the world; writing is sending an idea to another person.

Writing is touching another soul, moving that soul to respond with an "Aha! so that's what you mean" or "Why didn't I think of that?" or "Isn't that beautiful!" or "Such words to express so much fear."

As children, your reasons for writing were few: because you had to, because you had to, because you had to. It was the rare child who kept a journal (diary) or wrote to expresses their feelings before the social Internet came into their lives. The blog replicates a journal. However, much is lost when blog writers don't considered their *purpose* in writing.

PURPOSE IN WRITING

Knowing the reason for writing a particular item saves time and words when it comes to composing the business message. A child will think long and hard about the purpose of their writing. After all, they wouldn't want to waste their time writing something that didn't fulfill Teacher's assignment!

As grownups, the reasons for writing are many: to transfer information; to request information, material, time, etc.; to persuade or sell; to touch base or make nice; to document (cover your... backside); and because you have to.

> **Why Do You Write?**
>
> *Information*
> *Sell / Persuade*
> *Document*
> *Entertain*
> *Scratch the Itch*

Unfortunately, most adults just sit down and write. Somewhere near the end, if at all, a thought might appear that answers "why the heck am I doing this?" If that thought had been moved up front, the message would be much clearer. It's called putting the bottom line on top, a solid business strategy.

Putting the bottom line on top is the strategic way to express purpose. Too often a piece of writing begins with a clever word or phrase and continues through what is called "the thinking process" until the subject is well thought out. At that point, the "Aha" moment arrives and the writer draws conclusions or summarizes the thinking process. This results in "the bottom line". Now put that line at the top and start over!

For beginners, consider the purpose of your writing the next time you sit down to compose. Am I simply writing words? Am I providing data? Do I want something? Do I wish to change someone's mind? Am I expressing gratitude or maintaining contact? Is this for the record? By defining your purpose, you are one giant step closer to easier writing.

Writing must have a purpose to be worthwhile.

When turning on your business correspondence (yes, writing is a business) you'll reverse your fiction writing. Instead of "I'll whet their appetites with innuendos so they'll be waiting for my bottom-line message," get attention with an opening line, then lay out your project.

Why not begin with an intriguing statement:

Fifty million children went to bed hungry last night.
When will teachers receive the compensation they deserve?
What happens when a rich and beautiful teenager becomes an overnight sensation?
Did you know that alien creatures can write too?
Here is the manuscript I promised to send.

With this kind of straightforward writing, there are no doubts about what the document contains, thus saving the reader the time to sift through and guess. Busy business people appreciate this kind of message.

Bottom line? Put it on top! Intrigue? Hook 'em with it!

This technique works well in providing information, responding to requests, making requests, and documenting.

AUDIENCE

Once the purpose of your message is clear, good writers consider their audience. Who will be reading this message? The expected readers determine the tone of the writing, word choice, the degree of formality used. The audience must be identified before the writing begins.

Each message must fit the reader, must set the tone for receiving the communication that you wish to send. Writing for children is far different from teenage novel writing. Writing for men is different from writing for women.

FORMAL WRITING

Formal writing has a time and place of its own, and special guidelines that are about as far away from Twitters and emails as you can get. This is the writing technique you use when writing nonfiction: straightforward, omitting contractions and avoiding personal pronouns.

TERMS OF ENDEARMENT

Here's another place to rise up and be original. Eliminate the "terms of endearment", the "Dear whoever". Why on earth would a person you don't know be addressed as *dear*? And why would you waste all that time when you've finished a letter deciding whether you feel cordial, respectful, sincere, warmly regarding, truly or very truly? Surely you have better things to do with your time.

Shed some fresh light on your business correspondence by using innovative openings. Try using something you feel like writing.

Yes, Mr. Arliss,
I am delighted you want to read my manuscript.
Good morning, Toni Schultz,
You're right, Janice, few want to read about illness, but you may find my approach with this malady is more a message of hope than a run-of-the-mill tear-jerker.

CLOSINGS

More letters have been ruined by a namby-pamby closing than by any other part. If there is one sentence in the world that should be unlawful, it is this:

If you have any further questions please don't hesitate to ask.

Is there any doubt that a letter reader would hesitate if they had questions? Is there any doubt that the letter writer is trying to cover any oversights that may have been made? Or does the writer lack the brains to know when to quit writing?

Give your reader a break and use this valuable closing space to ask for what you want. And be specific.

May I send you a full proposal?
My revision will be in the mail in two days.

Sometimes a summary of the letter is all that is needed in this valuable spot.

SELLING YOUR IDEAS (PERSUASIVE WRITING)

The knack of selling an idea or a product with a written communication is highly prized in the writing world. Since we all use this skill, it seems important enough to include in this chapter about style.

Writers notoriously hate to write proposals; they hate to have to "sell" their articles, books, or ideas. By realizing you are the best sales person for your writing, you may attack the task with more confidence.

Writing a persuasive message has its own style, which utilizes some basic considerations — capturing attention, interesting the reader, describing the details, and asking for action by the reader. Persuasive messages also benefit from mechanical emphasis.

Student writers often balk at having to write a "sales" letter. "I don't like to sell," they whine. If you're married, have a close friend, have ever held a job, or belong to an organization, you have done a selling job — for yourself. Successful writers will tell you they have to sell themselves before they can sell their work.

If you're trying to persuade someone to publish your book, the art of writing a strong, positive message is invaluable. End with an offer they can't refuse. *"Would you prefer to look at a short proposal or a more detailed one?"*

WRITING FOR FUN (AND PROFIT)

The advent of the computer has triggered the writing gene in people around the world. The result is the opportunity to write down your story, share it with friends and family, and possibly with the rest of the world.

Book publishing has flourished. Where, a couple decades ago, a few hundred books were published each year, now thousands are published — daily! You write your stories on computers, your journals online, your opinions all over the Internet; you write out your lives, your dreams, and your emotions in many forms — stories, books, plays, songs, poems...

All of this is where writers have the most fun and consider the possibility of profit. *Someone will publish my book and make me rich. Someone will produce my play. Someone will read my poetry and weep. Someone will read my memoir and smile.*

HOW CAN YOU SATISFY THE WRITING ITCH?

Anyone with the answer to that question will attract the gratitude and everlasting riches of writers everywhere. Here are some guidelines, beginning with this qualifier: No one can teach you to write. You can read guidelines, the way someone else does it, helpful suggestions, and advice, but the "learning to write" is the sole job of the writer.

The best advice is this: Write. Write some more. Write again. Rewrite. Write it over. Write! Write! Write!

Listen to the published writers who admit they wrote for years before considering themselves "writers". Some write several novels, numerous poems, stories and more stories before even thinking of themselves as "writers". Every time you write something, you'll find it is better than the last thing you wrote. Listen to other writers, then write your own way.

Know that writing ideas do not come from "out there" (somewhere). They come from inside you — an idea that gnaws at you until you express it, an idea that screams to be shared. If you sit down to write expecting "inspiration" to appear instantaneously, you'll be disappointed. Instead, sit down and write — whatever comes into your head.

POINTERS FOR FICTION WRITERS

A few pointers when writing fiction:

Find characters that speak to you. Combine them with other characters that you feel comfortable knowing (or uncomfortable in the case of villains).

Let your characters do the talking. The best thing a writer can do is learn to listen to them.

Write out a story idea as fully as you can. Don't fuss with details, just lay out the story line. And, yes, dare to be yourself (which may be different from the author of the last book you read!)

Go back and add more details to your story. Expand scenes that show what is happening; reduce the "telling" aspect and increase the "showing" part. Often this is accomplished with dialog and description. Imagine you're watching your story on a screen as you write.

Keep adding the details to Your Style Manual. Some writers establish separate notebooks for each book or story. Know how your characters act and react; know how they got their names, where they went to school, some aspects of their childhood, how they vote, what they like for breakfast... and as much as you can dream up about them. Of course you won't use all that material, but you will know. It's like having friends that you feel you "know", even if you don't know how old they really are or how much schooling they had. You know how they act and react.

Go over your story again, this time noting idiosyncrasies, clues to drop before your readers, and background information to provide your readers with something they didn't know.

Check your inclination to record everything that you know into your manuscript. Leave enough for your reader to keep asking questions. This is similar to "leaving white space" in a painting. You want readers to keep reading, but mostly to find out for themselves what happens.

This monolog on writing could continue for days. However, as stated clearly above, you cannot be "taught" to write. Much like cooking, jazz music, and sex, you have to ***experience it*** to learn what it means to you, then improvise — your way.

Okay, just one more thing: ***write to please yourself.*** Enjoy what you're doing, how you're meandering around in another world, another time, with fascinating people. Do that and your readers will discover the same enjoyment.

Hold on, you're about to learn how to create *Your Style Manual*.

YOUR STYLE MANUAL

Understand that throwing out the "rules" leaves space to be filled. Your writing life is about to ease up. And the answer is so simple: create your own style manual.

While you may have a printed style manual on your bookshelf, take a good look at it. Style manuals offer a list of preferences for particular organizations to supply *their* writers with *their* preferences. "Their preferences" immediately suggests the possibility that other ways exist — no right or wrong way.

So write your own!

"Blimey nutter!" you react in surprise. "I have enough trouble just writing a decent sentence without writing an entire manual."

No, no, no — you don't have to write an entire manual. You'll end up with one, yes, but you don't have to write it all at once. You develop your manual one word at a time. Okay, maybe two or three words at a time, but definitely not all at once.

KNOW YOUR ONIONS

You can join anarchists in ranting and raging or you can make your own choices and create *Your Style Manual*.

The style manuals you find in bookstores and libraries are not written for you. They are written primarily for the reporters who work at particular newspapers or magazines. Many businesses, universities, and government offices, develop style manuals to guide their own writing staffs. The aim is to have all written material that emulates from a particular office follow a standard set of guidelines.

In other words, publications and businesses make *their* choices, select the guidelines *they* prefer, and turn them into rules for *their* style manuals. Some go so far as to publish their decisions (at $29.95 to $59.95 each), allowing you, the writer, to prepare your written material the same way as the *New York Times*, the Associated Press, the U.S. Government Office, the *Wall Street Journal*, the University of Chicago, or any number of other publication businesses.

But do you want to sound like *The New York Times* or the U.S. Government?

One way to develop *Your Style Manual* is to peruse other tomes and find the one that you agree with most. It's a bet you won't find a popular style manual that you agree with all the way; choose one that comes close. Observe the places where you disagree, and record your choices in *Your Style Manual*.

Here's another way: You can find many of these style manuals online. There you can download them (for a price) and edit them to fit your own preferences.

You don't have to compile *Your Style Manual* today; you can make your edits as you come across the need. Let's say you want to be consistent spelling words that once ended in "ue" (*catalogue, dialogue, monologue, analogue*). Some style manuals cling to the wonky British ending; others eliminate it (*catalog, dialog, monolog, analog*). Note your preference in the appropriate place in your chosen style manual — and get back to writing.

Or...

Begin today to write *Your Style Manual* from scratch. Prepare a log or recording spiral notebook (if you *handwrite* notations) or create a computer file. Title the file in large letters: *My Style Manual*; use your name if you wish (*Val's Style Manual*). Each time you feel confused about a "rule", check out the variations — most of which you'll find in this book — and make your decision. Record it in Your Style Manual, where you can easily check it out the next time you need it.

In a very short time, you won't have to refer to *Your Style Manual*. You will have incorporated your style preferences in your writing automatically. See how easy? You'll be surprised at how quickly your notebook or computer file fills up.

THE MANY LIVES OF YOUR STYLE MANUAL

Use *Your Style Manual* to keep track of other writing choices. *Do you use this word with this reader? Do you spell this word with a final "e" or not? Do you use a comma here? What was the name of the town you used in the last chapter? What color are the protagonist's eyes? How do characters in your story spell their names?*

Add your own spin to your writing by recording favorite words or extraordinary words you find in your extensive reading. When you have chosen a subject or theme, look up a corresponding section in an unabridged thesaurus. Make notes of the words that you may want to use as your writing progresses.

If you write in several different categories or write a variety of projects, you may want to create a Style Manual for each project. If you're writing a fiction novel, keep track of characters (their backgrounds, names, descriptions, ages), scenes (layout of a mansion, laboratory, palace, farm), and maps of a town, neighborhood, or region. Fiction writers in the throes of creativity often forget these details. Keepers of style manuals do not.

WHEN WRITING FOR HIRE, BELT UP

If you are writing for hire (for a magazine, newspaper, publisher), you *must* (oh, how this word galls) but you *must* follow the style manual of the publication. When submitting articles to magazines, for instance, learn which style manual is preferred, then follow it. You may wince, but the payoff is worth it.

Likewise, when seeking an editor for your work, discuss style manuals. If you want to maintain your own style, using *Your Style Manual*, this must be made clear at the start. Most freelance editors, unfortunately, cling to one of the commercial manuals. Educate them!

BE CONSISTENT

The key to creating and using *Your Style Manual* is consistency. Mark up the pages of this book and use your notes to create your own list of guidelines. Decide where you want to place punctuation, how you want to spell certain words, how you distinguish the people you write about and use that information throughout your work.

VAL'S STYLE MANUAL

You didn't ask, but yes, the author is writing *Val's Style Manual*. It includes such things as the following:

Yes, I prefer to use the comma before "and" in a series of three or more.
Yes, I use A.M. *and* P.M. *(small caps, rather than a.m./p.m. or A.M./P.M.)*
Yes, I spell dialog *and* monolog *without the "ue".*
Yes, I place punctuation that indicates a specific word or phrase outside quotation marks.
Yes, I capitalize President when it refers to the leader of the U.S.A.

YES! YES! Brilliant! The power of the writer is now clear — Writer, create your own style that reflects you.

ONE LAST QUESTION: DO YOU STILL BELIEVE EVERYTHING YOU READ?

I am certainly *not* telling you: "Trust me, I have all the answers." No indeed! I have only *my* answers, the ones I have chosen for *my* writing. After learning the truths of language in the U.S., where it comes from (all over), how it's taught (by preference), and how many choices a writer has to make (more and more every day), I chose to write my version of grammar in *The Anarchist's Guide To Grammar*. Read my views, sort out your preferences, and write your own bloody Style Manual!

Write on¡

GRAMMAR GLITCHES
A TO Z

Few languages have as many "exceptions to rules" as in the U.S. — mostly because our rag-tag language is composed of languages from around the world. While other languages have orderly rules set in stone, U.S. language struggles with a morass of iffy "rules" and their exception. A few helpful guidelines can put you out of your misery.

Here, alphabetically, are the red herrings that can throw off the best writers. These are some of the really really really crazy idiosyncrasies of U.S. language (the overuse of "really" is one of them), and some guidelines to help you remember how to deal with them. Use them... or not!

Sometimes grammar guidelines malfunction and you need some handy ways to write around them. Everybody—EVERYBODY—has words or phrases they always have trouble with.

In this section, you'll identify some of the more common problem areas and find some easy-to-remember ways to solve them. Some of these are simple spelling problems: *ible* or *able*; *accept* or *except*; *effect* or *affect*. Some are the old bugaboos of *who* or *whom*; *like* or *as*; *likely, apt,* or *liable*. Some will address some ordinary problems of punctuation, such as whether or not to use an apostrophe. While many of the "problems" will have been discussed in their corresponding chapters, this section provides a convenient review and reference.

ACCEPT / EXCEPT
If you accept a gift, you receive it, take it in. *Accept* is a verb that does something. *Except* is usually a preposition, meaning that something is left out. *She ate everything on her plate except the potatos.*

AFFECT / EFFECT
Most confusion between these words involves the verb *affect*, which means "to influence", and the noun *effect* that means "something that is caused to happen". The test is to ask, can the word *influence* be substituted? If it can, use *affect*. If it can't, use *effect*. You'll be right most of the time. *I wonder about the effect on my work habits; this thing could affect my whole life.*

ALL TOLD
The meaning of *all told* is everything taken into account. This is often misspelled *all tolled*. The phrase has also been spelled *all toled*, as if short for "all totaled".

ALOT / A LOT
Alot is a slangy form of the more traditional "a lot" (space included).

ALRIGHT / ALL RIGHT / ALTOGETHER
Know the difference between *all right* and *alright*, *all ready* and *already*, *all together* and *altogether*. The single words (*alright, already, altogether*) are adverbs and modify verbs and adjectives. (*The band played alright. They were already playing advanced music. They played altogether well.*) The combinations involve the pronoun *all*. The meanings shows that "all are right"; "all are ready"; "all are together". [Picky grammar pundits claim that *alright* is not acceptable. However, current usage shows this outsider has as much right to its existence as the other two adverbs (*already* and *altogether*). You decide.]

BESIDE / BESIDES
In most usage, *besides* means "in addition to", while *beside* means "next to". *Besides falling out of the race, the runner stayed beside the juice cart.*

BETWEEN / AMONG
Between involves two things; *among* involves more than two. *The argument was between the judge and the attorney; the jurors argued among themselves.* There is a time to use *between* with more than two items: if you wish the items to be considered separately. *The decision was between hanging the defendant, setting him free, or putting him in prison for life.*

BOTH / EACH
These words are not interchangeable. *Both* refers to two things together; *each* can be any number taken one at a time. *Both times we spoke, I told you about each of my children's activities.*

CAN / MAY
Can I eat an apple? You may if you can! The words depend on permission. *Can* says you are "able to"; *may* says you "have permission".

CAPS / AGENCIES
If you work for a government group, you probably will be asked to capitalize it (*city, county, state, federal governments*). Follow the advice given. Outside that agency, however, the words are not capitalized unless they're attached to capitalized names: *Pierce County, New York City, Washington State.*

CAPS / FAMILY
When talking about a family member and using an adjective modifier (generally a possessive — *my, your, his, her*) do not capitalize words like *mother, father, brother, sister.* If you do not use a modifier, capitalize the word as if it were a proper name.

> *She wanted to take her brother to the movies.*
> *He preferred Father to take him. But Mother got the job.*

CAPS / DIRECTIONS
Directions are capitalized only if they represent a specific place, such as the Northern Plains region, the Gracious South, the Wild West. Do not capitalize directions if they just point: *drive east 15 miles; the house is three blocks north; we live on the west side of the intersection.*

COMPARED TO / WITH
When you are showing a similarity between two ideas or things, use *compare to*. When you are examining, looking closely at people or objects, use *compare with*.

COMPLIMENTARY / COMPLEMENTARY
Easy to remember if you look at the letter that changes the meaning. *Complimentary* (with an *i* such as that found in *praise*) means "to say nice things about someone". *Complementary* (with an *e* such as found in *complete*) means "to add to, to make complete".

COMPOUND PLURALS
Compound words are made plural in two ways. If the first word is a noun, attach the plural on it — *brothers-in-law, fights-royal, gentlemen-personified*. If the first word is anything except a noun, attach the plural at the end — *back-ups, sleepy-heads, fast-talkers*.

CONTINUAL / CONTINUOUS
Continual means "recurring from time to time". *Continuous* means "without interruption". So make up your mind. Is this a *continual* nuisance or a *continuous* pain in the backside?

COUNCIL / COUNSEL
A *council* is a noun referring to "a group". *Counsel* is a verb meaning "to provide guidance".

CREDIBLE / CREDITABLE
Look closely when you meet one of these words. Is the word *credit* in there? *Creditable* is "worthy of credit". *Credible* simply means "believable". *Credulous*, on the other hand, is an adjective meaning "gullible, believing everything you're told".

DEFINITELY (NO "A")
Often misspelled as "definately", omit the "a" and double-up on the "i".

DISINTERESTED / UNINTERESTED
These words have separate meanings. *Disinterested* means "to be impartial, without interest for yourself". *Uninterested* means "to be without any interest at all, bored". *A psychologist must be a disinterested listener, but not an uninterested one.*

DIFFERENT FROM / DIFFERENT THAN / DIFFERENT TO
Those Brits again! They use "different to". In U.S. language, use "different from" when comparing two things or people. (*A house is different from a tent in many ways.*) The use of "different than" is usually followed by a clause (*A house is different than what a vagrant finds comfortable.*)

EXCESS / ACCESS
Excess is "too much"; *access* is "a way inside". *After gaining access to the banquet table, he ate in excess of his appetite.*

FARTHER / FURTHER
Use *farther* when indicating "distance". Use *further* when you mean "more". *If you wish to discuss this further, we'll have to move farther from this noisy crowd.*

FLAMMABLE / INFLAMMABLE
A conundrum in the world of language. Both words mean the same thing!

FOR / FORE / FOUR
When playing golf, you try *for* par; you yell out, "*Fore*", meaning "forward"; and when you count your putts, you may have to write *four*.

FORMALLY / FORMERLY
Two modifiers that get mixed up in pronunciation. *Formally* means "to wear a tuxedo and be stiff"; *formerly* means "once upon a time".

GOOD / BAD
In a crazy upside-down idiomatic world, *good* sometimes means *bad*, and *bad* means *good*. These words must be defined in context to the way they're used. Normally, they are adjectives. Slang has given them interchangeable meanings.

HE (MEANING ANYONE)

Avoid using the third person masculine pronoun *he* when you don't know the gender of the noun it replaces. If you don't know or are unsure, use any of the alternatives mentioned in the Unbiased Language Section. Or, use the third person plural. Avoid: *Anyone wishing to go may bring his friend.* Instead: *Anyone wishing to go may bring their friend.*

IBLE / ABLE

How do you decide which suffix to use? If you can complete your word with the suffix *ation*, use *able*. Try ending your word with such suffixes as *ive, tion*, or *ion*. If that works, use *ible*. This works enough of the time to be useful.

INFER / IMPLY

It takes two people to infer and imply. The do-er *implies*; that is, "the do-er suggests or hints at something". The do-ee *infers*; that is, "draws a conclusion". A speaker *implies*; a listener *infers*.

INSURE / ENSURE / ASSURE

These three words are close enough in meaning to be interchangeable. *Ensure* carries a slightly lighter shading of a legal guarantee. *Insure* stresses taking necessary measures ahead of time. *Assure* means to remove doubt and suspense.

ITS / IT'S

The difference between *its* and *it's* is more than an apostrophe. *Its* (without an apostrophe) is a possessive pronoun: *its fur, its surface, its value. It's* (with an apostrophe) is a contraction of *it is. It's that simple!*

IT IS I / IT IS ME

Because the verb *is* functions as a linking verb, the words on either side of it must complements each other. If one word isn't an adjective, that is, a description of the other, then both words must play the same role (complements). Since *it* is a subject (Column A word), then the pronoun complementing *it* must also be a Column A word, a subject. (You're right, *it is I*.)

LEAVE / LET
Leave means "to allow something to stay where it is". *Let* means "to grant permission". *Leave the house if you must, but let me go with you.*

LEND / LOAN / BORROW
While *lend* and *loan* as verbs are nearly interchangeable, *loan* is generally confined to finance. *I'll lend you my typewriter if you'll loan me $20.* Borrow applies to the action of taking the loan. *Give me the $20 and you can borrow my typewriter.*

LIKE (N / ADJ / ADV / V / PREP / CONJ / INTERJ)
An interesting word in that it may be used as any one of seven functions of language — noun, adjective, adverb, verb, preposition, conjunction, interjection.

> *Rae had distinct likes and dislikes.* (noun)
> *She preferred elegant clothes of like designs.* (adjective)
> *She likely wore them for everyday wear.* (adverb)
> *If Rae liked a jacket, she might buy it on impulse.* (verb)
> *Her appearance was like a fresh breeze in stylish circles.* (preposition)
> *People thought she was fashionable, like a movie star.* (conjunction)
> *They adored Rae, like for real!* (interjection)

LIKE / AS
Normally, *like* is a preposition that is followed by a noun or pronoun. (*The freedom of a bird is like a soaring updraft.*) *As* is a conjunction that introduces a clause. (*The freedom of a bird is as pleasant as one could imagine.*)

LIKELY / APT / LIABLE
Likely means "probable". (*The play is likely to begin on time.*) *Apt* indicates "a strong tendency". (*The actors are apt to over-emote.*) *Liable* predicts "a bad ending". (*The play is liable to draw strong criticism.*)

LOSE / LOOSE
O-o-oh! One *o* forms the verb meaning "It's gone! I've lost it." Two *o*'s means "Don't get uptight; remain cool (two *o*'s).

PAST / PASSED / PASTIME
The confusion here is in the sound of the words. Both *past* and *passed* are pronounced alike. *Past* is a noun or adjective that means "over and done with". *Passed* is the past tense of the verb "to pass". (*She passed the line of modesty in one of her past lives.*) *Pastime* is a single word, not a compound.

PERSECUTE / PROSECUTE
One can *persecute* (bring suffering to) without a lawyer. One can *prosecute* by going to court.

PRINCIPAL / PRINCIPLE
Principal means "chief", whether it's a person or a description. *Principle* refers to rules of conduct. (Note that *rules* and *principles* both end in *les*.)

RAISE / RISE
Somebody somewhere has to do the work of *raising* something. Something that *rises* may do so by itself. *You can raise the roof if you like, but the sun will rise tomorrow as usual.*

SHORT (N / ADJ / ADV / V)
Short is another word that can be used in many functions of language — noun, adjective, adverb, verb.

> *The short was noted in the year-end inventory.* (noun)
>
> *The materials were in short supply.* (adjective)
>
> *The entire process fell short of its goal.* (adverb)
>
> *"Don't you ever try to short me again,"* the owner shouted. (verb)

SIT / SET
When one *sits*, one puts one's bottom on a chair, bench, sofa, or other piece of furniture. When one *sets*, one places something somewhere. In other words, you may *set the chair in the middle of the room before you sit on it.*

THEIR / THEY'RE / THERE
Same sound, different words. *Their* is the possessive pronoun; *they're* is a contraction of "they are"; and *there* is the adverb showing location (*over there*).

THEN / THAN
Then is an adverb referring to time (*we walked, then we ran*). *Than* is a conjunction used to show comparison (*I walked faster than my friend*).

TOWARD / TOWARDS
However much some grammar technicians may try to muddy up these words, they both mean the same. They are interchangeable.

WAITING FOR / ON
When you are expectant, holding your breath, daring hardly to move, you are *waiting for*. When you are serving another person with food, slippers, or reading glasses, you are *waiting on*.

WEATHER / WHETHER
Weather is how the sun and rain perform when you decide whether to call off the picnic or risk the prediction of rain. *Whether* is a conjunction used to express doubt.

WHO / WHOM / WHOSE
These pronouns fall in succession in Columns A, B, and C of the Quick Pronoun Menu. *Who* is found in Column A, as a subject. *Whom* is found in Column B, as an object. *Whose* is found in Column C as a possessive.

> *The victim was one who liked to take risks.*
> *The accident occurred to the daredevil whom they chose to drive.*
> *Whose fault was it, really?*

YOUR / YOU'RE / YORE
This list belongs to Y-O-U. This is *your* (possessive pronoun) moment; *you're* (contraction of "you are") ready to write your story; in days of yore (noun meaning "long ago"), you hesitated. Now you are ready. Go for it!

ENGLISH TERMS

The following terms were used in this book, directly transported from England, to assuage the English purists who contend that U.S.ers speak "English". Are you convinced as yet of the absolute tosh of that belief?

English	U.S. Translation
Absobloodylootely	YES!
Absolute tosh	Complete rubbish
Belt up	Shut up
Bits 'n bobs	Various things
Blimey!	My goodness
Bloody	Damn
Bob's your uncle	There you go!
Bollocks	Slang term for "absolute rubbish". A load of tatt. Someone tells you a little white lie, tell them "bollocks to that!"
Brill	Short for "brilliant", means "cool"
Chivvy along	Hurry up
Codswallop	Baloney
Don't get your knickers in a twist	Don't get worked up
Easy peasy	Easy

Fancy	Like; be fond of
Keep your hair on	Calm down
Keep your pecker up	Remain cheerful; keep your head held high.
Know your onions	Knowledgeable
Leg it	Run extremely fast
Lost the Plot	Gone crazy
Nutter	Crazy person
On your tod	All on your own. Another expression is to say you were "nobby no-mates". Ahh, sad!
Plonker	Idiot
Rubbish	Garbage or "that's crap!"
Shambles	Bad shape, plan gone wrong; chaotic mess
Sorted	Arranged
Sprog	A baby
Suss	Figure out
Tad	Little bit
Throw a spanner in the works	Screw up; wreck something
Throw a wobbly	Have a tantrum
Tickety-boo	When something is going well
Uni	College / University
Whinge	Complain; whine
Wonky	Not right
Zonked	Tired, exhausted

ABOUT THE ANARCHIST

Val Dumond is an admitted word enthusiast, freak, buff, fan, aficionada, devotee, fanatic — all right, an addict. She can't stop putting words together and finding new ways to use them. In this book she offers some of her conclusions, as well as most of the choices that make up *Val's Style Manual*.

Her lifetime of writing includes years as a journalist, intermittent years writing advertising copy, and enumerable years jotting down ideas, putting them together, and fashioning short stories and books.

But it hasn't all been writing. She reared two children, raised funds for her favorite nonprofits, earned a couple of academic degrees, traveled up the Nile River, spent time on a Greek island, even stopped in London to hear Big Ben, and oh-sooo-much-more!

As this book goes to press, Val is editing several manuscripts for other writers, presenting another of her Tuesday Afternoon Writing Salons, and working on her *grande opus* — a novel to cap her long writing career.

P.S. She had an absobloodylutely great time in London and loves the Brits.

ACKNOWLEDGMENTS

This book has been in the making for many many many months, resulting in much time spent scouring grammar books, confirming quotations, rewriting the manuscript (so many times that the count has been lost), and then rewriting again.

My gratitude goes to the many linguists who confirm my work by understanding the dilemma of teaching grammar in the United States. Many of them reside in the UK; some reside in university towns in the U.S. Some live and work in China, Russia, Mexico, France, Australia, Israel, and Iran. Without the support of these professionals, especially among members of EuraLex and the North American Dictionary Society, I'd have quit long ago.

Most of my gratitude goes to Lisbeth Wheelehan who kept me in the 21st century and contributed the British slang for me to toss around. Without her nudging to "loosen up", this book might have been drowned in the swamp of U.S. grammar books that clot the Resource Books shelves in libraries and bookstores.

INDEX

A

accept/except, 266
Acknowledgments, 279
acronyms, 9
Action Verbs, 41-47
　active or passive, 46
　passive, good or bad, 47
　vs. Stop-action, 41
Adjectives, 68-83. See also **Phrases and Clauses**
　comparatives, 71
　compounds, 75
　even, 72
　infinitives, 79
　location, 70
　order, 74
　participles, 77
　possessives, 69
　problems, 79-83
　quantity/numbers, 73
　ultimates, 74
Adverbs, 84-91. See also **Phrases and Clauses**
　comparatives, 85
　without *ly*, 85
　with verbs, 85
　with adjectives, 86
　with other adverbs, 86
　with sentences, 86
　misplaced, 86
　infinitives, 87
　troublemakers, 87-91
affect/effect, 266
all told, 266
a lot/alot/lots, 81, 266
already/all ready, 90
alright/all right/altogether 266
America or U.S.? x-xi
Apostrophes, 175-178
　contractions, 176
　footnotes, 177
　in measurements, 177
　noun possessives, 175
　numbers and letters, 177
　plural possessives, 176
　pronoun possessives, 175
Articles, 117-118
　Exceptions with *"h"* and *"u"*, 117

Multiple duty, 118
Assembling the Parts. *See*: **Putting It All Together**
awful/awesome, 79
awhile, 90

B

beside/besides, 267
between/among, 267
Bling: Phrases/Clauses, 92-95. *See* Phrases/Clauses bling. *See* modifiers
both/each, 267
Brackets, 166-167
   for [sic], 166
   inside remarks, 166
British punctuation/words, xi
Building paragraphs. *See* Paragraphs

C

can/may, 267
caps/agencies, 267
caps/direction, 267
caps/family, 267
Clauses/Phrases. *See* Phrases/Clauses
Colons, 141-144
   more uses, 143
   quotations — long and short, 143
   something lies ahead, 142
Commas, 129-139
   after introductory adverb clause, 136
   after introductory verbal clause, 136
   after one introductory word, 137
   afterthought commas, 132
   how many are too many? 129
   in a complex series, 132
   in a series, 131
   in multi-modifiers, 137
   other uses, 138
   parenthetical ideas, 134
   The Reflective Pause, 129-139
   to clarify and interpret, 139
   to join sentences, 135
company names, 6, 9
comparative clauses, 71, 85
compared to/with, 268
complimentary/complementary, 268
compound-complex sentences, 215
compound plurals, 268
compound sentences, 213
complex sentences, 214
Conjunctions, 99-107
   adjective clauses, 102
   adverb clauses, 101
   and/but, 106
   but what, 107
   conjunctions, 99-107
   connectors in pairs, 100
   noun clauses, 104
   provided/providing, 106
   so/so that, 105
   unless, 106
   where/that, 107
   yet, 105
Connectors. *See* Little Words, *see also* Conjunctions, Prepositions, Articles, Interjections *Connotive/connotative*, 199
Consistency, 1-274
Constructing paragraphs. *See* Paragraphs
continual/continuous, 79, 268
council/counsel, 268
credible/creditable, 268

D

dangling verbals, 94-95
Dashes, 187-190
   m-dash, 187
   n-dash, 188
definitely (no "a"), 268
Denotive, denotative, 199
Diagonals, Virgules, 189-190
   and/or, 189
   backward diagonal/slash, 190
dictionaries, 198

based on English, 198
new words, 198
word labels, 198
different/from/different than/different to, 269
direct objects,
disinterested/uninterested, 269
Dots and Dashes, 173, 190
  See:
  Apostrophes
  Ellipses
  Hyphens
  Dashes
  Diagonals
Dots with Tails. *See* Semicolons *due to/ because*, 79

E

Ellipsis, 179
eminent/imminent, 80
Enclosures of the Word Kind, 161-172
  See:
  Brackets
  Parentheses
  Quotation Marks
English or U.S.? x, xi
English Terms, 275-276
excess/access, 269
Exclamation points, 158-159
  placing, 159
  the boy who cried wolf, 158

F

Fairy Tale Syndrome, 61
famous/notorious, 80
farther/further, 269
fewer/less, 80
flammable/inflammable, 269
for/fore/four, 269
formally/formerly, 91, 269
Four Parts of Grammar, 1-121
  Little Words
    Articles, 117-118
    Conjunctions, 99-107
    Interjections, 119-121
    Prepositions, 108-116
  Modifiers
    Adjectives, 68-83
    Adverbs, 84-91
    Clauses, 92-95
    Phrases, 92-95
  Action/Stop-action verbs
    Action, 41-47
    Stop-action, 48-63
  Things
    Nouns, 3-22
    Pronouns, 23-37
Full Stops. *See* Periods

G

good/bad, 80, 269
Grammar Glitches, 196, 265-274
Guidelines
  Caution (abbreviations), 149
  Combining Sentences, 135
  Commas in a Series, 131
  Commas, Necessary or Not, 133
  Company Rules, 7
  connotive/connotative, 199
  denote/denotative, 199
  Dictionary Spelling, 199
  Do Not Attempt To Memorize, 39
  Down, 115
  Evolution of a Compound Adjective, 76
  Fairy Tale Syndrome, 61
  Find Subject / Verb, 108
  Her birthday Is on the 15th, 138
  Irony (of typewriters), 199
  Johnny's in Trouble, 114
  Latin (media), 15
  Lazy Stop-action Verbs, 48
  Man/Woman, 246
  No Apostrophes, 27
  Nouns, 6

One "s" to a Noun, 20
One/Ten Thousand Exclamations, 158
Onomastic Nouns Place Modifiers Carefully, 109
Possessive Nouns, 18
Quick Pronoun Menu, 37
Ration the Quotes, 170
Sentences with Semicolons, 146
Short vs. Long Bling, 71
Verbs, 40
Who or Whom? 31
Who Owns What? 70
Why Do You Write? 253

H

hardly/scarcely/barely, 87
he (meaning anyone), 270
Headlights. *See* Colons *healthful/healthy*, 80
historic/historical, 81
hopefully, 87
How to write numbers. *See* Numbers
Hyphens, 180-186
   as word connector, 185
   as word divider, 185
   in compound words, 180
   with adjectives, 181
   with participles, 182
   with prefixes, 184
   with verbs and prepositions, 183

I

ible/able, 270
idiom, 198
Include "Them". *See* Unbiased Language
infer/imply, 270
insure/ensure/assure, 270
Interjections, 119-121
   it/there, 120
   like, 121
Introduction, ix-xviii

irregardless, 88
it is I/it is me, 270
its/it's, 270
it/there, 120

J

Johnny's in Trouble, 114
joining sentences with commas, 135, 213, 215
joining words with hyphens, 185
joining words. *See* Conjunctions

K

keyboarding, 199

L

labels, 6
later/latter, 80
leave/let, 271
lend/loan/borrow, 271
liable/likely/apt, 81
like (n, adj, adv, v, prep, conj, interj), 121, 271
like/as, 271
likely/apt/liable, 271
Little Words, 97-121
   See:
   Conjunctions
   Prepositions
   Articles
   Interjections
lose/loose, 271
lots/a lot, 81, 266

M

maybe, 91
Modifiers, 65-96
   See:
   Adjectives

Adverbs
Phrases and Clauses
Overview, 65-67
most/almost, 81

N

names, 3. *See also* Nouns
Nonsexist language. *See* Unbiased Language
Nouns, 3-22
   capitalizing, 6
      people, 8
      places, 8
      things, 9
   collectives, 13
   compound, 13
   connected with *and*, 20
   connected with *or*, 21
      gerunds, 19
      infinitives, 19
   Latin, 14
   names, 3. *See also* Nouns
   noun/verb agreement, 19
   plurals, 10-12
      ending o, 11
      ending y, 11
      simple s, 11
   possessives, 16
   proper nouns, 8-10
   verbals, 18-19
Numbers, 195, 237-243
   cardinals, 242
   in dates, time, 239-240
   measurements, 241
   money, 240-241
   ordinals, 242
   percentages, 242
   stock market quotes, 241-242
   streets, highways, 242
   temperature, 241
   weights, 241
   when to write out, 237-239

   one-ten, 236-237
   sentence beginning, 238

O

objects (direct and indirect), 23-37
onomastics, 4

P

Paragraphs, 194, 223-228
   computerized writing, 227
      brainstorming, 227
      organize material, 227-228
   definition, 223
   last is best, 228
   length, 223224
   topic sentences, 224-226
      placement, 225-226
      subject, tone, 224
   transitional words, 226
      give direction, 226
      parallel construction, 226
      repeat words, 226
Parallel writing, 209, 212, 216-218
Parenthesis, 161-165
   formal / legal, 164
   numbers and letters, 164
   to de-emphasize, 165
participles, 18, 57-60, 65, 77-78, 94-95, 182-183
past/passed/pastime, 272
Periods, 148-151
   abbreviations, 149
   decimal point, 150
   inside? outside? where to place, 151
   miscellaneous dots, 151
   The Complete Stop, 148-151
persecute/prosecute, 272
Phrases/Clauses, 92-95
   absolute participial phrase, 94
   adjectives, 92
   adverbs, 93
   dangling verbals, 94-95

summary, modifiers, 95
possessives, 16, 27, 175-176
    nouns, 175
    plurals, 176
    pronouns, 175
Prepositions, 108-116
    all, any, both, 111
    among/between, 111
    doubles, 109
    down, 115
    ending with, 110
    idiomatic expressions, 116
    in/into, 112
    like/as, 112
    per, 113
    troublemakers, 111-115
    up, 114
pretty, 88
principal/principle, 272
Pronouns, 23-37
    compound subjects, 34
    contractions, 17
    demonstrative, 32
    following *be*, 35
    gender, 34
    hints for writers, 36
    objects, 26
    plural, 28,
    possessives, 27
    pronoun-verb compatibility, 33
    Quick Pronoun Menu, 23-27, 37
    reflexive, 29
    singular, 28
    subjects, 25
    who/which/that/what, 32
    who/whom, 31
Punctuation, 125-190
    Apostrophes, 175-178
    Brackets, 166-167
    Colons, 141-144
    Commas, 129-139
    Dashes, 187-190
    Diagonals, 189-190
    Ellipsis, 179
    Exclamation Points, 158-159
    Hyphens, 180-186
    Overview, 125-127
    Parenthesis, 161-165
    Periods, 148-151
    Question Marks, 153-157
    Quotation Marks, 168-172
    Secret of Punctuation, 190
    Semicolons, 145-147
Putting It All Together, 193-263
    See:
    Numbers
    Paragraphs
    Sentences
    Spelling
    Unbiased Language
    Words
    Writing Style of Your Own
    Your Style Manual

Q

question authority, ix
Question Marks, 153-157
    another language, 157
    lesson in tact, 156
    more than one question, 155
    rhetorical questions, 154
    uncertainty, 157
    where to place the mark, 155
Quick Pronoun Menu, 23-27, 37
Quotation Marks, 168-172
    alternative uses, 169
    quoted words, 168
    single marks, 169
    special words, 170
    titles of newspapers, books, 171

R

raise/rise, 272
real good, 88

real/really, 82, 88
Reflective Pause, 129-139. *See* Commas
reflexive pronouns, 29
reoccurring, 82
rhetorical questions, 154
"rules"
    breaking, xii-xiii
    definition, xiv,
run smooth, 89

S

Secret of Punctuation, 190
seldom, 91
Semicolons, 145-147
    Choose-your-state Stop, 145-147
    connector, 145
    lists with commas, 147
    transition words, 146
Sentences, 194, 209-221
    clauses, phrases, 216
    complex, 214
    compound, 213
    compound-complex, 215
    definition, 210
    parallel writing, 216
    simple writing, 211, 212
    troubleshooting ideas, 218
        double verbs, modifiers, nouns, 219
        misplaced modifiers, 221
        too much, overload, 218
shall/will, 62
short (n, adj, adv, v), 89, 272
short/shortly, 89
simple sentences, 212
simple writing, 211
sit/set, 272
Spelling, 195, 229-236
    difficulty, 229
    ending in o, 234
    ending in y, 235
    Four Guidelines, 230-234
    look-it-up-&-memorize, 233
    prefix/suffix, 231
    root words, 231
    sounding out, 232
    "I before E...", 234
    long vowels, 235
    naughty jingles, 233-234
    note for northern users, 235-6
    other languages, 236
    short vowels, 235
s-shortage, 20
Stop-action Verbs, 48-63
    converted verbs, 51-52
    double verbing, 53
    is or *isn't*, 50
    modifiers, 49
    moods, 60
        demanding, 60
        Fairy Tale Syndrome, 61
        Plain, 60
    overview, 41-42
    regular/irregular verbs, 59
    shall/will, 62
    subject exchange, 49
    verb tense, 55
        complete (perfect), 58
        future, 56
        past, 57
        present, 55
        progressive, 57
    vs. Action, 41
    wimpy verbing, 54
Structuring sentences. *See* Sentences
surely, 89

T

technical language, 202
terrible, 82
The Grammar Anarchist, 277
their/they're/there, 272
theirs/yours/ours, 82
then/than, 272

Things. *See* Nouns, *also* Pronouns
   throwaway words, 205
too, 91
toward/towards, 273
Typewriter irony, 199
Typist or keyboarder, 199

U

Unbiased language, 195, 245-249
   diminish and demean, 247-248
      alternatives, 248
      importance, 247
      girl, 247
   man words, 246-247
   sexist, 245-246
   stereotypes, 248-249
   three forms of sexism, 245
uncool and illegal, 245

V

Verbs, 39-63. See Action, also Stop-action
   functions, 43-43
   overview, 39-45
very, 90
viable, 83
Voices of Writing, 153-159
   See:
   Exclamation Points
   Questions Marks

W

waiting for/on, 273
weather/whether, 273
well/badly, 90
who/whom/whose, 273
Wimpy and Wonderful. *See* Words
Words, 194, 197-207
   dictionaries, 198
   exercises, 207
   extraneous, 204
      better, 204
      too much, 204
   fun to try, 206
   make up your own, 200
   playing with, 200
   select carefully, 203
   technical language, 202
   thesaurus, 199
   throwaway, 205
      better, 205-206
      not so hot, 205-206
writing for hire, 261-262
Writing Style, 195, 251-258
   all your own, 251-258
   audience, 254
   bottom line on top, 253-254
   closings, 255
   formal writing, 254
   fun and profit, 256
   parallel writing, 216
   persuasive writing, 255-256
      proposals, 256
      seduce editors, 251, 256
   pointers for fiction writers, 257-258
   purpose, 252-254
      entertain
      persuade/sell
      request
      transfer information
   satisfy the writing itch, 257
   sell your ideas, 255-256

simple, grownup, pretentious, 211
  terms of endearment, 254

Y

your/you're/yore, 273
Your Style Manual, 196, 259-263
  be consistent, 262
  bookstores, libraries, 260
  buy or create, 260
  create your own, 259-263
  don't believe everything, everyone, 263
  how to create, 260-261
  learn from others, 260
  many lives of, 261
  one word at a time, 259-260
  throw out "rules", 259
  Val's Style Manual, 262
  writing for hire, 261-262

www.ingramcontent.com/pod-product-compliance
Lightning Source LLC
Chambersburg PA
CBHW060457090426
42735CB00011B/2019